JUSTICE FOR NATIVES
SEARCHING FOR COMMON GROUND

A collection of thirty-five essays and stories. *Justice for Natives* came together around the Oka crisis between Native people in Quebec and the government. Against the backdrop of this deep-rooted conflict, Native elders and leaders, provincial and federal government representatives, leading academics, lawyers, and judges from across Canada and the United States joined to explore various aspects of Native peoples' struggle for justice and to search for solutions.

The collection follows a cycle of remembering the past, learning from the present, and planning for the future. In the first section of the book, "Conflict, Self-Determination, and Native Peoples," contributors, including Mohawk activist Ken Deer, Judge Rejean Paul, and scholar Brian Slattery, look at the historical roots of the conflict between Native and non-Native people, problems in the current justice system, and the movement for Native self-determination. In the second section, "Lessons from Oka," Native leaders Elijah Harper, Matthew Coon-Come, and Diom Romeo Saganash respond to the crisis at Oka and scholars Bruce Clark and Robert Venables consider constitutional alternatives and compare Canadian policy with that in the United States. Looking into the future, the final section, "Justice for Natives?" offers practical alternatives for improving relations, reviews actual measures being taken, and proposes models for change. Some of the solutions raised include increased recognition of Crown fiduciary duties to Native people, co-management strategies for land use, and an independent Native judiciary as envisioned by scholar Leroy Little Bear of Saskatchewan. *Justice for Natives* makes an important contribution to Native, legal, and policy studies in Canada.

Andrea P. Morrison is a sessional lecturer in the Faculty of Law, McGill University, and a full-time practitioner in alternative dispute resolution, specializing in cross-cultural conflict and international transactions.

JUSTICE FOR NATIVES
SEARCHING FOR COMMON GROUND

Edited by

Andrea P. Morrison
with Irwin Cotler

Published for
InterAmicus
McGill University, Faculty of Law

by

McGill-Queen's University Press
Montreal & Kingston • London • Buffalo

The Aboriginal Law Association of McGill University gratefully acknowledges the
contributions made toward the first printing of this publication by the Department of
Indian Affairs and Northern Development, McCarthy Tétrault, InterAmicus, and the
McGill University Faculty of Law.

Canadian Cataloguing in Publication Data

Main entry under title:

Justice for Natives: Searching for Common Ground

Includes some text in French.
ISBN 0-7735-1635-2 (bound)
ISBN 0-7735-1645-X (pbk)

1. Indians of North America – Canada – Law – Conference proceedings – Essays 2.
Indians of North America – Culture 3. International Law 4. Constitutional Law 5. Civil
Rights 6. Canadian Charter of Rights and Freedoms 7. Criminal Law 8. Government
Relations 9. Alternative Dispute Resolution
I. Morrison, Andrea P., 1961-,

Associate Editors:

Bryan Sentes   Georg Wobbe

The editor wishes to thank the following individuals and organizations for their generous help with the book:

Irwin Cotler	Lorna Telfer
Margo Siminovitch	Anne Drost
Anjali Choksi	Christian Gagnon
Aurora Opazo Saez	Minelle D'Souza
Michelle Cumyn	Daniel Torsher
Mireille Dufault	Denise Langevin
Sarah McDonald	Renée Thériault

Ginette Compagna and the Canadian Embassy in Beijing

1990 – 1991 – 1992
Conference Organizers

Anjali Choksi, Andrea Morrison, Murray Mollard, Christine Deom, Mike Bush, Christine Bush, Darcy Edgar, Alison Wheeler, Karen Cadham, Margo Siminovitch, Ann Drost, David Kalmakoff, Steve Watts, Naomi Margo, Garth Wallbridge, Barbra Szeicz, Brian Cohen, André Brousseau, Chris Richter, Dirk Bouwer, Jocelyn Barrett, Cathy James, Tanya Perron, Chrystal Nicholas

Conference Sponsors

Department of Indian Affairs and Northern Development, Solicitor General, James O'Reilly & Associates, Hutchins & Soroka, McGill Law Student's Association, The Students' Society of McGill University, Quebec Public Interest Research Group (QPIRG), Air Creebec, Air Canada, The Montreal Gazette

CONTENTS

THE MEDICINE WHEEL

MAG-LA-QUE

Mag-la-que is a Yankton from South Dakota. He is involved in various educational programs in schools, and media. As well as extensive experience in the construction industry, he is a registered artist with the Indian Arts and Crafts Association of America. His goals are to help people understand and respect the Indigenous Peoples.

The medicine wheel design is of very old origin, predating the influences of Anglo-European colonialization.

The Wheel has great meaning to the Native Peoples.

The circle represents life and how everything must continue in the manner set by the Creator.

The crossed lines represent the following: the four winds, the four directions, the four seasons, and the four races of man.

The areas in between represent the secondary directions (NE, SE, SW, NW) as well as the elements, plants, animals, birds, and sea creatures.

The feathers hanging down represent the messengers to the Creator (Eagle, Hawk, and Raven). The upraised feather in the center is a sign of friendship.

Respect of the Creator's wishes are an integral part of the circle. No species could or should be destroyed or exterminated. Working together in balance keeps the Circle whole.

Artwork by
AKWEKS

THE 1990 CONFERENCE

(Photographs by Andrea Morrison)

BRIAN SLATTERY AND MURRAY MOLLARD

SALLY WEAVER

THE 1991 CONFERENCE

MATTHEW COON-COME

OREN LYONS

ELIJAH HARPER

THE 1992 CONFERENCE

OWEN YOUNG

LEROY LITTLE BEAR

JUSTICE FOR NATIVES

INTRODUCTION

ANDREA P. MORRISON and ANJALI CHOKSI

Conference Organizers

SEARCHING FOR COMMON GROUND

When our group of students, the Aboriginal Law Association of McGill University, first thought of the presenting this lecture series in the summer of 1989, our goal was to educate students of McGill University Faculty of Law, since only one course was offered bi-annually on Aboriginal law. However, we opened the conferences to the public in order to create greater awareness about the issues, controversies and conflicts surrounding the relationship between Aboriginal Peoples and Canadian governments and institutions.

The first annual Aboriginal conference was held at McGill only a few months before the crisis at Oka escalated into armed conflict. The crisis in 1990 arose when the Municipality of Oka sought to expand a golf course on land long claimed by the Mohawks of Kanesatake; this incident was the culmination of long-standing grievances of the Mohawks of Kanesatake relating to the manner in which the Seminary of St. Sulpice and the federal and provincial governments had dealt with their lands. The police and the army were called to bring down a blockade set up by the Mohawks, and the result was an armed stand-off for several months during the summer of 1990. The conferences contained in this book thus both preceded and attempted to respond to this critical historical point of Aboriginal and non-Aboriginal relations in Quebec and Canada.

Each year, conference participants explored questions relating to justice systems and Aboriginal Peoples. The topics range from local conflict resolution and criminal law, to international law and self-determination. Each conference was an event that brought together Aboriginal leaders, government officials, academics and the public, and the participants were from a variety of disciplines including anthropology, history, philosophy, spirituality, economics and law.

In 1990, *Conflict, Self-Determination and Native Peoples: Searching for Common Ground* began with an award ceremony for three courageous individuals who fought for the rights as Indian women to live in their communities with the same entitlement as Indian men. Participants in the first panel discussed the failures and weaknesses of the current justice system. It was followed by an analysis of the roots of the problem, and closed with a look at the possible manifestations of Aboriginal self-determination in the future, both at the local and international levels.

This cycle of "remembering the past, learning from the present, and planning for the future" was essentially repeated in the 1991 and 1992 conferences. However, the 1991 conference, *Lessons from Oka: Forging a New Relationship*, was held in the wake of the crisis at Oka, and the talks given by participants were charged with a special urgency and determination to protect Aboriginal rights, and were directed at a broader concern for Canadian-Aboriginal relations.

The third conference in 1992, *Justice for Native?*, emphasized actual measures that have been taken, or could be advanced for the further development of justice systems.

Finding a common ground for Aboriginal and non-Aboriginal Peoples will not be easy, and we do not purport to have found any through these conferences. In fact, the opinions revealed by the participants reveal extremely distinct and diverse points of view on vital issues. However, these views will have to be taken into account in the effort to effectively resolve the deep-rooted conflicts between First Nations and Canadian governments as well as the Canadian community at large. It is through the stories of speakers such as Sister Two Axe Early and Owen Young that we are able to "learn difference", an important step in finding solutions to current problems. All too often these stories have been ignored by the

Canadian legal system, even though it is becoming increasingly clear that deep-rooted conflict cannot be resolved until difference is recognized, accepted, and integrated into our justice systems.

Further, simply organizing and structuring each event was an important lesson for those involved. Our goal was to achieve a balance within the structure and process of the conferences, and to draw upon the teachings of Aboriginal Peoples as well as Canadians. We tried to live up to these principles by working together without carving out hierarchical positions and by making decisions on the basis of consensus.

Editor's Note:

A final comment should be made on the editorial process. Each conference was taped and then transcribed in its entirety. A rough draft was circulated immediately after each conference. However, for use in a book of wider distribution, considerable editing for clarity and continuity became necessary. With the exception of Bruce Clark, who I attempted unsuccessfully to reach in Bulgaria where, according to the Upper Canada Law Society, he is now living, each of the speakers were given the opportunity to review and further edit their talk. On behalf of the Aboriginal Law Association of McGill, I would like to thank the speakers for their continued interest and support.

Further, *researchers should be aware that we have not attempted to verify the statements, quotations, or pinpoint citations given by authors*. A Bibliography of legislation, cases and books is included at the end of the book, and readers should consult the materials in question directly for accuracy.

In closing, the true purpose of this book is to preserve the oral presentations given, and to share with a broader audience the original ideas and perspectives that came out of these talks. The issue of justice systems remains of vital concern to Aboriginal and non-Aboriginal Peoples alike, and it is hoped that this book will contribute to the search for effective conflict resolution.

The 1990 Conference

CONFLICT, SELF-DETERMINATION AND NATIVE PEOPLES: SEARCHING FOR COMMON GROUND

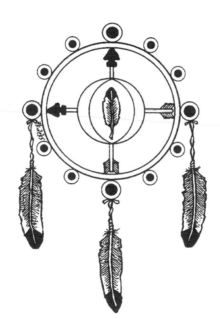

OPENING THANKSGIVING

TEKARONHIOKEN

Frank Tekaronhioken Jacobs is a teacher of the Mohawk language and a faith-keeper to the traditional Longhouse at Kahnawake.

Honoured and distinguished guests: before I begin the Thanksgiving Address, I would like to repeat some of it in our language, on behalf of my grandsons and my granddaughters who speak the Mohawk language. We are always teaching the youngsters the language so that they may carry on where we will leave off.

[address in Mohawk]

Now, it is our custom at every assembly, regardless of where it might be, to offer thanksgiving and acknowledgement to the Great Spirit. We shall begin this conference by honouring one another in this assembly, for we have much to do. So, we should greet one another and give thanks to one another. Let us now collect all of our thoughts and greet one another. Now our minds are as one.

Our grandfathers have given us what we know today. Our ancestors have passed on to us this very ritual of giving thanks and acknowledgment to the Great Spirit for all He has provided us. We must never forget that He alone has the power to keep the earth going.

Our grandfathers have said:

We should always remember our Mother Earth for She shall
provide everything, all our needs shall be fulfilled by Her.

We know today that She is having some difficulty, but, nevertheless, She continues to provide for us through the instructions of the
Great Spirit. It is unfortunate that She is suffering today as a result
of man's doing. Hopefully, there is going to be a turn-around so
that the Earth will be made a better place for all. So, let us bring all
our thoughts together and thank and acknowledge Mother Earth.
Now our minds are as one.

Our grandfathers have said:

Never forget to thank the roots of the plant life, for they shall
provide their power in time of sickness. We are of nature, and,
therefore, nature shall provide for us to cure our illness. Each
medicine has a specific duty: each root, each plant, each blade
of grass. Each of these plants has specific and special names.
Never forget them. Remember, for we shall not always be
here. You must carry on our work.

So, it is today that we carry on this work. We, too, are having much
difficulty, because our language is disappearing, but we are making
every effort to bring that language back, and we are being successful. We are all struggling for an identity.

Our grandfathers have said:

Each and every one of you shall be given a name, a sacred
name, so all these plant lives shall know you when you ask
for their assistance.

This is what they said to us, and this is what we must carry on today. So, it is our responsibility to care for Mother Earth. So, let us
thank and acknowledge the plant life and thank the Great Spirit
for providing the plant life for us. Now our minds are as one.

Our grandfathers have said:

There shall be lakes and rivers, large and small, where all
life on earth shall go to quench their thirst whether they are of
the smallest insect or the largest animal.

We, too, when we become thirsty, will go to these rivers and lakes. In days of old, this is how it used to be, but it is not so today. Can we take that gamble and go to the river and scoop a cup of water from it without risk to our health? This is why I say Mother Earth is struggling, but, nevertheless, She carries on. So, let us thank the Great Spirit for providing all the waters of the world. Now our minds are as one.

Our grandfathers have also said:

> *There shall be a variety of trees, but one shall be recognized as the leader, and that shall be the maple tree. There are other trees in the world, but the maple does not grow in all places of the world. But in this place, where you dwell, this is the tree that shall provide you medicine and provide you health. From this maple tree, the sap shall run and you shall turn it into syrup to be used as food. Remember to always thank all of the trees in the area that you reside, for they provide for you. They shall provide shelter for you; they shall provide warmth for you.*

So, let us collect all our thoughts and thank the Great Spirit for providing this for us. Now our minds are as one.

Now, within the forest there are birds of many varieties, of many sizes, of many colours, and of many songs. When we wake up in the morning, early in the morning, we hear their songs, and we see these beautiful birds of different colours. As they say in our language, they stir our minds up to see what a beautiful day it can be, what a beautiful day we can make it, and it is thanks to these birds that we have this feeling.

So, our grandfathers have said:

> *Always remember these are the gifts of the Great Spirit, for He provides all these birds of different sizes and colours. Many of them shall be used for food. When you take the life of a bird, you must apologize to it, since it has given up its life for you.*

This is what our grandfathers have said. So, let us collect all our thoughts and thank and honour the Great Spirit for providing the bird life.

Within the forest there are many animals of different sizes. If we go deep within the forest, we can see these animals running about. They stir up our minds. These are playful times and serious times: this is how we recognize life, life as it is. They are struggling for life as well.

Our grandfathers have looked at all the animal life and said:

> *Remember them too, since some of these animals shall provide food to supplement other food, so you must also apologize to these animals for the life they give up for you.*

So, it is that we thank and acknowledge the Great Spirit for providing this to man. Now our minds are as one.

As we go on, there are the other forces that make the world a good place to live, and they replenish the waters, the rivers and the lakes. We call them our grandfathers the rainmakers and the thunderers. When they come to replenish the rivers and the wells where we draw our water, we thank them, and we thank the Great Spirit for giving these forces the duties and responsibilities of life. So, it is that we thank and acknowledge the Great Spirit for all these natural elements that help Mother Earth live.

Our grandfathers have also said:

> *The windmakers, many of them come from different directions. Sometimes it is warm air, other times it is cold, but, nevertheless, this air is moving, and the old air is moved out of the way so that we may breathe better.*

As you all know, we are having problems with the air. Nevertheless, our grandfathers the windmakers, are constantly replenishing the air with fresh air. Let us thank and acknowledge the Great Spirit, for He has given the windmakers the duty and responsibility to replenish the air. Now our minds are as one.

As we move higher up, our ancestors, our grandfathers, grandmothers, aunts, uncles, cousins, and children who have gone before us have left us their knowledge and experience.

So, let us thank and acknowledge those that have gone before us. Now our minds are as one.

Now we come to the Great Spirit. The Great Spirit is not known to reside anywhere, but He resides in every one of us, every man, woman and child.

Our grandfathers have said that:

When we leave this earth, we shall go to the place that He has provided for us. We do not know where this place is, but we do know that there shall be a place for us in his Land.

So, let us thank the Great Spirit for all that He has provided for us, and let us take the time to look deep inside ourselves rather than out. There is a spiritual spark in all of us, and if we try hard enough we will find the spiritual happiness that the Great Spirit has intended for us.

May the Great Spirit shine a spiritual path for all man.

Tho niio wëñ:nake

NATIVE WOMEN AND THE INDIAN ACT: THE STRUGGLE FOR JUSTICE

(THE ROBERT S. LITVACK MEMORIAL AWARD)

IRWIN COTLER

Professor, McGill Faculty of Law

INTRODUCTION

I would like to say something about the award and the person in whose memory it has been established, Robert Litvack. Robert Litvack was a graduate of this law school and became a distinguished lawyer in Quebec. Shortly before his premature and tragic death from cancer, he decided to establish a human rights award, which we later decided to name in his memory, to recognize that the achievements of those whose struggle on behalf of human rights have made a difference.

I think it is not only fortuitous, but fitting, that our award recipients this evening are Native People, since one of Robert Litvack's first initiatives, before people were even aware of Native law, was to represent the Inuit at a time when there were no funds to do so. When he undertook the role as their advocate, as those of us who associated with him at the time knew, Robert Litvack not only undertook to represent them without a fee, but also paid the expenses, so that the initial injunctive remedy was made possible.

While the award was established to be given to any individual whose struggle for human rights has made a difference, in this instance, it is a matter of not only good fortune but almost of historical connectedness, that the award, in the name of one who himself struggled for human rights, should be given this evening to those who have become symbols for human rights.

I would like to add that Sister Mary Two Axe Earley, Jeanette Corbiere Lavell and Sandra Lovelace have each in their own unique way, and all three of them collectively, endured the triple jeopardy of discrimination: as Native People, as women, and as Native women. Each of them has advanced the cause of Native Peoples, women's rights, and Native women's rights through their struggle.

I first met Sister Mary Two Axe Earley here at McGill Law School, not long after she had founded what was in effect the first Native women's group in this country, Equal Rights for Native Women, and this group launched the struggle for Native women and their rights in this country.

At the time that Jeanette Corbiere Lavell was appealing her case from the Federal Court of Appeal to the Supreme Court of Canada, I had been acting as a special advisor to John Turner, then Federal Minister of Justice. For a variety of reasons, the Federal Minister of Justice and the Attorney General decided to character-ize the case as an internal case for Indians rather than as a sex dis-crimination case. Therefore, the Attorney General mistakenly, in my view, and perhaps soon by his own acknowledgement, decided to appeal the judgment of the Federal Court of Appeal to the Su-preme Court of Canada. That brought us to Sandra Lovelace, and there were a number of us engaged in Sandra Lovelace's struggle at the time. This is the first time that these women have been able to come together this evening and it is indeed an honour to take part in this award presentation.

SYLVIA LITVACK

AWARD PRESENTATION

There is a common theme which brings together these three women. Each one has advanced the cause of Indian women through her own individual effort and in so doing, contributed to the advancement of Indian rights and human rights as a whole. All three women took issue with a particular provision of the *Indian Act* which forced Indian women who marry non-Indians to lose their Indian status. I am referring to the infamous section 12(1)(b) of the *Indian Act*. No such stripping of Indian status applied to Indian men who married non-Indian women. The effect of this provision was in the words of the late Supreme Court Justice Mr. Bora Laskin:

> [T]o effect a statutory excommunication of Indian women from their society, but not of Indian men, a statutory banishment, a legal instrument of separation of an Indian woman from her Native society and from her kin, a separation to which no Indian man who married a non-Indian is exposed.

Some of you may remember that in 1987, the first recipient of the Robert S. Litvack Memorial Award was a young Chilean student, Carmen Quintana, who had been beaten by military police in Chile, set on fire, and left to die. She survived, spent many months here in Montreal for treatment, and then returned to Chile to testify against her attackers in a military court, something which took great personal courage because of the real risk to her safety. She was selected for the award not for being a victim, but for her courage in denouncing abuses and for the contribution she has made to the respect of the rule of law. All of our nominees remind us that human rights are fragile, that they need our vigilance, that our laws are not always perfect and that our courts are not always able to deliver justice. They remind us that it is determined individuals with a belief in the rule of law who can, and do make a difference.

SISTER MARY TWO AXE EARLEY

Mary Two Axe Earley was the first of these women to be offended by the notion that Indian women should be treated as a double minority with lesser rights in this country, first as Indians in a white society and secondly, as women within their own communities. She was born on the Kahnawake reserve, near Montreal, where she still lives. In 1967, she formed a movement called Equal Rights for Indian Women and the following year she presented a brief to the Royal Commission on the Status of Women. In 1972, she helped organize a national Indian women's organization called Indian Rights for Indian Women and has remained its Vice-President to this day. She has written, throughout the years, countless briefs to Ministers, task forces and Royal Commissions (of which we have many in this country) including a brief on the status of Indian women to the Task Force on Canadian Unity. In 1975, she was part of the Canadian delegation to the International Women's Year Conference in Mexico. In 1976, she was elected to the first Board of Directors of the Canadian Institute for the Advancement of Women. In 1979, she received an award from the Governor-General for her "tireless efforts to ensure rights for Native Indian women are equal to those of Native Indian men".

Firstly, I would like to mention that I come from the Kahnawake Mohawk Nation Territory, an Iroquois community that dates back to the earliest years of the sixteenth century. It was settled mainly by Mohawks and other members of the Six Nations Confederacy who, according to anthropologists and leading North American historians, had a socio-political system held together by a system of clans headed by a clan mother, who appointed the leader for the people. It was a true matrilineal social structure. Having been steeped in this culture by a grandmother born in the 1850s and by a grandfather who was a Medicine Man, I learned the proud history, legends and traditions and beliefs of my people.

These stories of our culture told to me when I was a child made it impossible for me to accept the manner in which the *Indian Act* governed my people, or its separate treatment of men and women. I felt it was in violation of the basis of my ancestral heritage, in violation of the intentions of the Great Spirit and in violation of the inalienable rights of every woman and man to be equal in the eyes of the law. In addition to my strong convictions and beliefs, a series of tragic episodes catapulted me into action. A childhood friend knocked on my door in the spring of 1965, anguishing over her eviction and banishment from her ancestral home. Her crime was marrying a status Indian from another reserve. After a long night trying to comfort her, she died of a broken heart in my arms the next morning. After this experience, I began networking with countless women across Canada.

As I met with these women, my eyes saw so much suffering, my senses were numbed by the words of anguish and despair from widows, mothers and daughters sharing the experience and pain of their exile. I became outraged by the grave psychological effects suffered by so many sisters because of their separation from their families and communities, stripped of their cultural identities as Indians. I was angry since I was made into a helpless victim and since I observed the devastating effects of this policy on so many women – many of whom sought refuge in drugs and alcohol, and escape through suicide. It was not only my Indian sisters who suffered, it was the Indian babies who, born in tents while their parents hunted and trapped, were never registered under the *Indian Act*. It was the war veteran who returned home to discover he was no longer Indian. It was the educated man who lost Indian status when he became a minister.

Let me give you a brief overview of our successful struggles to repeal section 12(1)(b) of the *Indian Act*. In 1965, I met with Judge Bonnelly of the United States Federal Court in Philadelphia who, as a young lawyer, had successfully overturned a ruling of the United States Customs and Immigration Service preventing Canadian-born Mohawks from working in the security-sensitive defence industry by using the *Jay Treaty* in their defence. He referred me to Professor John Humphrey at McGill University.

Professor Humphrey had been appointed to the Royal Commission on the Status of Women, and he was advised to prepare a brief of our case and present it to the Commission. In 1968, thirty Mohawk women travelled to Ottawa to present our brief. The Commission recommended that the discrimination in the *Indian Act* be ended. However, when the final report was published, that recommendation was deleted. In 1969, Equal Rights for Indian Women was founded as the first women's organization solely dedicated to the fight for the repeal of 12(1)(b). In 1973, the National Organization of Indian Rights for Indian Women was founded in Edmonton and in that same year, Jeanette Lavell had her case tried in the Supreme Court of Canada. Our hopes and dreams were shattered when her case was lost by one vote. In 1975, at the International Women's Conference held in Mexico City, in an unusual demonstration of international solidarity, the women of the world joined together to protest to the Canadian government the unjust treatment of Indian women in Canada. This protest was widely reported in the world press. In 1977, the government passed *Bill C-25*, a new human rights legislation which made no specific provision for the protection of the rights of Indian women. We protested. In 1979, several hundred women from the Tobique reserve, joined by women from every province, marched from Oka to Ottawa to protest discrimination. The Honourable Jake Epp, then Minister of Indian Affairs, promised us that a change would be made. That government was defeated along with our renewed hopes of emancipation.

In 1980, Premier René Lévesque, in defiance of the federal government's refusal to act upon the discriminatory practices of the *Indian Act*, declared that the Quebec government would always recognize an Indian woman's status and that it can never be abrogated. In 1981, the World Court of International Justice rendered its judgment in the *Lovelace* case and declared that Canada was in violation of its obligations under the United Nations Declaration of Human Rights. In 1984, *Bill C-47*, an *Act to amend the Indian Act*, was defeated in the Senate by Senator Charlie Watt and two other Liberal senators. In 1985, the newly elected government introduced *Bill C-31*, which became law.

In conclusion, we Indian women have travelled a long and arduous journey seeking justice and equality. Unfortunately, our journey must still continue as our work is yet unfinished. I am weary and would like to pass the fight on to the next generation of Indian women who will make that final climb to the top of the mountain. It is my hope that all the Indian nations of this land can work together to build an Indian unity within a Canadian unity. Together we can become an invincible force for peace and justice.

JEANETTE CORBIERE LAVELL

Jeannette Corbiere Lavell has an extensive background in education and youth work with her own people. She is of Ojibway/Odawa heritage and was educated in her own community, the Wikwemikong Unceded Reserve on Manitoulin Island, Ontario. She has completed courses in Social Work at Ryerson Polytechnical Institute, Linguistics and Psychology at University of Toronto, Anthropology at Laurention and Waterloo, and Education and Special Education at Western University. She obtained her teaching certificate in 1976 and has worked, first as a teacher and subsequently as a principal in the federal education system since 1980. Jeannette has, as well, extensive experience in counselling, social work and social animation, both at the grass-roots and management levels, beginning with the Company of Young Canadians in the mid 1960s, continuing through the Toronto Indian Friendship Centre, and Anduyaun, a Native women's residence in Toronto and, more recently, the First Nations Counselling Services in London. Jeannette was a founding board member and President of the Ontario Native Women's Association, as well as Executive Board Member of the Native Women's Association of Canada, Indian Rights For Indian Women, the Nishnawbe Institute, the Native Friendship Centre of Toronto and the North American Indian Travelling College in Akwesasne. She is currently employed in the Ontario Anti-Racism Secretariat, Ministry of Citizenship, and as a Senior Policy Advisor on Aboriginal Issues, she is responsible for developing an Aboriginal Anti-Racism Strategy in partnership with the Aboriginal Peoples of Ontario.

In 1970, Lavell came face to face, in a very personal way, with the issue of section 12(1)(b) of the Indian Act by marrying a non-Indian and losing her legal status as an Indian. She took the issue to court and argued the Canadian Bill of Rights, which precedes the present Charter of Rights, and which prohibited discrimination based on sex. She went before a County Court in Ontario and was told that the judge did not know why she was there because she had no legal standing and, after all, she should be glad that a white man had married her and taken her off the reserve. What was she complaining about? Undiscouraged, she took her case to the Federal Court of Appeal and there, three judges agreed with her position in a unanimous judgment. The Attorney General of Canada had the choice to appeal the case since he was faced with two pieces of federal legislation: the Canadian Bill of Rights and the Indian Act. He could have chosen to intervene in support of one or the other. However, he chose to support the Indian Act and appeal the case to the Supreme Court. There, the Court split five to four against Jeanette Lavell's position, over a strong dissent by Mr. Justice Laskin.

I would like to thank you for this award. It is a recognition that I personally feel quite honoured to share with my dear friend, Mary, who I have known right from the very beginning and who is one of our Elders, and an ideal for all of us. I just met Sandra for the first time today, since, for one reason, or another, we just have never had the opportunity to meet. So, this is quite an occasion. Sometimes I think we get a bit jaded when we are out there in the busy world and we do not think that people care. It is at occasions like tonight that we realize that there does come a time when people recognize our efforts. So, I thank all of you and, especially, Mrs. Litvack and her late husband for giving us this recognition tonight.

I would also like to thank and recognize my husband who has been very understanding and supportive over the past twenty years. We were married in 1970, and he is still here in 1990, so I guess we will survive into the next century. There is also our dear friend Dr. Thomas Naylor, a professor here at McGill, who has always encouraged us. Thank you for joining us.

I think there is one aspect of my court case that most people tend to overlook: the historical facts about the relations between Natives and non-Natives. I would like to briefly go over and share with you some of the historical facts ignored by a great many people and often disregarded by Native Peoples themselves.

Intermarriage with Europeans has been going on for quite a while, in fact, from the earliest times. The James Bay Cree married the Scots who manned the Hudson's Bay Trading Posts over several hundred years, giving us names like Sutherland, Stewart, McLeod, Kirsten, and Fiddler across the Canadian north. The Iroquois People have been intermarrying since the 1600's, leaving Welsh names such as Thomas, Summers and Henry or English names like Brant and Hill, as well as German and Scottish names like Doxtator or Jamieson. My own people, the Ojibway, had, since the earliest days of the fur trade, married the French, and later the Scots of the Hudson's Bay and Northwest Company. Although there has been no French influence in my own community since 1763, other than through the Catholic Church, we have French names like Trudeau, Recollet, Pelletier and Corbiere to this day. There is also considerable proof, through the work of Professor Barry Fell of Harvard University and others, that the Great Lakes at least were colonized extensively over the centuries by Norse and Celt traders as far back as 3000 B.C.

The point is that Native Peoples have always had relationships with the rest of the world and have intermarried, as do other ethnic groups, with other peoples of the world. Anyone denying this is doing so either through ignorance or for their own political and economic purposes. They are denying simple genetic and historical fact.

The original *Indian Act* recognized this intermarriage and defined "Indian" not only as someone whose parents were Indian, but also as anyone living in an Indian community and deemed by that community to be Indian. That was the original *Indian Act*. The entire notion of enfranchising Indians, either willingly or unwillingly, began around the turn of the century and was implemented probably for bureaucratic expediency, namely to administer as few Indians as possible and to assimilate even these as soon as possible. Giving status to the white wives of Indian men had the same thrust as missionaries, residential schools and the many poorly thought-out government programs since; to make the Indians more amenable to and dependent upon the dubious benefits of Western European civilization. When Canadians and Natives look at the question of marriage and Native women, we tend not to think about these historical facts.

I do not think I need to go back over the whole court case. As I said, I was married in 1970 and at that time, I was working with young Native People in Toronto. A friend of mine, Clayton Ruby, was quite active then with the rights of young people and I approached him for representation before the Department of Indian Affairs regarding my marriage.

During the course of our preparation, David obtained copies of the *United Nations Declaration of Human Rights* and the *Canadian Bill of Rights*. Both of these said that the individual is entitled to the protection of the law regardless of race, creed and sex. We thought this was clearly a point of law that should be looked into since section 12(1)(b) obviously denied my rights as a Native person and as a Canadian citizen.

I was not, nor was my husband, planning to take over the reserve and do all the terrible things insinuated by the media. My only interest was my right to be a member of my community. I was born and brought up on Wikwemikong reserve, all my relatives are there, and I speak Ojibway. Yet, all of a sudden, I was denied the basic right to even go back to my home. I could have been charged with trespassing had anyone so desired.

I went into the courts with the understanding that I should have the right to make a choice, an individual choice, as to whether I wanted to give up my rights as a Native person or not. That should have been my decision, not Indian Affairs' – who obviously had ulterior motives – or anyone else's. Not only was there section 12(1)(b) in the *Indian Act*, there were all those other sections that we tend to forget about and that Mary pointed out. I think there were fourteen other sections through which Indian Peoples lost their status. Research done by the Native Council of Canada found that half of all the Native Peoples in Canada at that time were not recognized legally as being Indian for these various reasons.

As Mrs. Litvack pointed out, Judge Grossberg made some very nice comments in the courtroom about how I should be happy to no longer legally be an Indian and glad that marriage to David took me away from the terrible reserves. He also said that I wanted to have my cake and eat it too. That was my introduction to the Canadian justice system. Prior to that, I was fairly idealistic about such things. I was educated in a convent by the Sisters of St. Joseph and I believed all the things that they told us. Now, all of a sudden, I was confronting a situation that was quite different. Although we won at the Federal Court of Appeal, it was overturned at the Supreme Court of Canada because of the pressure from Indian Affairs in cooperation with Native organizations, which were completely controlled at that time by men. The Attorney-General was pressured into appealing this case to the Supreme Court, and money was poured into a campaign against Native women. Native women were not very organized and had virtually no funds, unlike the Native "men's" organizations who were getting immense amounts of money to officially oppose us.

The campaign, quite aside from obvious sexism and racism, overlooked important points. For instance, information was "leaked" about white husbands going on the reserve, buying up property and taking over. This ignored the fact that no one other than a status Indian can own reserve land and that title has to be approved by the Band Chief and the Band Council. Furthermore, the reserve land, at that time and probably still to this day, is held in trust by the Crown through the Department of Indian and Northern Affairs. As Indian People, we do not own reserve land. It is held in trust for us. We are not landowners. We can build a house on our reserve and we can sell that house to another member of our community, but we cannot sell it to anyone off the reserve nor can we get collateral from a bank even if we spend a million on the house.

Another fear was that the reserves would be flooded by white husbands, but when we look at these reserves, they already had white women who had married Indian men and were living in the communities. These women were given Indian status and the same rights as Native People; they had the same rights under the *Indian Act* to reserve land as Indian men.

Most of the Native leaders within our Indian organisations, national as well as provincial, were men and most of them had white wives. Yet, they claimed that the Native women's movement was creating widespread division within Native communities, and they spread that impression. Although this was untrue, the effect of the campaign to discredit Native women's groups was that women's groups and human rights groups in Canada, in general, adopted a "hands-off" policy towards the "Lavell" case. They would not come out and say that this particular section was discriminatory to Native women, because they decided that it was a complex internal Native issue that they could not understand and, therefore, should not get involved with. In 1972, we approached then Prime Minister Pierre Elliot Trudeau, and he laughingly told us to go and convince our Indian men to accept us back and then the government would think about it.

In truth, there was no division in Indian communities over this issue prior to Indian Affairs' public relations campaign supporting the Appeal to the Supreme Court of Canada. In my own community, Chief John Wekegigig and the Band Council at the time supported me wholeheartedly. I still have their letters to prove it. The Chief had faced the same problem when his own daughter was in a similar situation, but he cautioned me not to think that I would have any success in the courts. Unfortunately, he was right. Before the case was decided, the Chief died in a car accident and his son, who was also his successor, listened to the media campaign and totally opposed me.

The Native Council of Canada representing non-status Indians and Metis was the only group other than the Native Women's Organization that came out in my support and made a presentation on my behalf. They did so in opposition to the National Indian Brotherhood, now the Assembly of First Nations.

Chiefs from across Canada were brought in by Indian Affairs to make it seem that Native Peoples were in support of this particular section. As Native women, we had to get there on our own. We did not have any funds or support from government, so we raised money through bake sales and bingos. We managed but we had to watch the big show put on by the National Indian Brotherhood, funded by Indian Affairs, and designed to persuade the Canadian public that there was division within the Native community over this issue.

The Supreme Court of Canada was obviously influenced by Indian Affairs as well as by Indian "men's" organizations and the media. The Supreme Court's decision said, in effect, that although the *Bill of Rights* guarantees Canadians equal protection under the law regardless of race, creed or sex, it did not apply to me because I was Indian. The extent to which the federal government had managed to manipulate the public mind was evident in the almost complete lack of public protest towards this decision. Essentially, the only reaction, other than from the Native Council and the Indian Women's groups, came from the late John Diefenbaker. I think he was quite disappointed with this decision and said in a letter to the Canadian people that he mourned the death of the Canadian *Bill of Rights*, which he had authored.

It is extremely difficult to imagine that a similar lack of public interest would have accompanied a case involving a Quebecois, Anglo-Saxon, black, or Jewish woman in this country. I do not think this decision or its impact would have been the same. What we had was another example of publicly-sanctioned discrimination towards Native Peoples.

It is hard not to question, in light of all this, whether anyone in Canada has a legal right to anything if it is not convenient for government, for big business or for any other vested interest. It is also hard to believe that the new constitution is going to bear any more weight than the *Bill of Rights* did in the long run. We shall wait and see. Indian Peoples see that the *Constitution* does not include them or recognize them in a fair way. I do not want to be too negative, but I question how so-called "self-determination" will be worked out within our communities, when this "self-determination" is to be financed and run by precisely the same alliance of federal government, Indian political organizations, and Indian political leaders that went to the Supreme Court of Canada to oppose Native women in 1973.

There is a somewhat happy ending to all this. In 1985, I was reinstated to my own community and my three children have also received their status. Looking back over the years, I realize that I did not take my "illegality" seriously. Sandra was saying to me that she also kept living as if she was not legally disentitled. Basically, that is what we had to do. Throughout this time, I was at home on the reserve and my children went to school on the reserve, although legally we were not entitled to do so. At least now we have that right, and it is not dependent on anyone making that decision for us. We need support from people like yourselves who are interested in making laws that fit real situations involving real people in real communities.

As Aboriginal Peoples in Canada, we are going to need a lot of support and a lot of understanding from the other citizens of this country regarding issues which are extremely important to all of us. These issues, like the rights of Native Peoples in general and Native women in particular, are complex and often painful to think about.

The importance of the *Lavell* case is not that it was a "woman's" issue, an "Aboriginal woman's" issue or even an "Aboriginal" issue. Its real importance, then and now, is that it shows very clearly to anyone who cares to look exactly how the Canadian judicial system functions; that a Canadian citizen can be denied the "protection of the law" for the purposes of political expediency.

As Aboriginal Peoples, and as citizens of Canada, we have specific legal rights and entitlements, which are established and clearly articulated in Canadian, British and international law. We do not need more government, "self-government" or otherwise, if it is to be a clone of the existing system; we do not need more costly, unworkable policies and programs if they are designed and implemented by bureaucrats or self-proclaimed Aboriginal leaders who neither know or care about our communities. From a broader prospective, all of us are aboriginal to this earth and subject to the ultimate laws of our Creator. Our legal system must reflect this recognition and we have the responsibility to ensure that it does.

SANDRA LOVELACE

Sandra Lovelace is a Malacite from Tobique in New Brunswick and she also lost her Indian status when she married. She did not even know she had lost her Indian status until she returned after a divorce.

She filed a complaint in 1977 with the United Nations Human Rights Committee arguing that Canada, through the Indian Act, was in violation of the International Covenant on Civil and Political Rights and that all domestic resources had been exhausted by the decision of the Supreme Court in the Lavell case. The wheels of justice move exceedingly slowly, but in 1985, much to the embarrassment of Canada, she won an opinion in favour of her position. That was also the year in which the Canadian government enacted the Charter of Rights, which would have made it even more difficult to defend the offending section. In 1985, the Canadian government finally repealed section 12(1)(b) and fulfilled the objective sought for so long by all three women.

I am also very pleased and honoured to be here this evening, and to meet my two sisters, Mary and Jeannette. I am also very happy to receive this Award.

I would like to speak about the effect of *Bill C-31* on the Tobique reserve. Section 12(1)(b) of the *Indian Act,* as we have heard, stated that all Indians of female gender, if they marry non-Indians, lose their status and also their right to benefits as Native People. This, of course, did not apply to Indians of male gender. I felt, when I returned to Tobique in 1977, that this was not right. So, when I was approached to lodge a complaint against Canada at the United Nations, I welcomed the opportunity and as a result, Canada was found to be in breach of its obligations under international covenant because the *Indian Act* denied my legal right to be in the community of my birth. As a result of my successful case, *Bill C-31* came into law in June 1985. The *Charter of Rights* had been enacted two months earlier.

Since the passage of *Bill C-31*, the population in Tobique has increased from a total of 800 to 1300 persons. Though *Bill C-31*, Indian women, their first generation children, and even some second generation children, have returned home. However, since Indians can no longer pass on Indian status to their non-Indian spouses and some non-Indians stay on the reserve even after a marriage break-up, these spouses have become a financial burden on the Band. The federal government does not pay for any of their expenses, such as medical costs. Further, because of *Bill C-31*, different categories of Indians have emerged: registered Indians with two Indian parents, and registered Indians with one Indian parent. The second type cannot pass on status.

I would like to see *Bill C-31* being looked on as a positive change instead of a negative one. However, even more, I would like to see national lobbying by our leaders and grassroot organizations to pressure the federal government into fulfilling their promise that no band will suffer as a result of the passage of *Bill C-31*.

PANEL ONE
NATIVE SELF-DETERMINATION AND JUSTICE

SAM STEVENS

Sam Stevens, a Native of Maniwaki, Quebec graduated from University of British Columbia Law School in 1983. He is both an instructor at the university and Director of their Native Law Program. Half of his time is spent in Native law private practice. He has also been an instructor at the Native law program at the University of Saskatchewan. This program is a pre-law summer program for prospective Native law students. Professor Stevens has published in the area of Native law, and among his publications are papers on the subject of custody of Indian children, Indian control of education and the effect of international treaties on Native Peoples. He is involved in a cross-cultural training project for justice personnel in British Columbia and is currently working on a submission on the same subject for the Manitoba Justice Inquiry.

NATIVE PEOPLE WITHIN THE JUDICIAL SYSTEM

During the past couple of years, we have had a great deal of media attention centered on Aboriginal Peoples and the justice system. In part, it is because of the Donald Marshall Prosecution Inquiry into the wrongful conviction of an innocent Aboriginal man. Increasingly, Canadians are becoming aware of the problems that Aboriginal Peoples face in the present justice system. They know that there is a disproportionate number of our people in federal and the provincial judicial institutions: statistics show, in fact, that almost ten percent of the population in our federal correctional institutions are Aboriginal People, although across Canada, Aboriginal Peoples only represent two percent of the population. In some of the prairie regions, the federal population numbers up to thirty-two percent. If you think that is bad, in our provincial institutions, especially in the prairies, it varies between forty-five to sixty percent.

To most Canadians, the present justice system is something to hold in reverence. It does a number of things: it seems to curb abuse of power, protect human rights, and resolve things fairly. For Aboriginal Peoples, the court system, the lawyers, the police, and the jails present a different image, one which they neither believe nor have any confidence in. It is a system which they say does not act as their protector, but one which denies their laws, forces upon them a foreign set of values and beliefs, and takes away their rights as Aboriginal Peoples. Why is there such a divergence in view between Aboriginal Peoples and non-Aboriginal Peoples in respect to the present justice system? Why is it that non-Natives seem to respect this justice system, while Aboriginal People are saying they have no confidence that it will ever give them justice?

To understand this basic difference, it is very important to look at history. History gives us some idea of the nature of the problem. When Europeans, primarily French and English, first made contact with Aboriginal Peoples in the Maritimes, Aboriginal First Nations had very well-developed institutions of justice, politics, and laws, as did the English and the French. Originally the French and the English lived with the Aboriginal First Nations on the basis of mutual respect. The First Nations continued to live by their own institutions, but as the European population increased, a basic problem had to be answered: how were these very different cultures going to live with one another? Which laws and institutions were going to apply, and where? Would each society continue to use their own justice system or would the English legal system apply to both the French and the Aboriginal First Nations?

The English colonial government proceeded to ignore the previously recognized Aboriginal way of life and imposed their law and justice system on all Aboriginal Peoples. By 1867, the federal and provincial governments divided between themselves the powers to make laws for all Canadians. The First Nations played no role in this decision. The federal government was given power by the *British North America Act* to make laws especially for Indians and their lands. In 1876, the first *Indian Act* came into force.

The *Indian Act* had the effect of controlling virtually every aspect of an Aboriginal person's life. It was an act which specifically forced Aboriginal Peoples, as individuals and as First Nations, not only to adapt, but also to conform to the Canadian justice system. It represented, and still represents, a tremendous change from Native customary justice systems. For example, in my province, the Nis'ga Indians of the northwest had highly developed systems of law with an entirely different philosophical basis than Canadian law. First, the Nis'ga were told they did not have any right to most of their traditional lands. Second, they were not allowed to care for their lands as they had been taught to do. Aboriginal customary law required the Nis'ga to treat the land in a stewardship role. They were taught to keep it in as good a condition as possible for the use of future generations. In contrast, the new colonial law allowed people to exploit the land.

The justice system imposed on Aboriginal Peoples was also foreign because of other basic legal concepts. Words such as "guilty", "innocent", "lawyer", "jury", and "peers" had no equivalents in Aboriginal languages. Furthermore, a central concept of non-Native legal systems is the adversarial process: the right to face your adversary before a neutral third person. In contrast, traditional Native societies valued conciliation and concern for the victim. They sought to restore peace and harmony to the community. In their way of resolving disputes, the two parties took the matter before the Elders and leaders of the nation in order to resolve the conflict and restore peace and harmony to the community. Even though Natives have been forced to live according to non-Native laws, they continue to practice their traditional ways.

Their customary law often conflicts with Canadian law. For example, Aboriginal Peoples continued to hunt and fish according to their customary laws even when federal and provincial laws forbade them. They were then charged and convicted for hunting and fishing illegally. The courts maintain Natives have no right to live in as they once did, nor to define their rights on the basis of different values and principles. Is it any wonder today that Aboriginal People do not believe in the present justice system?

What can be done to resolve some of the difficulties which Aboriginal People face within the present justice system? How can the present legal system accommodate Aboriginal beliefs and values? How can Aboriginal People regain the ability to resolve conflicts in a way which makes sense to them in their own communities?

First, let us look at how the Canadian court system can become fair for Aboriginal Peoples. Part of the problem is that judges and lawyers do not realize how much of a disadvantage an Aboriginal person faces in the courts. His beliefs and values may actually operate against him. Let me give you an example: most Aboriginal People still place great value in their Elders; it is very disrespectful in a conversation with an Elder to look directly into his eyes. As a result, the Aboriginal person seldom looks directly at the judge. When he comes into a court, he equates the judge with a person of authority, like his Elder. However, in this adversarial justice system, the Aboriginal person's body-language indicates to the judge that he is not telling the truth. Few lawyers and judges understand these problems and it is difficult for us to communicate that kind of thinking to our judiciary so as to make the trial process more fair.

Similarly, in traditional society, a non-interference ethic prevented an Aboriginal person from interfering in another's life. It prevented him from criticizing or giving advice to another; each person was free to make his or her own choice. This ethic prevented parents from telling their children when to do something, such as when to eat. It goes without saying that from a judge's standpoint, this absence of parental control goes against the Aboriginal person in a custody case. Losing your child is a disastrous result from a difference in ethics.

Solutions to cross-cultural differences

One of the ways of dealing with this problem is cross-cultural education. In order for a culture to take into account another culture's beliefs and values, each must learn to understand the other. When I talk to judges, it is clear that they realize that Canadian society is changing. In Vancouver, for example, the majority is no longer Anglo-Saxon. If we are to give any real assistance to people who come before our justice system, we have to understand the individual in terms of where they come from, their culture, their beliefs and their values. Future judges are going to have to know much more about different cultures than they presently know, and such cross-cultural insight would enable judges to accommodate Aboriginal beliefs and values in a practical way within the non-Native justice system.

Another way of resolving the problem of cultural difference is to give First Nations more responsibility in making decisions. For example, one of the options proposed by the the South Island Tribal Council was to give them a major role in the pre-trial diversion area. Section 4 of the *Young Offenders Act* allows for diversion programs to be developed; alternative measures that can be used to deal with our young offenders. The young offenders must consent to participate in the program, but, prior to this, the young offender must be advised of his right to counsel and accept responsibility for the offending act. The proposal put forward by the First Nations of the South Island Tribal Council would see the establishment of an Accountability Board composed of five prominent and well-respected members of the community. The members of the Accountability Board would interview the young offender, and a report would then be submitted as to whether the individual was a person that they could help. If the youth was accepted, they would then enter into a contract with the youth and assign an Elder to him. The youth would then be connected to his extended family for rehabilitation according to customary family principles.

The real advantage of this approach is that it provides an alternative within the present justice system. This process is not only culturally meaningful but also allows the community to play a major role in the rehabilitation of the youth. The same approach could be used for adult offenders, if the legislation were amended to permit it.

Another very successful model of how a court could involve a community dealing with their own people occurred on Vancouver Island last year. The judge was faced with a custody issue involving an Aboriginal child and two Aboriginal parents. The judge asked a Tribal Council of Elders to give him recommendations on how they would see the custody issue settled. The Council, after taking into account the lineage of the child and other cultural factors, found a way to settle the custody dispute. The judge then incorporated the Council's views into his decision. This model has been used in a number of places in Canada, particularly in the Northwest Territories, and it seems to work well.

Many of our Aboriginal leaders are going to say that these solutions are band-aid remedies. They will say that because of the inherent bias against visible minorities and the fact the system is based on different values and beliefs, they can never hope to receive justice within the present justice system. As you may know, the Marshall Prosecution Inquiry Report was released last week and the Attorney-General of Nova Scotia publicly apologized to Donald Marshall. The inquiry was regarding the wrongful conviction of a young Micmac Indian in Nova Scotia. The findings of that inquiry reinforced many of the beliefs of Aboriginal leaders in this country. The Commissioners found that the Nova Scotia justice system was riddled with racism; that a major factor in Donald Marshall's mistreatment was the fact that he was an Indian. It was very clear, they said, that Donald Marshall had told the truth and that his truth had been systematically disregarded.

The Commissioners proposed the development of a Native criminal court. In this system, an Indian Justice of Peace would hear minor *Criminal Code* offences: summary conviction offences such as assault. Indians charged with more serious offences, or offences that happened off the reserve, would still be heard by the present court system. Many of our Aboriginal leaders are going to say that this recommendation does not go far enough. What they really want is their own justice system.

Indeed, why should we not be allowed to resolve disputes in a way which makes sense to our own people? We cannot possibly do a worse job than the present justice system is doing. Even your own judges are telling us this. It is obvious that there is a problem with how the justice system treats Aboriginal People. The challenge now is for us, as Aboriginal and non-Aboriginal People, to work together and resolve the serious problems that Aboriginal People face on a daily basis within the present Canadian justice system.

Réjean Paul

Judge Réjean Paul is a Quebec Superior Court Judge. During the 1970s, he led an inquiry into organized crime. From 1976 to 1981, he was Director for Quebec in the Federal Ministry of Justice. In the early 1980s, he was appointed Commissioner, then Vice-President of the Law Reform Commission of Canada. He was then appointed Judge to the Superior Court of Quebec, as well as Deputy-Judge to the Supreme Court of the Northwest Territories. He teaches criminal law courses at the University of Ottawa and is the President of the Cree-Naskapi Commission.

L'ADMINISTRATION DE LA JUSTICE DANS LA PROVINCE DE QUÉBEC

Alors quel est le problème de l'administration de la justice dans la province de Québec? Dans son rapport de 1986 au Ministère de la Justice, un groupe d'experts faisait les constatations suivantes: de nouvelles orientations concernant l'administration de la justice auprès des Autochtones se doivent d'être élaborées. En effet, les efforts amorcés en 1972 par le Ministère de la Justice lors de la production du Rapport de la justice au-delà du 50ième parallèle et les multiples tentatives d'adaptation de la Cour itinérante du district d'Abitibi aux diverses réalités Autochtones nous forcent de constater que le bilan en matière de justice est plus ou moins satisfaisant.

D'une part, on constate que le personnel de la Cour itinérante, tout en reconnaissant fondamentalement les multiples barrières linguistiques et culturelles entre les Blancs et les Autochtones, souligne l'absence d'une organisation matérielle et logistique permettant à la Cour de répondre adéquatement aux besoins des diverses communautés. D'autre part, les Autochtones, tout en exprimant le désir de connaître davantage le système et de participer plus activement à l'administration de la justice, critiquent un système judiciaire dont les délais, la procédure et les sentences rendent inefficaces la justice dans les communautés. En effet, tant les Autochtones que les intervenants blancs dans ce domaine soulèvent des problèmes concrets.

À titre indicatif, soulignons les problèmes suivants: premièrement, un manque flagrant d'information et de communication dont souffrent les populations Autochtones; deuxièmement, une perte d'autorité familiale et communautaire vécue depuis le contact des Blancs commerçants, ministres du culte, enseignants, officiers de justice et autres à qui s'en sont remis les Autochtones; troisièmement, une criminalité nouvelle s'accroissant sans cesse en raison du nouveau mode de vie qui assaille les communautés et des sentences que l'on considère inadéquates; quatrièmement, de trop longs délais entre la commission des infractions, les comparutions et les prononcés des sentences; cinquièmement, l'absence de mise en application des règlements communautaires appropriés à ces communautés; sixièmement, une barrière linguistique presque infranchissable en raison du manque d'interprètes qualifiés et suffisamment informés sur les concepts de base de notre système judiciaire; septièmement, une différence de conception de la justice de la part des Autochtones qui souhaitent davantage aider un contrevenant que de le punir et qui saisissent mal les distinctions que nous apportons aux notions de culpabilité et de responsabilité et qui enfin, ne comprennent pas vraiment toute la portée de la notion de la présomption d'innocence.

Autres problèmes: la rapidité des voyages des membres de la Cour et les séjours absolument trop brefs dans les communautés; la préparation inadéquate de la défense de l'accusé tant en raison des barrières culturelles que des entrevues trop courtes avec les avocats de la défense qui ne passent dans la communauté qu'au moment de visites de la Cour; des sentences trop souvent indulgentes eu égard aux crimes commis, nonobstant le désir de conciliation; les taux élevés de récidive dans les communautés; l'impossibilité de la Cour de tenir vraiment compte des problèmes sociaux et d'intervenir à ce niveau; un manque d'intégration des services de justice et des services sociaux et de médiation; enfin, et pour toutes ces causes, on constate et on déplore la perte de confiance de la population Autochtone face à notre système de justice.

Un tel bilan justifie donc à plusieurs égards la remise en question par les Autochtones de l'autorité de la justice blanche dans leurs communautés. Ils illustrent de plus l'importance incontestable que des changements fondamentaux et urgents soient introduits au niveau du Québec et dans la région de la Baie James en matière de justice. Notre Commission Cree-Naskapi concluait au même effet dans notre rapport de 1988.

As we said in our 1988 report, the availability of a court is another major concern. Under the existing system, a travelling Provincial Court Judge visits each community, and in some cases, the visit is more regular than others. The Judge hears cases involving federal and provincial laws and regulations, and Cree or Naskapi by-laws, although the travelling prosecutor tends not to prosecute offenses under local by-laws. This travelling court has suspended its travel into some communities since August 22, 1988. The itinerant Provincial Court Judge Coutu refuses, and rightly so, to hear cases in those communities which lack proper facilities. As a result, persons with summons to appear in court must sometimes travel hundreds of miles.

The Cree and Naskapi have sought comprehensive changes in the justice system. They want a system of permanent local courts based on traditional Native dispute resolution systems. Their rationale is that their people will have greater respect for a system they perceive to be their own. Chief Billy Diamond of the Wiskaginish Band described the need for a comprehensive justice system in the community:

> First of all, you need some physical facilities, whether in the police station or in the proposed community centre. You need a court system that the people will respect. You need a facility where you can have an audience, where there is actually a court in place, that young and old people can see. You also need a system that works on a daily basis, where there is involvement of court workers, probation officers, people to monitor and counsel the offenders.

The issue of sentencing and incarceration was raised with the Commission, especially as it applies to young offenders. At present, communities are not equipped to deal with offenders who are sentenced to serve a period of incarceration in an institution. As a result, such offenders are sent to a non-Native community. Local offenders normally get sent away, and when they return, everyone is worse off. What we recommend is that incarceration be done within the community.

J'ajouterai à ces commentaires que nos Indiens ne reçoivent pas les services judiciaires dont les autres citoyens de notre pays bénéficient. Il n'y a pas de procès par jury dans les communautés comme c'est le cas dans les Territoires du Nord-Ouest. La division familiale de la Cour Supérieure, sa division civile et administrative, la Cour du Québec (sa division civile) ne siègent pas dans les communautés Cries. Pourtant une ville québecoise de deux milles citoyens a son hôpital, son centre sportif et son centre communautaire. Nos Cris doivent se déplacer à Val d'Or à un coût exorbitant pour faire valoir leurs droits. C'est une situation intolérable. Comment se fait-il que les premiers habitants du Canada reçoivent de nous tous un si piètre traitement? Il y a, à mon avis, urgence d'agir pour que nos frères indiens et nos soeurs indiennes se sentent à l'aise dans un système judiciaire conçu par eux, pour eux, géré et dirigé par eux.

Natives have lived in what we now call Canada for thousands of years before the English and the French colonized it. They had their own established ways of living and settling disputes. These mechanisms were based not on our adversarial system of confrontation, determination of guilt and then punishment of the offender by the state, but on mediation between the parties, with restitution to the victims and to the community. There was not just one person sitting in judgment. Community Elders and leaders settled disputes, based on what they believed was best for the whole community. This community-based approach to justice may be different than our method of resolving disputes but that does not make it any less valid.

Addressing Native concerns

The list of Native criticisms of our judicial system is long. They argue that it is not relevant to the daily lives of Native Peoples. The courtroom is an unfamiliar and intimidating institution, conceptually removed from Indigenous processes of social control based on mediation and restitution. Most courts are located some distance from the reserve, making it difficult for Natives to attend. In addition, many Natives, especially those from rural reserves, have problems understanding English. When you add that all the faces in the justice system are white, that Natives constitute a small minority of the population, and that Natives suffer from stereotyping and other forms of discrimination, you begin to understand why they are unhappy with the current system of administering justice.

The Royal Commission considered many possibilities for dealing effectively with these problems. One approach would be to deal with each problem individually. For example, language problems could be solved by Native interpreters available in court. Their lack of familiarity with court procedure and concepts could be tackled by establishing a professional court worker service. Their isolation from judges could be met by actually holding court on reserves. Their concerns about using their own traditional ways of settling disputes could be addressed by making some adaptation to the structure of sentencing.

However, this is a piecemeal approach. It does not address the differences between Native and white societies or the argument that justice for Natives must be on Native terms and according to Native concepts. Having looked at the problem and the options, the Commission believes the time has come to deal with these broader concerns by establishing, on an experimental basis, a Native criminal court that will allow Natives some measure of direct control over the administration of justice within their communities. The Commission described their proposal for the creation of community-controlled Native criminal court:

> We wish to make it clear that the Native criminal court we propose will administer the same law as applies to all other Canadians; we do not propose a separate system of Native law but rather a different process for administering on the reserve certain aspects of the criminal law. Laws enacted by Parliament or the legislative assembly will continue to apply to Natives, and as a safeguard for accused persons, the Charter will apply in any Native criminal court.

The Commission found two precedents of reserves in the province of Quebec that have established courts under this authority: Kahnawake and St-Régis. The Court of Kahnawake, which they took the opportunity to visit during their deliberations, is a positive example of how Native Peoples can successfully take some control over their own justice institutions. While limited in the scope of their authority by the terms of their appointment under section 107 of the *Indian Act*, the Native Justices of the Peace have managed to take account of the particular needs of Native People while still upholding the laws of the larger community. By using Native court personnel and court workers, an informal court process and sentencing with community and individual needs in mind, the Native Justices of the Peace appear to have struck an appropriate balance between the old and new ways. They are now attempting to obtain funding to include mediation and diversion facilities in the range of services provided. Under the Kahnawake model, the Court has jurisdiction over summary conviction offences committed within the boundaries of the reserve whether by

Natives or non-Natives. Appeals are either taken to federal or provincial courts depending on the offence.

Critics of the Court of Kahnawake feel that by simply enforcing the laws of the majority, the Court does not go far enough in recognizing the customary law of Native Peoples. It is true that courts established under the *Indian Act* do not provide an appropriate answer to the question of the full acceptance of Native justice mechanisms. However, with the benefit of the services recommended in the Marshall Report proposal, the Kahnawake model provides a good starting point for discussion.

That avenue is thus very interesting. I know that the Quebec Department of Justice is on the verge of tabling a proposal for reforms on the judicial system which, I hope, will deal with many of the Native concerns. At the Superior Court level, we will have to act rapidly following that reform. Furthermore, the judiciary will not only have to sit in these communities, but also to learn about the history, tradition, and culture of our Indian friends. The judges will have to go and live in the communities, discuss with the leaders, Elders and the younger generation.

Proposals for change

Here are some elements of solutions. First of all, let the Indians decide what kind of judicial system they want. Let them take into account their traditions and culture in order to create a judicial system that is up to their needs and expectations. The self-government which Aboriginal Peoples are so loudly demanding must not be allowed to turn into a puppet government with the strings being pulled by either Ottawa or the provinces. The same rule, from my point of view, should apply to the administration of justice and the judicial system.

Two: the alternate dispute resolution systems which have been in existence for years in the Indian communities should become the basis of a sound Indian judicial system. It worked well for years. Why do we try to impose our system which is not suited to their tradition and lifestyle?

Since the conflict between Aboriginal and European systems of justice seems to be most acute in relation to criminal law, I will start there. There has, in recent years, been some interest in the use of mediation in the field of criminal law. Projects have been set up to attempt, in certain cases, to bring the perpetrators and victims of the crime together for the purposes of resolving disputes that might never have escalated to the level of criminal charges if there had been communication in the first place. The focus in these mediation sessions is less on determining in a microscopic factual way exactly what happened and more on what the parties' perceptions of the conflict are and how the tension and, perhaps, fear that exists between the parties can be reduced.

Third: only those judges and lawyers who have an interest in Aboriginal law should be allowed to help our Indian brothers and sisters. It is one thing to know what the Supreme Court of Canada said in *Guérin, Calder, Simon, Drybones* and other important cases but it is quite another thing to sit in the communities and try to help the leaders to cope with a major problem like the drug and alcohol problem. The easy way is to send the offender to jail, but is it the right thing to do? Just imagine a young Cree, who speaks only Cree, sitting in his cell at Bordeaux in Montreal with all kinds of white criminals. What kind of future does he have?

Four: we have to change the rules of evidence to take into account the oral tradition of our Indian friends. For the sake of example: hearsay is important in the day-to-day operation of an Indian community. It is not because Lord So-and-So decided centuries ago in England that hearsay evidence is inadmissible that we should not invent special rules of evidence to adjust to the cultural background of Indians.

Five: education is essential in order to build a strong self-made Indian judicial system. Ottawa and the provinces should, from my point of view, invest massive amounts of money towards Native education in order to help our Indian brothers to build a strong and up-to-their-expectations judicial system.

Finally, I dare to hope that in Canada, in the very near future, *La Presse* newspaper will not need to publish a commentary such as the one published on August 12, 1988, and I translate:

> We know that the First Nations of Canada are the least of our worries; it is so obvious that we have a fatalistic attitude towards them. Nevertheless, for a country that does not appear anywhere on a black list as a human rights violator, it makes it that much easier for us to interfere with the human rights of our Aboriginal People.

Harry LaForme

Harry S. LaForme is a lawyer who, while in private practice, specialized in the area of Aboriginal rights law. Mr. LaForme is an Anishinabe from the Mississauga of New Credit First Nations in southern Ontario where his family continues to be active in the First Nations government.

Mr. LaForme has extensive experience in the area of Indian land claims. In his former position as the Indian Commissioner of Ontario, Mr. LaForme submitted a discussion paper to the governments of Canada, Ontario and First Nations on First Nations land claims. He subsequently served as Co-chair to the National Chiefs Committee on Claims which contributed significantly to the development of the new specific claims initiative under the government's Native Agenda.

A graduate of Osgoode Hall Law School, Mr. LaForme was called to the Ontario Bar in 1979. His law experience includes special emphasis on Aboriginal and treaty rights issues as well as constitutional matters, including the Charter of Rights and Freedoms. In addition to his current duties, Mr. LaForme teaches the "Rights of Indigenous Peoples" law course at Osgoode Hall Law School in Toronto.

FAIRNESS AND PARTNERSHIP IN JUSTICE SYSTEMS

I have found that there are three specific components to justice: the first is his Lordship, the title given to a Superior Court Judge; the second is the system which deals with the conflict; and the third is underlying equity or fairness. It is this latter aspect, the fairness component, which I turn to and rely upon in my private practice of Native law. I would like to share with you reflections upon my experience as an Indian Commissioner facing the problem of violence on reserves.

Justice is much more than a fair criminal trial. "Fairness" comes into play long before someone is taken into custody and charged with criminal or quasi-criminal offenses. Individuals, particularly Native People, must be looked after before they get arrested and before they find themselves in the judicial process. Increasing the number of Native Justices of the Peace is not the solution since they treat the individual only after-the-fact and their powers are limited to sentencing. So, our concern must take us into the communities and see how their fight against violent crime can be supported.

My experience in court has repeatedly shown that Native People wonder whether there is any justice or fairness to this system. When the issue is treaties and their basic right to fish and hunt as was their custom, they have to pay a tremendous price in order to exercise their rights. In most cases of Indian fishermen that I have represented, they supplemented their income annually by only several hundred dollars. However, it seemed more important to the system to spend tremendous amounts of money to prosecute these people and cut their incomes by a few hundred dollars. I still find that extremely offensive. In all the years that I have defended Indians in court on treaty rights issues, I cannot honestly say I felt we ever won. It was not a victory if my clients did not have to pay the full fine. A judge would say, "You are guilty, but I find the offence in keeping with the traditional methods. So, a fifty dollar fine is in order" or "I am going to suspend sentence". That was not a victory, nor a system recognizing the rights of these people.

It is not enough that they deny the right to hunt and fish to Indian Peoples, notwithstanding that this right is specifically set out in treaties as clearly as possible. It is a concerted and on-going effort to prevent the treaties from being interpreted in a way favourable to Indians. The prosecutors and the courts do not want to give favourable interpretations. In fact, the most creative arguments on earth are not going to render decisions favourable to Indian hunting and fishing rights. If that is justice, then it is wrong and must change.

I was a child advocate for the Official Guardian's Office in Ontario and I was particularly delighted with that position, given the province of Ontario's initiative in the area of child welfare. They had passed a statute which recognized the special and unique characteristics of Indians and their heritage, and the statute spelled out that recognition in legislation. One would think that this was progress, except that words are not sufficient to ensure that justice is done. It was really disheartening and actually frustrating to learn that in most cases in the court system, judges and lawyers representing the Children's Aid Society or the parents all thought "An Indian is an Indian: if you place a Mohawk child with an Ojibway family, what is the big deal? They are still Indian." They just did not seem to want to understand. It was not only so with the lawyers, but also with the courts and with the judges themselves.

Once we brought a Chief and family worker in from the community to the courtroom, where they gave poignant, sincere evidence as to the good of their community. They were litigating against the child being placed with an Indian woman living in

Toronto, and the Children's Aid Society was fighting for the placement of this baby with its maternal aunt on the reserve (the legislation says that priority will be given to the extended family). The opposition evidence was as follows: in that community they have facilities to deal with drug and alcohol abuse, they have facilities to deal with young offenders, and they have counselling. The lawyer representing the non-Indian interest therefore argued that these facilities were evidence of the kind of problems that exist in that community. They have to have drug and alcohol abuse centres and they have to have counselling units for their kids. Do you want to send the child up to that community? That is how they interpreted the evidence presented by the community. What I am impressing upon you is the fact that attitudes and conduct today still allow people to argue this way in the courtroom.

I was involved in several land claims and I again question the fairness or justice of the system. For example, with respect to my own First Nations: the federal government validated our land claim to two hundred acres of land in Mississauga which they agreed was taken from us without proper authority, surrender, or lawful process, and sold to someone 130 years ago. However, they said, "It does not matter. You do not have a claim to that land." And when we asked why, they answered, "It is simple: even though we unlawfully took that land from you and sold it out from under your feet, and even though the Treaty said we were not to do that, we put money for the sale into your account one hundred and fifty years ago, so, you do not have any grievance now." Yet, is it true that somebody can take your house from underneath you and sell it, and so long as they put the money in your bank account, you do not have a cause of action? That is ridiculous. Where is the justice in that? Where is the fairness? Where is the equity?

There has been some discussion about alternative dispute resolution. When I first accepted the position as Commissioner to the Indian Commission of Ontario, I thought that my function was to initiate alternative dispute resolution processes. Instead, my role is to attempt to identify who is responsible for the issue. Virtually every issue that comes to the Commission is one which everybody agrees is bad for Aboriginal Peoples and needs to be addressed, but no one agrees about who is responsible for doing something about it. That is where we come in.

The Indian Commission of Ontario and policing programs

What have we done in the Indian Commission? It was established in 1978. The first Commissioner was Justice Patrick Hart; the second, Roberta Jamieson, a Mohawk Indian from Six Nations, who is now the Ombudsman of Ontario; I am the third. In the history of the Commission, there is one significant program that has evolved, and that is the policing of Indian reserves by Indian People. It is an excellent program, though not a perfect one. Recently, the Department of Indian Affairs issued a report on Indian policing across Canada. In that report, the Ontario police program is recognized as perhaps the best in Canada. Beyond that, I do not know whether the Indian Commission has really accomplished anything, because serious change comes through change in attitude.

The policing program presently has 132 constables to police some 122 reserves in Ontario. The OPP have done a study that says to properly police, there need to be 218 constables. The reason we do not have 218 is the jurisdictional problem of who is responsible for the cost of policing Indian reserves. The federal government claims that, according to the *Constitution*, the provinces are responsible for the administration of justice, which would include policing reserves. So, they fight back and forth about who is going to pay for the additional constables that both agree are necessary.

There are several reasons why these problems are turned over to the Indian Commission. One, governments do not want to set a precedent. If they took direct responsibility for a decent program in one geographical area, they might be required to put that same program in other areas across Canada. The second reason is the whole jurisdictional question. The third reason, of course, is money.

Twenty-two percent of Canadian status Indians live in Ontario. Thirty-eight percent in Canada live off the reserves; although, in Ontario, this percentage is as high as forty-five percent. Violent crimes on Indian reserves are six times the national average. Given the presence of those populations, what is the justification for arguing over whose jurisdiction it is? Surely, there is an overlap of jurisdiction. I do not care whether the federal government is sixty-five percent responsible for policing, or ninety. The answer is simple, collectively, we can work out a solution in the near future if we choose to. Give the jurisdiction to the Indians.

I agree there should be separate justice systems. We must, in the meantime, look to improve the existing justice system. When asked in a recent interview whether or not there should or could be an independent justice system for Native Peoples, the Justice Minister concluded "no". He felt that the problem could be addressed simply in other ways. For example, the program in Saskatchewan to get more Native People in law. He said that he wants to concentrate on those kind of programs because they are "do-able", to use his words. Yes, they are do-able – in fact, they have been done. We have Native courtworkers and we have had them for years. We also have six or more Native Justices of Peace. As far as lawyers, I recently received some statistics on the Saskatchewan law program. That program was started in 1973, and the statistics to date suggest that there were 939 Native applicants; 515 were accepted into the program and, of these, only 118 have been called to the Bar. This low percentage of graduates suggests that the program is not as effective as hoped. Some other alternatives must be explored. What the Justice Minister is suggesting has already been attempted by programs in place since 1973, and, still, Indians are disproportionately represented in the penitentiary population, and Indians reserves still have a violent crime rate six times that of the national average.

There has to be rethinking: there has to be a partnership, and that partnership simply cannot be in terms of blaming the other group for not taking responsibility. We all have responsibility, each and every one of us, and that includes the provinces. Our task is to share this responsibility, and we have seen how the government can take action when it has to, so they must show the same commitment to solving Indian problems as quickly as possible. They have not only a moral obligation, they have a legal obligation.

The Ontario Declaration of Political Intent

In 1985, the Minister of Native Affairs in Ontario, Ian Scott, and the Minister of Indian Affairs and Northern Development, signed a document called the *Declaration of Political Intent*. A lot of people suggest the document is nothing more than a re-commitment to sit down and resolve recognized problems. I say they are wrong. It is more than a re-commitment. It is a legal obligation. It reads:

> The parties declare their commitment to enter into tripartite discussions to resolve issues relating to Indian First Nations' self-government mat-

ters and arrangements with respect to the exercise
of jurisdiction and powers by First Nations' governments in Ontario ... The parties agree that the
matters with which the tripartite process on Indian First Nations' self-government may deal,
with the approval of the participants, shall include: the forms, institutions, legal and constitutional status, source of jurisdiction, land issues
and financial base of First Nations' governments
in Ontario and the clarification of areas of jurisdictional overlap and arrangements with respect
to the exercise of jurisdiction by governments in
Ontario.

There is more than a mere declaration of political intent: there
is a legal commitment to sit down and talk about alternatives, including justice and jurisdiction for Indian Peoples. Governments,
whether provincial or federal, are responsible for the circumstances that we are in today. They are responsible because it is
their programs, their courts, their laws. We are what we are today
because they have "taken care" of us. They should, then, do the
necessary financing to correct that. So, it is not a question of jurisdiction, rather it is a question of sharing responsibility for changing the direction of programs. The actual management of that
change belongs to us.

JANE DICKSON-GILMORE

Jane Dickson-Gilmore is a lecturer in Law at Carleton University. Her work with the Mohawk Nation at Kahnawake toward the development of a separate, tradition-based legal system continues, and has been elaborated in detail in her recently completed doctoral dissertation in Law at the London School of Economics, entitled "Resurrecting the Peace: Separate Justice and the Invention of Legal Tradition in the Kahnawake Mohawk Nation".

THE INCENTIVE FOR SEPARATE JUSTICE SYSTEMS

The reasons why Amerindian People in this country are seeking self-determination in regards to the administration of justice have been abundantly clear. Basically, Amerindian People feel that they are not well served by our justice system, and it is very hard to argue with the statistics that verify that feeling. They often feel that this system is removed from their communities, both physically and conceptually, and it is antithetical to Indigenous worldviews and to their juridical needs. Amerindian People also recognize that without activating an appropriate justice process free from outside interference in their territories it will be impossible to fully activate self-determination in those territories.

We have taken many initiatives, both Aboriginal and non-Aboriginal People working separately and together, to try and ameliorate the problems with the administration of justice to Amerindian Peoples in this country. We have tried to work around the system, through programs focusing on diversion, and Amerindian resolution programs. We have tried to work within the system, through indigenising it, which essentially means taking non-Amerindian structures and populating those structures with Amerindian People in hope that it will in some way render this system more effective and more relevant to Amerindian Peoples. If you think that it is possible to move into a system which is as intensive and bureaucratic as the criminal justice system and not be, to a certain extent, co-opted by that system, then indigenisation may be a good program. At this point, however, little or no benefit has been demonstrated.

We have tried to get communities more involved in the administration of justice by, for example, having Elders sit with judges when they make their decisions and by obtaining the input of those people with regard to the offensiveness of the act or the dispute within the cultural and community context. We have developed Aboriginal programs, and while some of these are very good programs which can, in fact, help Amerindian People move through the Canadian criminal justice system in a way which hopefully mitigates to some degree the negative impact of that system, for the most part, those programs suffer from under-funding, high staff turn-over and a lack of training across Canada. We have tried Amerindian Justices of the Peace, and, while these initiatives have potential, they are still essentially a form of in-digenisation and therefore, are prone to the same sorts of problems as the current system.

One more recent initiative suggests that we should take non-indigenised courts and place them in Aboriginal communities and that will, in some way, bridge the cultural and information gap be-tween the system and the community, foster a sense of community investment in the system, and remove problematic elements as-sociated with circuit court systems and non-attendance due to geographical distance. These initiatives have, for the most part, met with varying degrees of success.

It would be completely inaccurate to say that all Amerindian Peoples within this country are demanding a separate system. There are Amerindian People who feel that the system to varying degrees works for them and that improvements can be made within it. Therefore, when you hear radical statements in the media, such as that we are looking at forty to fifty separate systems working in this country, you should be highly skeptical.

There are groups that are focusing on separate systems and those individuals focus primarily on the fact that the criminal jus-tice system in Canada is an alien system. It is based on what is, for many of them, a very ambiguous value system, and, if that is not enough to motivate a separate court, the simple fact that the courts were imposed on them without their consent and with highly deleterious results should justify moving towards a separate sys-tem of their own.

I would like to speak to you very briefly about the initiatives of two groups in Canada who are working to set up separate sys-tems within their territories: the Dene Nation in the Northwest Territories and the Mohawk Nation of Kahnawake, outside of Montreal. Both of these groups, while separated geographically and manifesting very different levels of pre-contact traditional so-cial organizations, are necessarily united by the fact that they are taking their traditions and attempting to revitalize them in a modern justice system.

Traditional Dene dispute resolution

The Dene Nation was a simple band-level society prior to the intrusion of European influences and the fur trade. It was a society which very definitely focused on individual autonomy, and there were very few defined social institutions or means by which an individual could demonstrate or achieve some kind of authority. Disputes arose rarely, because they were prevented by the harshness of the northern environment, by a profound respect for individual autonomy, and by the fact that you have to cultivate a certain amount of personal discipline to live in a very small society where everything you achieve, both as an individual and as a member of a group, is premised upon your reputation and the respect gained within the community.

I am going to outline traditional dispute resolution techniques in a way that is perhaps most easily understandable to those of us who are taught about law based very clearly on legal strata. From that perspective, the Dene system was traditionally a very loosely structured three-tier system. The first level was the private level. This was the level where two individuals would come into conflict, and they would try, of themselves, to resolve that conflict. If they found that they were unable to do so, they would then approach a common older person whom they would ask to mediate this dispute. That person, however, could refuse to become involved if he or she felt so inclined, or could tell them to go away and deal with it themselves, if it was thought that outside input was not necessary.

If, however, that common older relative did intervene, he or she would work with the disputants to mediate the dispute, and if mediation proved impossible, and the dispute threatened to fester to the point of potentially disrupting the community, then the community would become involved and the dispute would assume a public quality. The public system, as it was understood then, was simply the force of public opinion. Everybody knew what was going on, and the dispute was resolved as soon as public opinion, as regards to who was right and who was wrong, was formed and readily apparent. At that point, the individual who was in the wrong would know so clearly, and would be forced to take appropriate measures to deal with the offense. Most commonly, the individual would either make some kind of restitution for the act committed or opt for self-imposed banishment by simply leaving the community for a period of time.

In their 1987 statement, *Public Government for the People of the North*, the Dene and the Metis stated their desire to assume control over the administration of justice through the resurrection of a traditional legal system. There is a problem that comes into play for a lot of non-Amerindian when we view these assertions, namely, we are unsure whether or not the traditions are still in place and sufficiently developed to be translated to a modern context as the basis of a legal system. More simply, the question is whether those traditions can deal with the modern imperatives that are placed upon a criminal justice system.

If you freeze-frame culture, or if you expect Amerindian culture to be like what you see in Hollywood movies and take it no further, then you are going to say the traditions are gone. Amerindian People have cars, dishwashers and coloured televisions, and that is not traditional. If that is the way you feel, then you are going to say that these systems are not possible.

However, if you realize that traditions, as part of a culture, can evolve and incorporate alien technologies without compromising their cultural core; if you realize that what is traditional is really a decision of what will work for a people, made by those people living the traditions rather than someone who is outside them; if you are willing to and capable of removing your own cultural blinders to respect Aboriginal definitions of their traditions and be flexible in regard to the form and content which they propose their modern institutions will assume, then traditional systems are possible and workable.

How the Dene and Metis will shape their traditional system is, at this point, uncertain. They signed the *Promise of Agreement* with the federal Conservatives in 1988, and the next step to be taken in the following two years, between 1988 and 1990, was for self-government proposals to be worked out between the Dene, the Metis and the re-elected Conservative government. It would appear, however, that step has not been taken.

Unfortunately, the 1987 statement on Public Government of People of the North did not specify what form of system should be put into place. It is possible to postulate that they may look to the formation of a tribal court system. A model that might be open to them would be, for example, the tribal system in place, I believe, in Alberta.

This particular model is a two-tier system involving a peace-maker, commonly an Elder, who would intervene in a dispute as early as possible in order to avoid reaching a point where formal resolution is required. If the peacemaker is unable to resolve the dispute, then the dispute would go to the second tier, which is a tribunal of three members who are appointed by a larger tribal justice committee and who hear disputes and resolve them based upon traditional dispute resolution philosophies. The system they are proposing would have jurisdiction extending to criminal law, civil and family law, land disputes, disputes among Band members, and bylaws. They hope to create remedies that include fines, restitution, compensation and banishment.

Banishment has become, of course, a more problematic type of penalty, given the intensity of modern population. You can no longer send someone out to a great vast wilderness. Thus, it may be that "banishment" will be affected through contracting out with larger criminal correction agencies in order to achieve the same actual effect of removing the person from the community. It is also possible that banishment could be incorporated into sentencing in the form of a "no-go" probation order.

Village courts in Papau New Guinea

Another model which the Dene might wish to consider is the village courts in Papua New Guinea. These courts were established around 1975 and are essentially mediation-based structures which have jurisdiction over all persons in the village. That would seem to imply that if a non-Amerindian person came into the community and became involved in a dispute, they would be subject to the dispute resolution techniques of the village courts.

These courts are administered by magistrates who are appointed by the local residents for a three-year term. They do not require any special qualifications, although some knowledge of the community and of traditional dispute resolution techniques is considered necessary. Mediation always precedes formal adjudication, and the effectiveness of the mediation is demonstrated in the fact that adjudication of disputes at this level is twice as common as formal court sittings.

There are a range of possibilities for the Dene Nation. The important point, however, is that any system that the Dene may ultimately set up or whatever system they aspire to must be one that comes from them. We, as outsiders, must hold back criticizing their systems on the basis of our own alien and potentially irrelevant legal traditions.

The Mohawk justice system: Two Row Wampum

The Mohawk Nation is a nation which has a very high probability of achieving a separate justice system, because they do have a viable constitutional basis for such a system. In their traditional, pre-contact state, they had a highly complex social organization which not only had very clearly defined political mechanisms for dealing with international disputes, but also very clear institutions for resolving disputes within the community itself. It is important to note that there was a treaty signed in the 1600s with the Dutch and later with the British, which guaranteed the Mohawk Nation, as part of the Six Nation Iroquois Confederacy, the right to retain and practice their own law. The central concept was set out as two boats going down a river together. In one boat are the laws, customs and politics of the European system. In the other boat are the law, customs and politics of the Mohawk nation, and these boats carry on side by side down the river. You do not jump from boat to boat or rock each other's boats; you just allow each other to move smoothly down this river of life and, in so doing, you co-exist in a pacific way.

On the basis of that Treaty, the *Two Row Wampum* Treaty, it is interesting to note that the current situation in regard to the administration of justice in Kahnawake is in many ways effectively that of two systems, although the relations between them are not quite pacific. Kahnawake currently has a section 107 *Indian Act* court and Long House justice based on a pre-contact mode of dispute resolution.

Similarly to the Dene, Mohawk social relations were regulated by the importance of individual autonomy, mutual respect and responsibility to the group. This responsibility was rooted in the basic social institution of the clan. When an individual acted, they did so as a representative of their clan. If an individual acted in a deviant manner or committed what would be regarded in our society as a criminal offense, then the whole clan had to accept responsibility, and the whole clan would have to make reparation for the offense. In that regard, an individual was rarely placed in a position where they could throw their hands up in the air and say, "I have nothing to lose if I kill the person I hate", because they had to consider how much the entire clan had to lose. This pressure had a very strong deterrent effect on individual behaviour in the community.

Based upon traditional dispute resolution philosophies of communal responsibility, restitution and restoration of the *status quo*, the "Longhouse Justice System" attempts to resolve disputes in effectively a five-tiered system. The first tier is a private tier (as in the Dene context), where the individuals try to resolve the dispute themselves without taking it into the community and disrupting the affairs of others. If they are unable to do so, they might approach an Elder or a clan leader and ask that person to help them mediate the dispute and to reach some kind of positive determination. The Elder may agree to assist them, or they may send the dispute back to the two people and say: this really is not important enough, you should be able to deal with this, go and deal with it.

When the offense is very serious or part of a persistent pattern of deviant behaviour in the community, they may move the dispute up to the next level, which would involve all the clans in a community meeting. Again, if the clan leaders cannot resolve the dispute, it moves automatically to the next level. At the Community Council level, representatives of the entire community, sitting in clans within the Long House, deliberate over the nature of the offense and an appropriate remedy in terms of how serious the offense is and how acceptable the solution would be to the parties and the community.

If the conflict is not resolved at this level, it may then go on to the next level, the Nation Council, where the process would effectively be repeated with the exception that, at this level, if the Nation Council believes that they are unable to resolve the dispute because of an inadequacy of evidence or because additional information is available but cannot be brought to the tribunal at that time, they can set that dispute aside for a period of time and then resume consideration of it at a later date in light of the additional information.

If the Nation Council is unable to resolve the dispute, there is a "court of last resort". This is the "Supreme Court" of the Mohawk Nation and, as with most senior courts, you apply to this court to be heard and, if accepted, they will hear your dispute and attempt to resolve it through the same process used at the lower level, but having the additional advantage of being able to determine the best compromise and to impose it in order to return the community to pacific relations.

What makes this system somewhat more difficult to manage than, for example, the Canadian criminal justice system, is that you do not simply make a decision and impose it on the people who come to you with the dispute. The dispute must always be resolved in a way which is to the mutual satisfaction of both parties. So, if you have a victim and an offender, not only the victim must be satisfied, but also the offender. The offender must feel that justice has been done to the same degree as the victim. In this way, the need for an appeal court system is effectively obviated by the fact that appeal is implicit in these structures. The message is: if you do not like it at this point, then we will stop and we will work it out. We are not going to send you off to another structure to have them work it out.

Based on that very brief elaboration of a traditional system, it is possible to see that there are two effectively competing proposals with regard to separate justice in Kahnawake. The first is the traditional system detailed above. The second is based on the section 107 *Indian Act* court. This court has very limited jurisdiction, which is clearly defined in the *Indian Act*. What has been suggested in the community is that this court would exercise its jurisdiction in a way that allows it not only to adjudicate disputes which are beyond its technical jurisdiction but which allows it to incorporate traditional remedies and Mohawk communal law as well. It has also been suggested that as part of this movement, a section 107 court would eventually move itself completely out from underneath the auspices of the *Indian Act* and of Canadian legislation, notwithstanding whatever amendments might be made to the *Indian Act*, some of which are currently under consideration.

It has also been suggested that the section 107 court may be able to evolve into what is essentially the bureaucratic arm of the Long House justice system, and, in that regard, mesh the Canadian system and the traditional Mohawk system. While that may seem like an agreeable compromise to some of us on the outside, to some traditional people in the community it is a basic violation of the constitutional principles of the Six Nations Iroquois Confederacy. A man who tries to stand with one foot in either boat gets wet, and that is effectively the analogy that would apply to this system.

The establishment of Long House justice would be based on what would be effectively a replication of the traditional legal value system. I think this is viable because the processes are there, the physical structure is there, and the Long House is there. We are not talking about a major monetary investment to build a courthouse. The Long House is already used by the clans. Traditionalists believe that the Long House justice system could evolve as the sole juridical body, in effect by-passing the need for a section 107 court.

It is important to note that in order for systems anywhere in this country to be effective, Amerindian Peoples must have the primary voice in the establishment and formation of alternatives to the Canadian justice system. Not all Amerindian People want a separate court. Not all Amerindian People want a parallel justice system. It is not for us to decide what they want. We must also, for the same reasons, not tell them how to go about getting what they want. It is not for us to say whether or not a system will work based on our experiences with our system. These are different systems. We must respect the differences and be open to alternatives based on very different cultural values.

It is also very important for people in the legal profession to be aware that non-Amerindians must cease enlisting their own legal system and rule of law to deny the rights of First Nations to self-determination in general, and separate justice in particular. Ameridian self-determination is not a matter of legal technicalities. It is a matter of social justice. It is in this context that justifications for Amerindian institutions designed by and for Amerindian People exists, and it is in this light that proposals for separate justice must be entertained.

The Alternative Dispute Resolution Movement

Amerindian People are not the only people who find our justice system inappropriate in many cases. There is a widespread movement for reform of the justice system both within the system and outside the system, and this movement has come to be called ADR (Alternative Dispute Resolution). It is a dramatic explosion of technology where we move to multiple options to effectively resolve disputes. Aboriginal Peoples are actually ahead of us; they have already arrived at our planned destination.

There is thus a potential common ground which creates the opportunity of sharing and mutual benefit. I suggest that we focus on these processes as a very important part of that common ground before trying to resolve deep-rooted conflicts. Prior to leaping into

the fray, where we often become frustrated, it is often best to com-
mence with a common ground. Agree to disagree on substance, if
we must, and begin by agreeing on processes. One of the experiences gaining acceptance in the United States and somewhat in
Canada is the multi-door courthouse, whereby the courthouse is
being redefined and perceived in a different way. It becomes a
place where justice is granted, not only through judgments, but
through multiple options. We need to recognize that there are
many doors to justice for First Nations within Canada and we have
no rights to close them.

(Postscript: 1993)

Separate justice at Kahnawake: three years after

Since giving the above presentation three years ago, I have
focused solely on my work with the Kahnawake Mohawks and the
articulation, critique and realization of a separate system of traditional justice within Kahnawake. During this time, the traditional
"Longhouse Justice System" has reached a much higher and more
detailed level of development and is poised to offer a real and substantial alternative to the imposed Canadian criminal legal system
within the community.

To a degree, however, implementation of the system has been
stalled by those very events which may also prove, ultimately, to
have heightened the potential for its realization, namely, the crises
at Kanesatake and Kahnawake in 1990. For in the same moment
that these crises disrupted life in Kahnawake and Kanesatake to
such a degree that full recovery is still not realized, they also went
far to mend the enduring internecine competition between the
Mohawk Council and the Nation Office – between "conservatives"
and "traditionalists" – which had for so long limited the ability of
the community to work toward a shared goal of self-
determination.

In the "post-Oka" Kahnawake, these two groups have been
seen to be working cooperatively on a number of ventures, including those related to the achievement of local control over the administration of justice through the development of a separate legal
system. Where "Peacekeepers" and "Warriors" were once often
locked in a fundamentally oppositional relationship, they now pa-
trol the community together; where research by the Nation Office
directed to the elaboration of a "traditional" system was once
viewed with suspicion by the Mohawk Council (and vice-versa),

they are now active partners in the support of such projects. These groups once shared only a superficial agreement on self-determination and battled fundamentally on the best means to accomplish a form of self-determination which is felt more deeply and clearly defined. Inasmuch as internal conflicts over laws and tradition stood as one of the most profound barriers to the realisation of separate justice in Kahnawake, the potential for a "resurrection of the Peace" in the community is greatly enhanced.

QUESTION PERIOD: PANEL ONE

Question: GARTH WALLBRIDGE
McGill Law Student

As a resident of Yellowknife in the Northwest Territories, I listened to your comments as Deputy-Justice of the Superior Court with much interest. I am wondering how you envision a system that allows only lawyers and judges interested in Aboriginal issues to become involved? I am not challenging you. I am just wondering how you envision that policy being adopted or is it something unofficial?

Answer: REJEAN PAUL

It is highly unofficial, nonetheless my experience is that only those who have a keen interest in Aboriginal law should represent or judge such cases. You have, for sake of example, judges sitting in Aboriginal matters who do not know anything about Aboriginal law, tradition, culture, etc. They go strictly by the black letter law and apply the rules of evidence as we know them in the criminal court system. That is absolutely unacceptable nowadays. You are not taking into account the background of these people, and you are not rendering justice at all. At a trial in Labrador, one of the Elder women wanted to say what happened to her community, but the judge said it was not admissible under our rules of evidence. It is distressing to see things like that happen. That is why I am urging that our rules of evidence and law be changed. The first step is to change our minds as judges and lawyers.

Question: ROSEMARY HNATIUK
McGill student

I would like to ask Jane a question. Where would women fit into the system that you outlined, because I understand the Dene and Iroquois Nations, particularly at the time of contact, had women play a very strong role in the society, and that is still the case. I come from Manitoba, and speaking to Native women there, they are very concerned with instituting a justice system where men would be the people resolving disputes, when often Native women are victims of abuse within the community. There was a report that came out last week, I believe, that showed a really horrendous degree of abuse of Native women within their community.

Answer: JANE DICKSON-GILMORE

Assuming that you are talking about a traditional or a Long House justice system, my assessment is based on my experience in the community. If you look back to the pre-contact state, the male government of Mohawk society was appointed by the women, who held the traditional offices, based on a matrilineal line. They decided which men would be offered a position, and they could pull him out of that office if he did not do the job. One could argue that such a process could be replicated when appointing people to work in the new system. Clan leaders would be removed by the women participating in a mediation process, for the same sorts of reasons and in the same way that they would have been removed if they were inadequate political leaders.

There is also a possibility that women would have a place, if for no other reason than the prominent role that Native women in Kahnawake are taking now to promote self-determination in the community. I would say that women would definitely play a role in that system.

Answer: SAM STEVENS

Aboriginal Peoples have to play an important role in the development of any new systems and in any cross-cultural training. In British Columbia, the Western Judicial Education Conference is responsible for the continuing legal education of western Canadian judges. Last year, the WJEC started a program for cross-cultural training that will continue for another couple of years. At least eighty provincial court judges, twenty federally-appointed judges, and an equal number of Aboriginal People will participate. In other words, we need to ensure that judges understand this culture, where it came from, how it has adapted, and the laws today that we call Native law, both from an Aboriginal perspective and from a Canadian legal perspective.

Aboriginal People also need cross-cultural training. They do not understand this system, its principles, beliefs or values. It is important, if they are to come into this system, that they know what they are up against.

One of the current projects we have at the university uses principles of customary law. The present government says they do not know what effect customary law would have, for example, on the *Charter*. The federal government, for example, is obliged to protect individual rights under the *Charter*. Unfortunately, it is difficult to study, since customary law, by its very nature, was never written down. It is something which responded to the circumstances, and as circumstances changed, the tradition or custom would change as well. For the most part, in many of our communities, that traditional or customary law has been blocked for some time. As I mentioned before, the imposition of law forced them to conform to new laws, and, over a long period of time, customary law fell out of use. In fact, in many of the communities, it has fallen out of memory.

There is also a problem bringing custom forward into a modern context, but in three of our communities in British Columbia, one very remote community, one in the interior of British Columbia, and one in a fairly urbanized setting, they have agreed to go through that process. It will take us about three years, but we expect at the end of the three year period to have developed some approach which allows the community to use as much of their customary law and as much of the dominant law as they feel necessary to create a context which allows their culture or their society to continue to exist as a society.

PANEL TWO
ABORIGINAL TITLE AND LAND CLAIMS

Jean-Paul Lacasse

Professor Jean-Paul Lacasse teaches at the Faculty of Law, University of Ottawa. He is both a lawyer and a geographer, and holds a doctoral degree in mining law. Professor Lacasse has been a faculty member at the University of Ottawa since 1975, specializing in mining law and in resource taxation. He has published extensively in the areas of energy and natural resource law. He was a speaker at seminars on the Canada-US Free Trade Agreement and is presently giving a graduate course on the topic. Professor Lacasse has also been extensively involved in Aboriginal law as a teacher, researcher and consultant. As a member of the Dorion Commission in the 1970s, he was the main writer of its report on the "Domaine Indien". In 1989, he spear-headed a feasibility study on the establishment of a pre-law program in French for Native People. He is now Director of the program.

ISSUES RAISED BY ABORIGINAL TITLE AND LAND CLAIMS

One of the problems we are faced with in a panel discussion on Aboriginal title and land claims is the abundance of data, both legal and non-legal. This analysis is further complicated by the prior occupation of the land by one Aboriginal group vis-à-vis other groups, different legal standards of Native and non-Native groups competing for the same territory, the quasi-disappearance of the legal system of a Native group, the recognition in international and constitutional law of Aboriginal rights, and the spatial and geographical variations of rights as affected by treaties and legislation.

The *Constitution Act, 1982* does not mention Aboriginal title as such, but it does entrench Aboriginal rights, Aboriginal title being, presumably, one of its components. The concept of Aboriginal title has evolved considerably in recent years. Prior to 1973, Aboriginal title was usually thought to be derived from the *Royal Proclamation of 1763*, and *St. Catherine's Milling* was heavily relied upon. However, in the *Calder* case in 1973, the Supreme Court of Canada went beyond *St. Catherine's Milling* and stated that Aboriginal title existed in Canada independently of the *Royal Proclamation*. In 1984, the Supreme Court of Canada went further in *Guerin*, stating that the interest of Indians in their lands was a pre-existing legal right not created by the *Royal Proclamation* nor any other legislation.

The nature and extent of Aboriginal title has been the subject of many comments, both in case law and in our scholarly literature. It has been described as a personal and usufructary right, a right to hunt for food, or, more recently, as the legal right of Indians to occupy and possess certain lands, the unltimate title to which is in the Crown.

Where such Aboriginal title exists, there may be a non-judicial recourse for its recognition as a land claim under the *Federal Government Comprehensive Claims Policy*. According to the federal government definition, land claims may be comprehensive or specific, but they are almost always comprehensive when derived from Aboriginal title. Some agreements have been arrived at through the comprehensive claims negotiation process, although many feel that the process is too slow. One reason for this slowness is, perhaps, that each side views entitlement to a comprehensive claim differently. Indeed, the broad approach to Aboriginal title adopted by Native groups is often confronted by the narrower federal government view based on continuous occupation of the land in a traditional way. That is, if the land is not occupied as it was three hundred years ago, the tendency is to reject the claim. Natives argue the reverse.

Many questions and problems remain unresolved. For instance, to what extent does Aboriginal title extend to mines and minerals? Will section 35 of the *Constitution Act, 1982* be interpreted to entrench Aboriginal title? To what extent is it possible under section 35 to revive customary law under the doctrine of Aboriginal title? During the process of negotiating a comprehensive claim, what does one do when the Crown, the owner of the land under Canadian law, disagrees on the area to be recognized as Indian lands? What can be done when the courts decide in a specific case that no Aboriginal title exists? Should other Aboriginal rights such as self-government be invoked in order to arrive at the desired result? Is self-government itself an Aboriginal right? Are comprehensive land claims viable alternatives? Should the courts decide against the existence of an Aboriginal title? Or would a specific claim, based on the federal government's failure to meet its legal obligations, be a better route to follow?

RENÉ MORIN

René Morin détient un baccalauréat des arts, un baccalauréat en droit, et une maîtrise en sciences politiques. Il est membre du Barreau du Québec et oeuvre au sein du Gouvernement du Québec depuis 1972. Il a d'abord oeuvré au Ministère des Affaires intergouvernementales et est maintenant au Ministère de la Justice. Me Morin est un spécialiste en matière de droits Autochtones au sein du gouvernement du Québec. Il a également participé à toutes les conférences constitutionnelles fédérales-provinciales de 1982 à 1987. Il a plaidé pour le Gouvernement du Québec, plusieurs causes se rapportant aux droits Autochtones à tous les niveaux judiciaires, y compris à la Cour Suprême du Canada. Me Morin est le conseiller juridique du Gouvernement du Québec dans les négociations avec le Conseil Montagnais relativement à la revendication globale des bandes amérindiennes du Québec.

LES DROITS ANCESTRAUX ET LES TITRES AU CANADA: ÉVOLUTION OU RÉVOLUTION?

Le présent colloque s'inscrit va dans le sens de la recommandation 28 adoptée en août 1989 par l'Association du Barreau Canadien à partir du rapport intitulé "Les droits des Autochtones au Canada: du défi à l'action", laquelle recommandation se lit comme suit:

> Les barreaux (ou sociétés d'avocats) des provinces et territoires canadiens, ainsi que les divisions provinciales de l'Association du Barreau canadien devraient encourager de façon active leur séminaire de formation juridique permanente à mettre sur pied des séminaires et des ateliers sur les questions juridiques concernant les Autochtones.

Avant de déterminer si la reconnaissance des droits ancestraux (ou titre indien) dans l'ordre juridique canadien est le fruit d'une évolution ou d'une révolution, il convient de souligner que cette notion a été consacrée par les tribunaux dans l'affaire *Calder* et qu'elle témoigne d'un nouveau phénomène au Canada, soit celui où les Autochtones revendiquent de plus en plus leurs droits par la voie judiciaire.

Longtemps, les litiges devant les tribunaux ont opposé les gouvernements fédéral et provincial sur l'application des lois provinciales à l'égard des Indiens et des terres réservées aux Indiens. À cet égard, les arrêts *St. Catherine's Milling*, *Seybold* et *Dominion of Canada*, montrent bien les préoccupations des gouvernements fédéral et provincial au tournant du siècle dernier sur la question des terres indiennes.

Dans l'arrêt *St. Catherine's Milling*, le Conseil Privé avait établi que les terres cédées par les Indiens dans la cadre d'un traité ne devenaient pas des terres publiques fédérales mais retournaient dans le domaine public de la province, libre de tout intérêt ou titre indien. Quelques années plus tard, dans l'arrêt *Seybold*, le Conseil Privé dégagea les conséquences pratiques de l'arrêt *St. Catherine's Milling*, en indiquant que le fédéral ne pouvait créer des réserves indiennes à partir de terres cédées, même s'il s'y était dûment engagé par traité. Enfin, en 1910, dans *Dominion of Canada and Province of Ontario*, il a été décidé que le fédéral ne pouvait réclamer de la province bénéficiaire d'une terre libérée de son titre indien le montant de l'indemnité qu'il devait payer aux Indiens en vertu du traité de cession. En d'autres termes, même si la province pouvait bénéficier d'une terre libre d'un intérêt indien, le fédéral ne pouvait réclamer à la province une indemnité à cet égard.

Soulignons que ces trois décisions se situaient dans le contexte d'un territoire réservé ou visé par la *Proclamation royale* du 7 octobre 1763.

Je constate que ce genre de débat a cédé la place à un autre enjeu, soit celui des droits ancestraux et des titres indiens vis-à-vis les lois fédérales et provinciales. Ainsi, l'ancien problème qui impliquait deux niveaux de juridiction en implique maintenant trois, à savoir le fédéral, le provincial et les Autochtones.

Par ailleurs, le débat sur la *Proclamation royale* a été remplacée par le débat sur la notion de titre indien. Vous vous rappelez que la *Proclamation royale*, en plus de créer de nouvelles colonies, entre autres le Québec de 1763 qui couvrait la vallée du St-Laurent, a laissé pour le bénéfice des Indiens des terres à l'extérieur de ces colonies, communément appelées le territoire indien, tout en réservant aussi des terres pour les Indiens à l'intérieur des colonies.

Cependant, coup de tonnerre en 1973. Monsieur le juge Judson dans l'affaire *Calder* (1973), a clairement indiqué que la *Proclamation royale* n'était pas l'unique fondement du droit Autochtone au Canada. D'après lui, les Autochtones pouvaient également s'appuyer sur la notion de titre indien qu'il décrit comme suit dans un passage désormais célèbre,

> Je crois qu'il est clair qu'en Colombie Britannique, le titre indien ne peut avoir pour origine la *Proclamation de 1763*, mais il reste que lorsque les colons sont arrivés, les indiens étaient déjà là, ils étaient organisés en sociétés et occupaient les terres comme leurs ancêtres l'avaient fait depuis des siècles. C'est ce que signifie le titre indien... (p. 328)

Cette position a été réaffirmée par monsieur le juge Dickson dans *Guérin* (1984) et encore récemment dans *Canadien Pacifique* (1988).

Ainsi, le droit territorial des indiens n'est pas limité aux seules terres de réserves au sens de la *Loi sur les Indiens* ou encore au territoire dit «réservé» au sens de la *Proclamation royale*.

On comprend le choc que cette décision pouvait provoquer pour les gouvernements lorsque l'on songe qu'en 1867 le Canada ne comprenait à toutes fins pratiques que le Haut et le Bas-Canada, réunis dans ce qu'on appelait le Canada-Uni (la *Proclamation royale* visait à peine la moitié des territoires actuels de ces deux provinces), la Nouvelle-Écosse et le Nouveau-Brunswick. Or, quelle était en 1867 la situation dans toutes ces provinces?

En Ontario, la plus grande partie du territoire au 1er juillet 1867 était libérée par traité de tout titre indien, notamment par les deux grands traités de 1850 dits *Robinson-Supérieur* et *Robinson-Hudson*, qui prévoyaient la mise à part de terres pour le bénéfice des indiens.

Quant au Québec, la Nouvelle-Écosse et le Nouveau-Brunswick, il y avait déjà plusieurs lois qui prévoyaient la mise à part de terres pour le bénéfice des indiens. À titre d'exemple, je vous réfère à l'*Acte pour mettre à part certaines étendues de terres pour l'usage de certaines tribus de sauvages dans le Bas-Canada*, qui est une loi de 1851.

Comment fait-il qu'aucune cession, qu'aucun traité n'avait été nécessaire au Québec, en Nouvelle-Écosse, au Nouveau-Brunswick? Peut-être que les choses seront un jour clarifiées dans un sens ou dans l'autre par les tribunaux, mais on peut supposer qu'à ce moment-là, on pensait que le droit français applicable sur ces territoires ne reconnaissait aucun droit ancestral ou titre indien, ou encore que le droit des Indiens sur ces territoires avait probablement été éteint par l'arrivée des colons et des bûcherons dans l'arrière-pays, les lois adoptées sur la question des terres indiennes étant alors destinées à compenser cette perte. De toute façon, les Indiens eux-mêmes à cette époque ne faisaient aucune revendication de terres prenant la forme de traité. Je ne veux pas dire que j'endosse ces positions, mais je constate qu'en 1867, il était plutôt dans l'esprit du temps qu'en référant aux terres réservées aux Indiens, à tout le moins du côté gouvernemental, on visait des terres qui avaient été mises à part pour le bénéfice des Indiens. Ceci est tellement vrai que le juge Boyd, qui dans *St. Catherine's Milling* (1885) avait rendu la décision en première instance déclarait:

> There is an essential difference in meaning between the "reservations" spoken of in the *Royal Proclamation*, and the like term in the *B.N.A. Act*. The *Royal Proclamation* views the Indians in their wild state, and leaves them there in undisturbed and unlimited possession of all their hunting ranges, whereas the *Act* (en parlant du B.N.A Act) through giving jurisdiction to the Dominion over all Indians, wild or settled, does not transfer to that government all public or waste lands of the provinces on which they may be found at large.

Et, il ajoute en conclusion:

> The territorial jurisdiction of the Dominion extends only to the land reserved for them. (p. 228)

Ainsi, pour monsieur le juge Boyd, la notion constitutionnelle de terres réservées ne pouvait signifier que les terres mises à part par les lois à cet effet. Cette appréciation a été reconnue par plusieurs juges de la Cour d'Appel et de la Cour Suprême, et a même été soutenue par le procureur général de l'Ontario devant le Conseil privé. Cependant Lord Watson dans cette décision du Conseil privé a réfuté cette thèse en ces termes:

> The argument might have deserved consideration if the expression had been adopted by the British Parliament in 1867, but it does not occur in section 91(24), and the words actually used are, according to their natural meaning, sufficient to include all lands reserved, upon any terms or conditions, for Indian occupation. (p. 59)

Peut-être cet énoncé de Lord Watson annonçait-il déjà l'ouverture de monsieur le juge Judson dans l'arrêt *Calder*. D'une certaine façon, on peut dire que monsieur le juge Judson dans *Calder* a bouclé la boucle par rapport à ce que Lord Watson annonçait presque 90 ans plus tôt. Mais de déclarer que le titre indien existe, qu'il peut avoir une existence indépendante de la *Proclamation royale* ne constitue qu'un début. Il reste encore beaucoup de questions à clarifier en rapport avec cette notion de titre indien.

Many fundamental questions must be resolved by the courts. We can put them in three categories. First category: what are the requisite elements necessary to establish the existence of an Aboriginal right or Indian Title? Are these elements applicable on territory given by the *Royal Proclamation*? Do they apply to territories already under French sovereignty in North America?

Second category: does the exercise of an Aboriginal right imply the existence of an Indian Title?

Third category: how can Indian title and Aboriginal rights be extinguished? Is it necessary to have a treaty to extinguish these rights? Can a law extinguish such a right expressly or implicitly? What about the simple passage of time?

Je pense que les tribunaux vont avoir un très grand défi à relever face à toutes ces questions-là. On voit déjà les difficultés auxquelles les cours sont confrontées pour résoudre des problèmes en droit Autochtone. Revenons juste à la notion de titre indien. Me Lacasse, tout à l'heure, vous mentionnait qu'on avait qualifié ce droit de droit personnel de la nature d'un usufruit dans l'arrêt *St. Catherine's Milling*. Soit dit en passant, Lord Watson était un Écossais et c'est peut-être en ayant à l'esprit un concept de droit romain, qui est la source du droit écossais, qu'il a parlé de la notion d'usufruit. Quoi qu'il en soit, je pense qu'il a employé cette notion à titre d'analogie plutôt que d'assimiler le titre indien à un veritable usufruit au sens du Code Civil.

Mais cette notion a été quelque peu mise de côté par le juge Dickson dans l'arrêt *Guérin*; selon lui, cette notion était empruntée à la terminologie traditionnelle de droit des biens. Finalement, la réponse, ou peut-être un aveu d'impuissance, est venue de *Canadien Pacifique* où la Cour déclare:

> The inescapable conclusion from the Court's analysis of Indian title up to this point is that the Indian interest in land is truly *sui generis*. It is more

> than the right to enjoyment and occupancy, although, as Judge Dickson pointed out in *Guérin*, it is difficult to describe what more in traditional property law terminology. (p. 678)

En d'autres termes, l'honorable juge ne le sait pas. Il y a quelque chose, mais il ne sait pas quoi. Alors, en espérant que les tribunaux vont en dire plus, je vais tenter d'élaborer sur les trois question déjà mentionnées.

Relativement à la première catégorie de questions, à savoir quels sont les éléments requis pour établir l'existence d'un droit ancestral ou d'un titre indien, vous vous rappelez l'énoncé de monsieur le juge Judson dans *Calder* où, pour lui, les Indiens étaient déjà là au moment de l'arrivée des colons, vivaient en sociétés organisées, et occupaient un territoire comme leurs ancêtres l'avaient fait depuis des siècles. Le juge Mahoney dans *Baker Lake* c. *Le ministre des affaires indiennes et du Nord canadien* (1981) a peut-être systématisé ces énoncés, en disant:

> Voici quels sont les éléments que doivent prouver les demandeurs pour établir un titre aborigène que reconnaîtrait la *common law*:
>
> 1. Eux et leurs ancêtres doivent avoir été membre d'une société organisée. Donc, il rejoint là une des préoccupations du juge Judson.
>
> 2. Cette société organisée doit avoir occupé le territoire précis sur lequel ils prétendent exercer ce titre aborigène. Là aussi monsieur le juge Judson parlait d'occupation de terres.
>
> 3. Cette occupation doit avoir été à l'exclusion de toute autre société organisée. Il n'est pas évident que cette exigence faisait partie de l'énoncé de monsieur le juge Judson. Cette notion d'exclusivité ajoute peut-être une contrainte assez difficile à satisfaire.
>
> 4. L'occupation devait être un fait établi à l'époque où l'Angleterre imposa sa souveraineté.

Soit dit en passant, monsieur le juge Steele dans *Attorney General for Ontario* v. *Bear Island Foundation* (1984), a appliqué ce test afin de déterminer si la bande indienne de Temagami en Ontario pouvait prétendre à un titre indien.

Il ne fait pas de doute que la preuve de ce titre peut s'avérer difficile à faire, surtout si la notion d'exclusivité mentionnée dans les critères de monsieur le juge Mahoney s'avérait tout aussi essentielle que les autres critères. En effet, qu'entendons-nous par "cette occupation doit avoir été à l'exclusion de toute autre société organisée"? On peut penser que les incursions des non-Autochtones ou l'arrivée d'autres bandes indiennes sur le territoire sont des facteurs susceptibles d'affecter ce titre indien. Il est également possible que l'occupation exclusive des indiens dans l'ouest du pays ait été plus stable qu'au Québec et qu'en Ontario. Or, s'il fallait appliquer intégralement cette notion d'exclusivité, à la lumière des grandes luttes qui ont opposé les Iroquois et les autres nations indiennes en Ontario et au Québec, on peut comprendre que ce critère serait susceptible de poser des problèmes s'il devait s'appliquer de façon rigide.

Il est possible que la Cour suprême du Canada revienne sur cette question dans l'arrêt *Sparrow* (1990) qui est en délibéré devant la Cour depuis le 3 novembre 1988. En effet, la Cour d'appel de la Colombie Britannique a trouvé dans l'existence de dispositions législatives ou réglementaires au sujet des pêcheries visant les Indiens depuis plus d'un siècle une preuve que le droit ancestral devait exister. Plus précisément, elle écrit: *what possible reason can there be for the continuous regulation for a century of Indian fishing except recognition of an Aboriginal right?*

Si on devait appliquer cette remarque, force serait peut-être de conclure qu'il existe beaucoup de droits ancestraux et de titres indiens au Québec parce que les lois de chasse et de pêche du 19ième siècle et du 20ième siècle ont souvent contenu des dispositions spécifiques concernant les Autochtones. De sorte que cet énoncé de la Cour d'appel de la Colombie Britannique peut peut-être fournir des arguments aux Autochtones pour établir leur titre au Québec, voire dans les provinces maritimes.

Deuxième point: Est-ce que la notion de droit ancestral ou de titre indien est applicable sur le territoire visé par la *Proclamation royale*? Je vous dit immédiatement que je n'ai pas de réponse catégorique sur cette question. Je constate cependant que les arrêts *Calder* et *Guérin* qui parlent d'un titre indien et d'un droit ancestral, de même que *Baker Lake*, visent des territoires situés à l'extérieur de terres réservées au sens de la *Proclamation royale*. Même monsieur le juge Steele dans *Bear Island Foundation* semble dire que lorsque la *Proclamation royale* s'applique, la notion de titre indien ne peut pas s'appliquer. Bien que selon lui il s'agisse finalement d'un même droit quant à sa nature. Il dit:

> With respect to the small area north of the height of land, I find that the land was not covered by the *Royal Proclamation of 1763* but that the rights of the Indians and Crown at common law are in all ways the same as in Proclamation lands, except that the relevant date for determining Aboriginal rights is the coming of settlement. (p. 373)

Alors, monsieur le juge Steele semble n'en faire qu'une question de date, quoique dans son esprit ça semble être une question qui se divise. Lorsque la *Proclamation royale* s'applique, on ne parle pas de titre indien, et vice-versa. À l'inverse, on pourrait se demander si les droits découlant de ces deux sources de droit ne se superposent pas sur le même territoire. En effet, monsieur le juge Hall dans *Calder* n'a-t-il pas dit que la *Proclamation royale* était déclaratoire d'un droit ancestral? Monsieur le juge MacKeegan de la Cour d'appel de la Nouvelle-Écosse dans *Isaac* (1975) a soutenu la même position.

Je laisse à d'autres, peut-être à monsieur le professeur Slattery, le soin de donner une réponse à cette question mais il semble qu'il y ait encore une ambiguïté devant les tribunaux à cet égard.

Troisième question: est-ce que la notion de droit ancestral ou de titre indien était applicable sur les anciennes possessions françaises en Amérique du Nord? Les tribunaux ont qualifié le titre indien de droit reconnu par la *common law*. Cela pourrait signifier que dans l'ordre juridique britannique, le droit "découlant de l'occupation et de la possession historiques par les Indiens de leurs terres tribales" était reconnu. C'est ce qui a expliqué l'achat des terre par les Britanniques qui a pris la forme d'un processus conduisant à la conclusion des traités, processus repris de façon solennelle dans la *Proclamation royale*. Or, si c'est cela la notion de titre indien, d'après moi, ce système n'a jamais existé sous le régime français. Les autorités françaises ont plutôt octroyé les terres aux Indiens par le biais de communautés religieuses. Il y aurait donc pas eu, à ce titre, de reconnaissance de titre indien ou de droits ancestraux sous le régime français, de sorte qu'il n'existerait pas, au moment de l'arrivée des français, de droit équivalent à celui que semble développer la *common law*.

Très récemment, monsieur le juge Frenette de la Cour Supérieure du Québec, dans l'arrêt *Decontie* (1989) a conclu que les Français, je cite:

> ... n'ont jamais reconnu le droit à l'occupation du territoire par les Indiens après qu'ils eurent imposé leur souveraineté en Amérique.

Monsieur le professeur Brian Slattery, dans un intéressant article intitulé "Understanding Aboriginal Rights", soutient que la notion de droit ancestral ou de titre indien ferait partie du droit public fondamental ou du droit constitutionnel britannique et qu'en conséquence, il se serait appliqué au Canada au moment de la conquête de 1760.

On peut objecter à cette théorie les deux questions suivantes: si les titres indiens ou droits ancestraux n'étaient pas reconnus sous le régime français, ça voudrait donc dire que le droit britannique l'aurait créé de toutes pièces en 1760? S'il avait été éteint sous le régime français, cela signifierait-il que le droit britannique l'aurait alors ressuscité?

Peut-être le débat devient-il académique dans la mesure où la *Proclamation royale* et le titre indien, en tant que sources distinctes de droit ne s'appliquant pas sur le même territoire conféreraient de toute façon des droits analogues sur le territoire.

Autre question fondamentale à être débattue devant les tribunaux: un droit ancestral implique-t-il un titre indien?

Dans l'arrêt *Kruger et Manuel* c. *La Reine* (1978), monsieur le juge Dickson parle d'un titre indien mais dans l'arrêt *La Reine* c. *Derriksan* (1976), monsieur le juge Laskin réfère à un droit aborigène de pêche. Dans ce dernier cas, il situe néanmoins ce droit dans le contexte d'un territoire lorsqu'il dit:

> [T]here is an Aboriginal right to fish in the particular area arising out of Indian occupation

Je vous souligne que monsieur le juge Johnson de la Cour d'appel des Territoires du Nord-Ouest a été encore plus explicite dans *Sikyea* (1964) lorsqu'il énonce:

> The right of Indians to hunt and fish for food on unoccupied Crown lands has always been recog-

nized in Canada in the early days as an incident of their "ownership" of the land, and later by the treaties by which the Indians gave up their ownership right in these lands. (p. 152)

Il semblerait donc que le droit ancestral implique un titre.

Dernière question: comment un traité indien et un droit ancestral peuvent-ils s'éteindre? Depuis la mise en vigueur de la *Loi constitutionnelle de 1982* le problème est plus compliqué. En effet, avant cette date, outre le cas où les Indiens pouvaient volontairement céder leurs droits par traité, il ne faisait pas de doute qu'une loi pouvait éteindre un titre indien. Le problème consistait à savoir si cette loi devait le faire de manière expresse ou implicite. La Cour suprême, dans *Canadien Pacifique Ltée* c. *Paul* a succinctement résumé les positions des juges Judson et Hall dans l'arrêt *Calder*.

Je me demande si l'arrêt *Paul* de la Cour suprême n'a pas apporté une certaine réponse à ce problème d'extinction des droits puisque dans cette affaire, il fallait déterminer si l'acquisition par la Compagnie de chemin de fer de Woodstock d'un droit de passage sur des terres d'une réserve indienne avait eu pour effet d'éteindre le droit de la bande sur le fief sousjacent que la Couronne continuait à détenir.

La Cour réfère alors au droit de la bande sur la terre afin de déterminer si le droit de passage de la compagnie de chemin de fer était incompatible avec ce droit indien. Or, comme la Cour ne pouvait qualifier ce droit ancestral au moyen "de la terminologie traditionnelle du droit des biens", elle ne répond pas directement à la question. Elle fait cependant le commentaire suivant:

> Si le droit de la bande n'en était qu'un de jouissance et d'occupation, on peut certes soutenir que le droit de passage de la Compagnie de chemin de fer de Woodstock était incompatible avec la subsistance du droit de jouissance et d'occupation de la bande. (p. 679)

On pourrait donc conclure de ce passage que l'intention du législateur d'éteindre le titre indien n'aurait pas besoin d'être énoncé expressément. Il suffirait de démontrer une incompatibilité entre la loi et le droit indien en cause.

Il est possible que la Cour suprême se penche sur la notion de l'extinction du titre indien dans l'affaire *Sparrow* parce que plusieurs gouvernements intervenants et associations intervenantes ont argumenté que le fait que l'on ait un règlement de pêche ne pouvait avoir d'autre signification que d'éteindre un droit ancestral de pêche, le règlement constituant un code en soi. Je peux vous dire que le procureur général du Québec n'a pas du tout pris part à ce genre de discussion; il ne s'est intéressé qu'au degré de protection que l'article 35 de la *Loi constitutionnelle de 1982* conférerait au droit ancestral de pêche. Il a pris pour acquis qu'il n'avait pas été éteint par un règlement fédéral.

Enfin, est-ce qu'un droit ancestral peut s'éteindre par le simple effet du temps? La Cour suprême a dit dans l'arrêt *Paul*:

> [I]l semble que sur le plan constitutionnel, une législation provinciale en matière de prescription ne s'applique pas aux terres des Indiens:(p. 296)

Cependant, il faut situer cet énoncé dans un contexte de terres réservées au sens de la *Loi sur les Indiens*; une loi provinciale, même d'application générale comme peut l'être le Code civil, ne peut pas aller à l'encontre de la *Loi sur les Indiens* puisque le fédéral doit protéger les terres des Indiens. Mais qu'en serait-il en dehors des réserves où il peut exister un titre indien ou un droit ancestral? Est-ce qu'on pourrait appliquer l'article 479 du Code civil qui énonce que "l'usufruit s'éteint ... par l'expiration du temps pour lequel il a été accordé"? Ou encore, l'article 488 du Code civil qui énonce au titre de l'usage et de l'habitation que ces droits se perdent de la même manière que l'usufruit?

Je pense qu'on ne peut pas appliquer ces deux dispositions puisque le titre indien n'est pas à proprement parler un droit d'usufruit, d'usage ou d'habitation au sens du Code civil. Peut-être que la réponse se trouve dans les conditions requises pour établir l'existence d'un droit ancestral ou titre indien. Il faut une occupation continue de sorte que s'il y a eu interruption pendant une certaine période, le droit devrait s'éteindre. Il reviendrait à la Cour d'apprécier cette question en fonction des faits historiques, anthropologiques ou autres.

Nous venons d'esquisser à grands traits quelques éléments de réflexion et de solutions en regard des questions que nous jugeons fondamentales en ce qui concerne les titres indiens ou les droits ancestraux. S'agit-il d'une évolution ou d'une révolution dans notre droit? Une chose est certaine, les causes de droit Autochtone sont beaucoup plus nombreuses depuis une quinzaine d'années et mettent en cause les droits des Autochtones eux-mêmes et non les conflits fédéraux-provinciaux sur des questions de compétence.

Les tribunaux devront donc inévitablement, un jour ou l'autre, apporter des réponses à ces questions. L'arrêt *Calder* a créé une nouvelle dynamique en droit Autochtone en référant à la notion de droits ancestraux ou titres indiens. S'agit-il d'une révolution?

Ce serait le cas si la notion de titre indien ou de droits ancestraux constituait un concept nouveau. Or, cette notion plonge ses racines dans l'histoire des communautés Autochtones qui sont les premières nations du Canada. Qu'ils n'aient pas été exprimés aussi clairement par les tribunaux avant 1973 ne signifie pas que ces droits n'existaient pas. Toutefois, les clarifications que les tribunaux pourront apporter à ces grandes questions pourraient avoir un caractère "plus révolutionnaire". Jusqu'à maintenant toutefois le développement du droit des peuples Autochtones au Canada nous apparaît davantage le fruit d'une évolution que le signe d'une révolution. Il serait donc plus juste de parler de "continuité dans le changement".

BRIAN SLATTERY

Brian Slattery is a professor at Osgoode Hall Law School, York University, where he teaches courses in Constitutional Law, Indigenous Rights, and Legal Theory. He holds a Bachelor of Arts degree from Loyola College, Montreal, a Bachelor of Civil Law from McGill University, and a D. Phil. in Law from Oxford University. He has many publications dealing with Aboriginal rights and Constitutional Law.

THE RECOLLECTION OF HISTORICAL PRACTICE

Perhaps you have had the experience of clearing out your garage on a Saturday morning and, amidst other relics of the past, coming across an object that, for the life of you, you cannot identify. You look at it and wonder why you kept it and what purpose it could have served. Was it part of an old washing machine or perhaps a remnant of a discarded lawnmower? You turn it over and over in your hands, waiting for that flash of inspiration that will place the object in its proper setting and tell you what it is.

The question of setting is an important one, for it is only within a certain context that an object exhibits its nature and significance. What is true of objects is equally true of legal terms, which, notoriously, have the capacity to change their colours like chameleons to match the prevailing tones of their surroundings. How, then, are we to understand a term like "Aboriginal rights" as guaranteed in section 35(1) of the *Constitution Act, 1982*? This section states that the existing Aboriginal and treaty rights of the Aboriginal Peoples of Canada are hereby recognized and affirmed. While the term "Aboriginal rights" is not mysterious in itself, we are left uncertain as to which legal setting displays these rights in their best and truest sense.

We run through the four main possibilities. Are Aboriginal rights an emanation of traditional Aboriginal law and custom, as practiced in Native American societies upon contact? Or are they somehow grounded in French or English law, as imported into Canada at the time of settlement? Should we look beyond domestic legal systems to international law as the true setting for Aboriginal rights? Or should we look rather to "natural law" and fundamental principles of justice?

While all of these possibilities can shed light on Aboriginal rights to some degree, I believe that, in the final analysis, none of them can provide a completely satisfactory answer. We have to look to another alternative, one that does not exclude the other possibilities, but rather draws on them and places them in a larger and more comprehensive framework.

Possible legal settings to Aboriginal rights

Here I will briefly discuss the four main alternatives just mentioned and then consider a further possibility, which may in the end provide the best solution. In doing this, I am recounting to you my own "intellectual odyssey", to give a dignified name to a rather erratic journey. Perhaps I should call it, in Oscar Wilde's phrase, my voyage from darkness into darkness. At one time or another, I have thought that each of the following alternatives was the best. I no longer do, but then again, perhaps I have gone astray.

The first possibility is customary law. Aboriginal rights have a clear connection to the original laws, customs and practices of the First Peoples of Canada. What else could Aboriginal rights be if not Aboriginal custom? How could we understand these rights apart from Aboriginal world-views, cultures, and practices? Clearly, there is much to be said for an approach grounded in customary law.

There are, however, some drawbacks to this approach. For example, what is the legal position when an Aboriginal group, under its traditional notions, did not claim "ownership" of the lands it used and occupied? Suppose, for example, that the group viewed itself as part of the land rather than as "owning" it, or held that the land belonged to the Creator and was only given to the people on trust. Does this mean that the group cannot claim Aboriginal title to the land today?

More generally, are Aboriginal Peoples confined to their original uses of the land, so that a people that traditionally lived by hunting and fishing must remain hunters and fishers forever, like living exhibits in an anthropological museum? Or can they live like other modern Canadians, developing their lands for agriculture, grazing, tourism, or whatever other purposes they see fit?

There is another significant difficulty with this approach: the relationship between customary legal systems and other systems of law, such as French or English law. What happens when these systems interact or conflict? For example, which system of law applies when an Aboriginal group purports to transfer some of its lands to a member of the English community: Aboriginal law or English law? What happens when an outsider trespasses on

Aboriginal lands? What sort of remedy would the group have? And where could that remedy be enforced and under what legal system? These are difficult questions, which take us beyond the customary law of a particular Aboriginal group. In short, we have to consider the relationship between customary legal systems and incoming systems of French and English law.

This brings us to a second possibility. If you are presenting an Aboriginal land claim before a court staffed by people educated in English common law or French civil law, you may find it useful to persuade them that Aboriginal title is not some unusual and exotic species of right but, in fact, finds its roots in familiar principles of English or French law. For example, Professor Kent MacNeil, my colleague at Osgoode Hall Law School, has argued persuasively that Aboriginal land rights are supported by ancient principles of English land law under which a person in factual occupation of land is presumed to hold valid title. Others have pointed out that English law has always allowed for the application of local custom in certain cases, such as a custom of the county of Kent, whereby fishermen are entitled to spread and dry their nets on the beaches.

An attractive feature of this approach is that it renders Aboriginal rights more accessible to lawyers trained in European-based legal systems. However, this approach also has its drawbacks. First, there is something inherently paradoxical in tracing the root of Aboriginal title to English or French law. One can, of course, see the point of looking for parallels and supporting lines of thought. It seems, perhaps, a little strained to look to Europe for the ultimate foundation of Aboriginal title when all the relevant elements of the situation are found here in North America and have been the subject of continuous practice and accomodation from ancient times. Second, there is a problem in trying to force Aboriginal rights into conceptual categories that evolved in response to social conditions found in Europe under different circumstances. However appropriate those categories may have been to the situation in Europe, we should be wary of assuming that they are applicable to the situation of Aboriginal Peoples in North America.

A third possible approach is to look for the root of Aboriginal title in international law. Here, surely, we are on the right track, since international law deals with the law and practice prevailing between independent nations. If you examine the history of European settlement in North America, you will find that relations between Aboriginal Peoples and the representatives of France and Great Britain were in many cases conducted in a spirit of rough equality, especially during the early stages of settlement in the sixteenth to eighteenth centuries. The terminology that was used, the protocol that was followed, and the type of alliances and treaties that were concluded often tend to suggest the existence of genuine international relations.

Again, there are difficulties. In dealing with early periods, such as the sixteenth and seventeenth centuries, where does one look in order to discover the law of nations? Most textbooks assume that early international law was generated by the practice of European states among themselves, as reflected in the writings of such European authorities as Grotius and Vattel. According to this approach, then, the only rights held by Native American peoples under international law were those that European states were willing to concede to them in the context of inter-European relations. However, in dealings among themselves, as opposed to direct dealings with Native Peoples, European states tended to disregard Aboriginal rights. So, for example, in 1763, France purported to cede to Great Britain an enormous stretch of territory in North America, most of which France did not actually possess or control and which was in fact under Aboriginal control. So, if international law is based on inter-European practice, Aboriginal rights tend to sink below the horizon.

This is not, of course, the only approach that can be taken to early international law. One can, for example, broaden out the inquiry and look to the practice of non-European nations. However, even if we do so, we face another hurdle. Which nations should be recognized as genuine international entities, capable of contributing to the formation of international law? In particular, should we recognize Aboriginal groups in North America in the sixteenth to eighteenth centuries as international entities? To answer that crucial question, we cannot look to international practice without falling into an infinite regress. For we again have to determine which international entities merit to have their practice taken into account, which yet again raises the question of the original status of American Aboriginal Peoples.

So, for example, if you look exclusively to the practice of European states, you have already answered the question. You tacitly hold that Native American Peoples did not constitute international entities, capable of contributing to the formation of international law. By the same token, if you expand the inquiry to include the practice of American Native Peoples, you have once again answered the question in advance. You think that such peoples are international entities, with the capacity to generate the practice that sustains international law.

How does one escape from this dilemma? I believe that the only possible way out is to appeal to basic principles of international justice, or what the early European authorities, such as Victoria and Grotius, called "natural law". These authors were attempting to construct universal principles of international law that reflected fundamental principles of justice and rights, albeit from a Christian and West European perspective. In this endeavour, they did not rely exclusively on state practice, they also considered what justice demanded in the circumstances, according to their best lights. If we today would disagree with some of their conclusions, we would nevertheless do well to recognize the merits of their approach, one that was rooted ultimately in principles of justice and fundamental rights.

We have arrived, then, at our fourth possibility: that Aboriginal rights are a species of natural or fundamental human rights and derive from basic principles of justice. Following this approach, one can develop abstract arguments identifying the conditions necessary for the survival and flourishing of the individual within communities and then trace the link between the welfare of communities and their access to land and other needed resources, both material and spiritual. While such abstract exercises are essential and fruitful in a general sort of way, nevertheless, in my experience, they do not readily lead to the kind of specific conclusions that one needs in order to develop a workable concept of Aboriginal rights. Or, if such conclusions are arrived at, they often have an air of improvisation and prove to be rather contentious.

We have exhausted, then, the four main possibilities identified at the start. We have looked in turn at Aboriginal customary law, English and French law, international law, and natural law and found that all four had drawbacks of one kind or another. Is there anything left?

Historical practice as a constitutional framework

Let me suggest one further approach, which over the years I have come to favour. I am inclined to think that the proper setting for understanding Aboriginal rights in Canada lies in historical practice: namely, the practice generated by relations among Aboriginal Peoples and incoming European states over a period running from initial contact to about 1763. That historical practice was created by Aboriginal and European nations alike and often presumed a rough equality among the parties, albeit within a context of growing European power and European pretensions to overall hegemony. The body of practice was not wholly European in origins, nor, on the other hand, was it wholly Iroquois, Cree, or Micmac. It was the joint product of the complex and multiple relationships that developed historically among Aboriginal and European nations in the course of trade, alliance, and war. The prime expression of that practice is to be found in treaties and parleys of various kinds, but it is also reflected in such documents as the *Royal Proclamation of 1763*.

What can this practice do for us today? Basically, it can provide us with a concrete constitutional framework for relations between Aboriginal and non-Aboriginal groups in Canada, to supplement the more abstract principles of justice considered under our fourth approach. I have identified on other occasions what I take to be the main attributes of this body of historical practice, and so will not say much about the subject here, given the little time remaining. Nevertheless, in broad terms, it could be said that the historical practice recognized a *principle of continuity*, whereby Aboriginal nations, as they fell increasingly under the sway of the Crown, were acknowledged to retain the right to govern themselves within their own territories, under their own systems of law.

This is not to say that conflicts did not arise in the interpretation and application of the practice. For example, under standard British constitutional doctrines, Aboriginal rights were considered to be modifiable by Parliament without the consent of the peoples concerned. By contrast, most Aboriginal groups considered that such modifications could only be carried out by treaty, with the full concurrence of the peoples affected. The entrenchment of Aboriginal and treaty rights in the *Constitution Act, 1982* has gone some distance to resolving this particular dispute. However, other points of disagreement over the nature and scope of Aboriginal rights remain. In resolving these disputes, I suggest that the legal community should pursue an approach that blends consideration of basic principles of justice with respect for the more concrete principles emerging from historical relations between Aboriginal Peoples and incoming Europeans.

In part, the process involved is one of recollection. As noted earlier, when we come across an unfamiliar object, we turn it over in our hands, we consider it from different angles and we try to "place" it in our memory. With Aboriginal rights, we have to go through a similar sort of process, except that the memory involved is collective rather than personal. We have to draw upon our collective history: the history of the various founding peoples of Canada and their links with one another, including First Nations, the French, and the English. Here, above all, we have good reason to say: "Je me souviens".

MARY LARONDE

A member of the Caribou Clan of the Teme-augama Anishnabay, which means "People of the Deep Water", Mary Laronde studied philosophy at University of Toronto and journalism at the University of Western Ontario. At the time of the Conference, she was in her third term as an elected official of the Teme-augama Anishnabay, and Public Information Officer for the Tribal Council since 1982. She has produced several video-documentaries and radio shows, and has acted as spokesperson for the Teme-augama Anishnabay as their 112 year-old struggle for justice continues.

THE TEME-AUGAMA ANISHNABAY AT BEAR ISLAND: CLAIMING OUR HOMELAND

The Teme-augama Anishnabay have occupied our homeland surrounding Lake Temagami (now north-eastern Ontario) for six thousand years of documented history. At the time of the *Royal Proclamation* in 1763 to beyond the signing of *Robinson Treaty* in 1850, the People of the Deep Water were a self-governing nation possessing over 3,800 square miles of geographically-defined lands. This land and their civil affairs were regulated by a communal system of law. Each of fourteen families maintained its own tract of between 200 to 300 square miles.

In June of 1990, 113 years will have passed since we first initiated our claim, or as we prefer to call it, "our land defence". At that time, lumbermen were on the Montreal River, which forms our eastern boundary. Fearing this encroachment, our Chief sought protection for our people through a reservation and compensation for the surrender of the remaining territory. He saw this as a way of having a landbase to provide, in his own words, "for the children and that, forever". Only in 1883 did the federal government recognize that the Teme-augama Anishnabay had been omitted from the *Robinson-Huron Treaty* of 1850. They then put the Temagami Indians on the annuity pay lists and began the process whereby a reserve would be surveyed and a deal hammered out, as Professor Slattery described, in a treaty of cession whose terms would be approved by the band council.

In 1884, a one hundred square mile reserve at the southern end of Lake Temagami was surveyed by the federal government for our reservation. That summer, an Ontario representative promised to come up and finalize a treaty, since provincial concurrence with a treaty was necessary. He simply did not show up and so the treaty did not take place.

In 1894, the federal government represented the Teme-augama Anishnabay at a board set up to arbitrate outstanding land issues as of Confederation. In its representation, the federal government spoke on behalf of the Temagami Indians and claimed that the lands were subject to the interest of the said Indians and that the province ought to allow a reserve to be set apart or prove surrender of Indian title in the remaining portions of the tract. Emilius Irving, counsel for Ontario, successfully argued on a technical issue that the case was a matter for treaty and not a proper matter for arbitration by the board. Therefore, the issue was deferred.

In 1901, Ontario established the Temagami Forest Reserve, and, about this time, the Ontario government's presence was first felt strongly in our area. When the Forest Reserve was created, the Department of Indian Affairs acted on our behalf, requesting, once again, that land be set aside for a reserve. The Crown Commissioner of Lands for Ontario said that the reserve of one hundred square miles was more than the Indian population needed, therefore, no action was taken. In 1910, the Department of Indian Affairs again asked Ontario for a reserve, and again the Ontario government decided the land was too valuable as a logging resource. With the establishment of the Forest Reserve, harassment and oppression began in earnest. The fire ranger demanded that the Temagami Indians buy licenses to cut firewood, for example. They were threatened with jail should they fail to comply. Around the turn of the century, the prospects for an Indian person in jail were not very good. People believed that if you went there, you might never come back.

In 1911, Ontario established the Temagami Game and Fish Reserve, and the harassment escalated. There were a number of families who had to remove themselves from their traditional territories because they were being prosecuted and jailed for fishing and hunting on their own traditional lands. When people travelled from one section of their territory to another on main waterways, agents of the Ontario government confiscated their nets, guns, furs, and any kind of food supplies that they had. The wild game that they had in their canoes would all be confiscated. In 1912, the White Bear family was flooded out from their family grounds, and, in 1921, another family was flooded out at Cross Lake. The lakes were raised fourteen and twenty-one feet, completely destroying the beaver habitat, as well as Temagami settlements, buildings, gardens, and even a graveyard.

In 1929, people forced off their traditional family grounds came to live at Bear Island, close to the Hudson's Bay post. There, they had seasonal work as guides and workers for the Hudson's Bay Company. Already living on Bear Island was a white community, therefore the Ontario government decided that they would charge the Temagami Indians rent for living on Bear Island. We protested to the federal government, and, again, our representatives in the government restated that we had no treaty settlement and that we deserved some kind of recognition and a land-base. Ontario replied that, with the passage of time, there seemed to be less and less reason why land should be set aside for the Temagami Indians. However, the federal government insisted that the province had a moral, as well as a legal, obligation to provide a reserve.

In 1939, the value of the land as a timber resource was again used to argue that the area was just too valuable. Even if the people were allotted a portion of Bear Island, we could not get a guarantee from the federal government that we could stay there. In 1939, we were also forbidden to trap without purchasing Ontario licenses, and the trapping areas were cut down to the size of the townships: thirty-six square miles. Some of the Temagami men overseas fighting the Second World War had their trapping grounds licensed out to non-Indian trappers, and lost both their cabins and their hunting territory.

In 1943, where the Temagami Indians would have a reserve was still a question; the federal government was still persisting and the Temagami Indians were still demanding a treaty settlement. Bear Island was then purchased by the federal government from Ontario for three thousand dollars so that we could stay there rent-free. In the conditions of that sale, Ontario insisted that when the Temagami Indians became extinct, the land would revert back to the province. Throughout the years, the Chiefs have annually petitioned the federal government to secure a treaty.

In 1948, another family was flooded out of their territory at Diamond Lake for a Hydro development project. It is interesting to note that when the lake was flooded, a non-Indian man who had occupied an Indian cabin received compensation for a cabin he did not build, while the Indian family that lived there received no compensation.

The response of the courts

As time went on, the band at Bear Island continued attempting to secure a treaty. However, in 1970, the band decided to open up a tourist development. Since Bear Island was not an Indian reservation as defined in the *Indian Act*, since it was just land held by the federal government in trust for the Temagami Indians, the federal government passed an Order in Council to create Bear Island Reserve Number One. That is how the Temagami Indian band secured their reserve at Bear Island – through an Order in Council in 1970.

Then in 1973, the Ontario government began planning a major tourist resort on Maple Mountain, the second highest point in Ontario. To us, the name of the mountain in our language means "where the spirit goes after the body dies" and it is the most sacred site. We filed cautions on one hundred and ten townships within our traditional lands. These cautions, which are still in effect today, are against all unregistered lands – so-called Crown lands.

In 1978, the province of Ontario sued the Teme-augama Anishnabay in the Supreme Court of Ontario. In June 1982, the trial commenced and proceeded for 119 days, ending on March 15, 1984. On December 11, 1984, we received the judgment of Justice Steele, and one of the comments he made, among others, was that our history was pieced together by a small, dedicated and well-meaning group of white people. We had asked a number of academic witnesses to show that we had been on the land for six thousand years, and this was his response. He also said that, in 1763, George III had not granted ownership of vast tracts of land to Indian bands subject to a limited right of repossession by repurchase, surrender or conquest. The judge found that Europeans had never considered Indians equal to themselves, and it was inconceivable that the King would have made such vast grants to undefined bands thereby restricting his European subjects from occupying these lands in the future except at great expense. Our argument was that King George did not grant anything, and, seen in a historical context, the King was simply responding to what was already a fact: we had possession of the lands and were self-governing.

Justice Steele also lists nine Aboriginal rights that he admitted existed when the *Royal Proclamation* was signed. In the context of changing perceptions of Aboriginal rights over the last twenty years, his list is a decided step backward. We had the right to hunt animals for food and personal use. The individual family had the right to trap fur and to fish; to use berries, herbs, roots and so on; to use stones for tools, but not for mining; to use clay for pottery, pipes and ornaments; to use trees for housing, but not for lumber, firewood, canoes, sleighs or snowshoes. Of course, they also found that we had no Aboriginal title to the lands, and that we were, in fact, signatories to the *Robinson-Huron Treaty* of 1850, although there was overwhelming evidence to the contrary.

We appealed the decision to the Court of Appeal of Ontario. The Appeal Court upheld Justice Steele's decision pretty much point for point, and they said that, although we did not sign the Treaty, a man whom we had never heard of before had signed the Treaty on our behalf. Further, if that was not the case, we had adhered to the Treaty by receiving annuities and by receiving our reserve in 1970. Thirdly, even if we had not consented, the intention of the Crown to take those lands could extinguish Aboriginal rights unilaterally.

Usually, whenever a Chief or someone signed on behalf of a band in a land cession, this representation was always expressly stated on the face of the document. In our case, that had definitely not happened. In our favour was a map produced in the 1980s by the Department of Indian Affairs, which clearly shows the Temagami lands outside the boundaries of the *Robinson-Huron Treaty*. So, we feel that the judge erred in his decision and his decision is completely unacceptable.

Steele also found the annuities and the Bear Island reserve constituted adherence to the *Robinson Treaty*. We argued that there is neither documentation to support this finding, nor any grounds to conclude that a treaty can be adhered to in this way. The Court of Appeal of Ontario replied that the aspect of the *Royal Proclamation* stating that Indian lands may be acquired through cession was repealed by the *Quebec Act* of 1774. The learned judges referred to a case in Idaho to support their decision that Aboriginal title is not a property right. They did not refer to any of the more recent and stronger cases in Canada.

We have had two losses and were informed by the Supreme Court of Canada last October that they will hear our appeal, but no court date has yet been. For ninety-six years, we have petitioned government agents for a treaty and after sixteen years of legal actions, legal expenses and frustration, we are still seeking justice and fair treatment. We do not think that surrender of Aboriginal title is necessary for settlement of land claims. Aboriginal Peoples have been in a situation where governments would only recognize Aboriginal title if it was to be surrendered. We would like to maintain title to our lands and develop a new way of settlement of land claims in a treaty called a "Treaty of Co-Existence".

With Aboriginal title intact, we could forever maintain our interest in the land and thereby have a large say in what uses the land would be put to. Therefore, we could ensure the continuity of the land and of ourselves.

We would like to see the public insist that human rights abuses, and theft of land and resources be stopped in Canada and that honour, integrity and justice be revived in dealing with outstanding Aboriginal land claims.

QUESTION PERIOD: PANEL TWO

Question: JACK MILLER
Conflict Resolver, Interlex Group (an ADR firm)

Picking up from Professor Slattery on the possible sources of Aboriginal title, I would like to suggest to you that there is at least another one: namely, that Aboriginal title is founded upon the internal sense of justice and fairness that each one of us feels. I would like to suggest to you that this may possibly be the only basis for resolving deep-rooted conflict. Judgments of courts can only serve as information – they could never resolve such matters in a definitive way.

This internal sense of fairness and justice is the foundation of the Alternative Dispute Resolution movement which has led us to a different view of law and conflict. The law, under these circumstances, does not play an authoritative role in deciding matters, but rather a normative role.

What we have seen are developments in assertiveness as a basic approach for the establishment of Aboriginal interests, leading to an interaction based on cooperation rather than competition, arrived at through principled negotiation. I think that the adjudicative approach can only play a very limited role by generating information, since real change comes through interaction of people face-to-face. I would like to hear your reaction and comments.

Answer: RENE MORIN

I agree with your statement, but let's take two examples. The *James Bay Agreement* came about not only because Quebec was generous, but also because they had a gun to their head. The James Bay project had to go ahead and they were able to make a general agreement of five hundred pages in less than a year. In another example, we have been in negotiation with the Montagnais for the last eight to nine years, but because there is no gun to our head, we have no agreement. So, I think that legal procedure, although frustrating for Aboriginal Peoples, can force negotiations up to a certain point. There are at least two or three cases where litigation may help Indian Peoples to negotiate. I agree that we need good-will and a political context, but I am not too sure it is enough.

Question: JACK MILLER

Well, thank you, because you have actually illustrated the point I was making. It was not resolved in the courts despite the gun at their head.

Answer: RENE MORIN

I think that the legal context can put Aboriginal Peoples in a position to negotiate. Where did the "gun" come from? We lost in front of Judge Malouf in 1973; we won at the Court of Appeal, but just an interlocutory injunction, and there was a chance to go up to the Supreme Court, which would have taken many years to "wait and lose". Or, we could sit down and negotiate.

So, the legal context was crucial. I was not there at that time, but my reading is that there was also a lot of pressure from the millions and millions of dollars waiting in New York to pay for the James Bay project.

Question: CHRISTOPHE EICK
Masters student, McGill Faculty of Law

It has been suggested by Mr. Morin that the French did not recognize territorial rights of the Indians when they arrived in this country, since they did not conclude any land cession treaties. I would suggest to you that this is a question that has to be answered by the international law of the time. If you look at the records, you will find that the French did treat the Indian nations as sovereign entities, and the fact that there were no land cession treaties can be attributed to the fact that the French dealt with no-madic nations rather than sedentary tribes, as the English did further south. Further, the French were very few in number, while the English had more people to settle. The French were more interested in the fur trade, so, they actually wanted the Indians to keep the land so that the Indians could hunt for the furs.

Answer: BRIAN SLATTERY

In my opinion, the land rights of Aboriginal Peoples were recognized in practice during the French Regime. The evidence that I have looked at, which includes the official Royal Commissions and Letters of Patent issued for French Canada and the various documents issued by the King in relation to Native Peoples, does not suggest that the French Crown necessarily had the intention of extinguishing Aboriginal title. To the contrary, the health and wealth of a colony in New France depended upon the fur trade. The fur trade depended upon Indians coming regularly to Quebec, Montreal and Trois-Rivières with furs. The furs were gathered by Indians from their territories. The French were trying to solicit the cooperation and alliance of the Indians. Normally, you do not do that by saying: well, we want your help, we want your furs, we want you to fight with us against the English, but, of course, by the way, we have just taken your lands. More recent historical writers, such as Professor Eccles from the University of Toronto, have supported this newer point of view. The older view was based on the few documents setting aside reserves for Native Peoples and did not take proper account of the large mass of documents dealing with direct relations between the French and Indian Peoples.

Question: DALE TURNER

Could you inform us on how the band relates to the Temagami Wilderness Society or environmentalists?

Answer: MARY LARONDE

The environmental issue in the Temagami area has posed a number of difficulties for us. We, of course, have the recent example where environmentalists and the Indian People have gotten together. However, the fight for Aboriginal title is being forgotten. We have had a lot of interest in the area because it is one of the last large ecosystems of White Pine forests in North America and certainly the last accessible wilderness in Ontario. Nonetheless, we have found that the environmental issue has given the government a diversionary tactic in dealing with the issue of Aboriginal title.

Meanwhile, in December, we were manning a roadblock to stop logging in the last 5 % of our traditional lands that have not been logged. While we were manning this roadblock, the minister deferred 585 hectares of Red Pine forest for an environmental study on a lumber road south. Then we are asked the question: is this not a good thing?

The point is that the Aboriginal title issue has been outstanding for 113 years, and, for us, that is the issue. It is very difficult to give reasons in a short news spot of why we do not think something is a good idea. The whole environmental movement in our area has been a problem for us simply because it is used as a smokescreen for the real issue, and the government uses this tactic to its advantage. We are having a hard time saying whether we are with the environmentalists because we have to keep the issues separated.

In response to questions of land use, the province has put together this thing called the Temagami Advisory Council, composed of citizens, people in industry and residents. They also offered a seat on the Council to the Temagami Indian band. We could not accept because we do not recognize Ontario's jurisdiction on our lands, and we do not think that they have free and clear title to the lands to do with it as they wish. So, they offer us these political seats and then because we refuse, they say that we are unreasonable about this whole issue of the environment. The attention directed at Temagami has turned into a real public relations war, a media war, and it is been very difficult for us to keep our issues focussed so people understand that for us, our homeland is the issue and not the environment.

PANEL THREE

SELF-DETERMINATION IN THE NATIONAL AND INTERNATIONAL CONTEXTS

JOSEPH SANDERS

Joseph Sanders was Constitutional Adviser to the Assembly of First Nations from 1981 to 1991, and has advised them in their deliberations in Geneva at the International Labour Organization and at the Working Group on Indigenous Populations. He served for several years as an international legal advisor and diplomat at the United Nations. Before that, he taught law in England and was a journalist-broadcaster and producer with the BBC. He negotiated and participated in drafting several international legal instruments, including the Code of Conduct for Law Enforcement Officials and the Convention on the Elimination of Discrimination against Women. As well, he has acted as President of the United Nations Security Council.

THE INTERNATIONAL COMMUNITY AND SELF-DETERMINATION

Is self-determination a right? From 1946, self-determination began to grow as a principle in international law, and it was enshrined in the *United Nations Charter*. As a result of widespread application and frequent reference, this principle has become a right according to customary international law. In addition, since the independence of countries like India, in 1947, and the African countries, beginning with Ghana, in the 1950s, new nations in the United Nations have referred to it as a right rather than a principle. In 1950, for example, a General Assembly resolution required the Commission on Human Rights to study ways and means to ensure the right of peoples and nations to self-determination. In 1952, another resolution said that the right to self-determination is a prerequisite to the full enjoyment of all fundamental human rights. In 1960, the famous *Resolution 1514*, which is the "Bible" on decolonization, said for the first time that all peoples have the right to self-determination. It was adopted by eighty-nine votes, without opposition and with only nine abstentions. A year later, *Resolution 1654* emphasized that *Resolution 1514* was more than a moral declaration. In 1966, the United Nations completed and adopted two covenants, one of which was the *International Covenant of Civil and Political Rights*. We had enshrined in plain language that all peoples had the right to self-determination in binding covenants. Canada, by the way, is party to these conventions.

In the *Western Sahara* case, the International Court of Justice made reference to this right to self-determination, and we have evidence, in practice, that states have accepted the right to all peoples to self-determination. One could look, for example, at the United Nations involvement in the conflict between the Dutch and the Indonesian nationalist forces, when the Indonesians were struggling for their independence. The United Nations intervened because they believed that those peoples had a right to self-determination. The United Nations also backed the struggles in Morocco, in Tunisia, in Algeria; they set up the Decolonization Committee which took a very active interest in independence struggles in Mozambique, Angola, Rhodesia and Namibia.

That is not to say that there have been no failures. The United Nations does recognize the right to self-determination. However, Tibet, Palestine and Timor continue to be dominated by alien forces. During the time I was involved in the Security Council, I had the dubious honour of piloting the resolution calling for the removal of remaining Indonesian forces from Timor. Not only are they still there, but the territory is now practically an integral part of Indonesia.

The meaning of self-determination in international law

Despite these failures, international law protects the right to all peoples to self-determination. So, what does it mean? The two international covenants say that all peoples have the right to self-determination and, by virtue of that right, to freely decide their political status and to pursue their economic, social and cultural development. Nevertherless, how do we implement this right to self-determination? In the *Friendly Relations' Declaration, Resolution 2625* of 1970, article 5 states some ways:

1. The establishment of a sovereign and independent state;

2. The free association with an independent state;

3. Integration with an independent state; and

4. Emergence into any other political status freely determined by the peoples.

Well, what does it mean? As law students or lawyers, we know that no right is absolute. *Resolution 2625* says categorically that any attempt aimed at the partial or total disruption of national unity, the territorial integrity of a state, or its political independence, is incompatible with the purposes and principles of the *United Nations' Charter.* There is, in the same resolution, a caveat about how far this right should extend and an indication of what kind of support the United Nations would give a people seeking to exercise its right to self-determination. Two countries, Canada and Italy, sponsored the following paragraphs:

> Nothing in the foregoing shall be construed as authorizing or encouraging any action which would dismember or impair totally or in part the territorial integrity or political unity of sovereign and independent states conducting themselves in compliance with the principle of equal rights and self-determination of peoples and thus possessed of a government representing the whole peoples belonging to the territory without distinction as to race, creed or colour.

How would one exercise the right to self-determination with these caveats in mind? The test, I suppose, is one of reasonableness. As with any right, whether individual or group, we have to weigh and balance conflicting rights and seek the best solution in the particular circumstances. Where you have a people claiming to have a right to self-determination and wishing to exercise it, that has to be balanced in international law by the rights of the dominant state. Remember, when Bangladesh, or East Pakistan as it was called then, wanted to exercise its right to self-determination, this was fiercely resisted by Pakistan, then West Pakistan, and they actually went to war.

So, how would Aboriginal People exercise this right to self-determination in Canada? At the First Ministers Conference on Aboriginal Constitutional Matters in 1983, then Prime Minister Trudeau said in his opening remarks something to the effect that assimilation may be out since Aboriginal People do not want to be assimilated; however, independence or total sovereignty was also out, meaning by that Canada would not permit it. Let us find the option in the wide in-between range. Something between assimilation and total independence.

Next question: how is this right to self-determination to be enforced? There are basically two ways: by peaceful means or by violence. Many member countries of the Commonwealth and the United Nations have exercised their right to independence by peaceful means. Those in the Caribbean come to mind. However, there were others that had to fight, and are fighting today for their independence. It is still continuing in parts of Africa and the Middle East. The famous *Friendly Relations Declaration* forbids states to use force against peoples seeking to exercise their right to self-determination. It also says that if force is used, such peoples have the right to seek and receive support in accordance with the principles and purposes of the *Charter*.

Who has the right to self-determination? The answer is: all peoples. Having said that, the problems begin. What is a people? Perhaps, Professor Sally Weaver may give us some enlightenment from an anthropological perspective. Certainly, international lawyers have no fixed definition of what a people is. Further, the government of Canada says that the Aboriginal Peoples of Canada are not "peoples" in the sense of international law, as former Minister of Justice, Mr. MacGuigan, told the National Chief of the Assembly of First Nations in my presence, and as is said by Canada in discussions at the United Nations. The position of the government of Canada is that Aboriginal Peoples, while "peoples" in the domestic sense and protected by the *Constitution* of Canada, are not "peoples" in the international sense and are, therefore, not entitled to a right to self-determination. Many attempts have been made to arrive at a definition, and these share certain common features. The most important features would be history, ethnicity or race, culture, language, religion, ideology, geography and economics. All of these must be present if one is going to identify a people. Theorists of international law have agreed, at least, that these features are important. Most have agreed on one other indispensable, but subjective element for a people, and that is that the group itself must have become conscious of its own identity and must assert its will to exist as a group. In other words, no one group can say to another that the latter cannot be considered a people. It is a subjective test recognized by international law.

International agreements on the right to self-determination

In the last couple of years, attempts have been made to do something real about self-determination and Indigenous Peoples. In 1957, the *International Labour Organization Convention No. 107* came into force. This convention was drafted way back in 1954, and it was intended to take care of the labour and social problems of Indigenous populations in Central and South America. Very few other countries paid much attention to it. Should you look at the original convention, you will see that it was integrationist in tone, and it was being used by Latin American governments to integrate their Indigenous populations.

In 1986, the ILO called a meeting of experts to look at this convention and to decide whether it should be revised, and if it was going to be revised, whether totally or partially. I attended that meeting. The decision that emerged was that it should be revised. Some of us argued that it should be revised totally, but then we discovered that we were treading on dangerous ground, since many were afraid of a total revision. The compromise – and the UN is a great place for compromise – was a partial revision.

During the course of the two sessions, in 1988 and 1989, it became evident that we were going to have problems with the term "peoples". *The Convention Concerning Indigenous and Tribal Populations*, as it was called, was controversial partly because of the word "populations". Many countries reasoned that the word "peoples" was connected to the right to self-determination, and the right to self-determination includes the right to secede and to form an independent state. Therefore, it would invite trouble to describe Indigenous "populations" as "peoples". This sounds silly, but believe me, the argument went on throughout the summer months when the convention was being revised. In fact, it continued right up into 1989.

The Indigenous Peoples present were not part of the decision-making structure of the ILO. They were there to make their views known to the delegations present, and the delegations could choose to take into account their views, if they wished. Only some delegations had Indigenous advisors. Canada was one; the Canadian Labour Congress had an Indigenous advisor. If you look at article 1, part 1 of the General Policy of this Convention, you will see the compromise:

> [T]he use of the term "peoples" in this Convention shall not be construed as having any implications as regards the rights which may attach to the term under international law.

A second process is taking place within the General Assembly of the United Nations in the drafting of the *Universal Declaration of Indigenous Rights*. There is an influence from the ILO already apparent in that exercise. The revised ILO Convention has been adopted with the clause stating that "peoples" does not mean "peoples" in the sense of international law. The Ambassador for New Zealand opened his remarks on the draft *Universal Declaration* by repeating the same distinction.

> We cannot recognize indigenous populations as peoples, otherwise, we will be opening the door to independence movements, secession and that sort of thing.

The statement made by the Assembly of First Nations immediately following that of New Zealand was to the effect that self-determination does not automatically lead to independence. There are sufficient safeguards within the covenants themselves. One safeguard is the necessary recognition as a nation-state by the international community. For example, Biafra tried to secede from Nigeria, and only Tanzania recognized it. Where is Biafra today? In Cyprus, only Turkey recognized the part of Cyprus that tried to become independent. Without recognition from the United Nations, the game is up. Look at the so-called independent homelands in South Africa. They are recognized by no other country than South Africa. Peoples with the right to self-determination therefore have to reflect upon this need for recognition.

The situation now in the Soviet Union is very interesting. The *Declaration of the Rights of the Peoples of Russia*, passed in November 1917, laid down a policy for the minorities in the Soviet Union as part of the USSR Constitution. It recognized the equality and sovereignty of the peoples of the Soviet Union, including their right to the establishment of independent states. Lenin likened this right to self-determination to the right to divorce: claiming that supporting the freedom to self-determination meant encouraging separation is as foolish and hypocritical as accusing advocates of freedom of divorce of encouraging the destruction of family ties. In other words, the fact that you are supporting a right to self-determination does not, in itself, mean that you are supporting a right to secession. Mr. Gorbachev might be gambling on the fact that, by enjoying a large measure of self-government, the peoples of the Soviet Union would not want to secede. Many multi-ethnic countries are watching the situation in the Soviet Union very carefully.

KEN DEER

Ken Deer participated in the International Labour Organization (ILO) drafting process for the revision of the Convention Concerning Indigenous and Tribal Populations, as well as the Working Group on Indigenous Populations that worked on the draft Declaration of Indigenous Rights. He is a Mohawk from Kahnawake and has lived there. He worked in the Kahnawake education system for sixteen years as an education counsellor and Director of the Kahnawake Survival School. He is past Chairman of the National Indian Education Council out of the Assembly of First Nations' National Office. He is presently the Coordinator of the Mohawk Nation Office, which is a secretariat for the traditional Longhouse in Kahnawake, and editor of the Eastern Door newspaper in Kahnawake.

THE FAILURE OF INTERNATIONAL LAW TO ASSIST INDIGENOUS PEOPLES

No matter what takes place at the United Nations, as a Mohawk person, I believe that I have the right to self-determination and the right to secede from Canada or any other state. As a Mohawk, I belong to a nation of people, the Iroquois Confederacy. Our people have a stable population, and, like most countries, we have a homeland that goes from the St. Lawrence River down to Albany, New York, from the watershed of the Vermont mountains to part way up Lake Ontario. We have laws within our Mohawk Nation, and we have the ability to enforce those laws. We have made agreements with other nations that must be considered treaties, since treaties are international instruments used only between nations. Most importantly, we have a living, breathing constitution that predates European contact and that still exists today as it did five or six hundred years ago.

This constitution, called the *Great Law of Peace*, gives us the ability and the power to take care of our political structures and our spiritual ceremonies. It gives us everything that we need to exist, to defend ourselves, and to co-exist with other nations. The three words our constitution is built upon are: righteousness, reason and power. "Righteousness" means that justice is practised among the people using the purest and most unselfish minds in harmony with the flow of life. "Reason" means the soundness of mind and body and the peace that comes when minds are sane and bodies are cared for. "Power" means the authority of law and custom backed by such force as necessary to make justice prevail.

These are the principles that our people have lived with for centuries.

We continue to this day to exercise these powers. The Confederacy has made a statement regarding Canada's *Constitution* and its international position, and I quote:

> The Confederacy has no desire to be governed now or in the future by the *Indian Act* or by any Canadian form of Indian self-government. The *Indian Act* as it stands today and as it has always been over the years in its various forms is a detriment to our people and our Confederacy.

In December 26, 1982 the Confederacy also passed a resolution concerning lands and government, and one of the points was the sovereignty of the Confederacy in the international community, not within the Canadian or American communities. The Confederacy has no desire to separate from Canada, but we have never been part of Canada either. We have always had our own country and our own government. We meet the fundamental requirements of nationhood by having a permanent population, a definite territory, a government and an ability to enter into relations with other nations. As nations, we are subjects of international law, not Canadian or American Law.

We draw our authority from the *Great Law of Peace*, not the *Constitution* of Canada. Like the many nation-states and their institutions, the Confederacy encompasses the following: principal objectives for political life, a definition of the main institutions of government, a definition of divisions of power, and a definition of the relationship between governments and the people. We are no different than the people of Canada, the people of the United States or of any other sovereign nation in the world, and our constitution is, if not the oldest in the world, pretty darn close.

We feel, as a separate nation, that we come under the protection of the *Declaration of Human Rights*, the *International Covenant on Economic, Social and Cultural Rights*, the *International Covenant on Civil and Political Rights* and the *Declaration of Principles for the Defense of Indigenous Nations and the People of the Western Hemisphere*. We seek only the rightful recognition of our historic, current and future rights as one of the original confederations in the world.

The position that the Confederacy has taken is not new. Anyone who is familiar with our history knows that the relationship between ourselves, Great Britain and France is long. I am not going to give you a long history of our activities and our relationships. I would rather talk about the present and about how Canada continues to ignore our right to self-determination and perhaps by extension, how the United Nations has not fulfilled its promise to Indigenous Peoples.

The discussion of the International Labour Organization for the revision of *Convention 107*, now called *Convention 169*, gives us an example of the kind of difficulty that Indigenous Peoples have faced in the international arena. Despite the justness of our cause, governments continue to deceive and manipulate countries into subduing Indigenous Peoples. Canada is right up there with the worst of them, and despite Canada's reputation as a fighter for human rights in the international field, their human rights practice is an embarrassment when it comes to Indigenous Peoples. My first-hand experience with the Canadian delegations have been negative, to put it mildly.

The International Labour Organization

Before I talk about the Canadian government, I would like to talk about the International Labour Organization (ILO) and how Indigenous Peoples are completely shut out of their decision-making processes. The International Labour Organization is made up of three parts: member governments, labour organizations and employee associations. It is the only international forum where governments share power with anybody else. There is no room in there for Indigenous representation – none. Yet, these people are passing international covenants that directly affect the relations between governments and Indigenous Peoples. At the ILO meeting I attended, some countries, such as the United States, brought an Indian with them, but those Indians definitely toed the government line. Countries saw that the delegation includes an Indian and said, "Hey, there's that Indian speaking for the United States. What they're recommending must be pretty good, because the Indians agree with it." Nothing could be further from the truth.

The only avenue close to direct participation that Native Peoples have had that has been in the labour faction of the ILO. Native People were, in some delegations, allowed to take part directly. Nonetheless, they could not truly represent Native Peoples.

Two of us Mohawks went to a recent ILO convention and tried to register as a government. We certainly were not a labour organization, and we were not employers. We were a government, and we decided to demand to be registered as a government. It caused quite a fuss. They did not know what to do with us; they asked what countries recognized us, and stuff like that. They tried to draw Canada into the negotiations to accommodate us, but we refused to accept that. We said, "Either you recognize us as a Mohawk Nation or as part of the Iroquois Confederacy, or we refuse to register." And since they would not recognize us as a government, we did not register. However, we were allowed into all the meeting rooms; the security guard would give us a wink and a nudge, and we would be in. We never had I.D. cards, but we attended all of the sessions anyway. A lot of people supported us, and we took a very active part in the meetings. Some countries openly congratulated our stand. So, at least they were helpful by not throwing us out of the conference. Canada was not that helpful; Canada was not happy with our behaviour. However, I was not happy with theirs either.

Joseph Sanders explained Canada's position and why they do not want to recognize the Mohawk Nation or other nations as a people despite all the moral and logical reasons of why we should be. Other "great" countries, human rights advocates like Chile, India and, perhaps, Bolivia, gathered around Canada and supported the idea that we cannot be recognized as a people. Since Canada and these countries did not want to be embarrassed by a vote on the floor in favour of Indigenous Peoples, they worked the backrooms and managed to negotiate the compromise of our rights as a people. As Joseph said, the word "peoples" in the Convention cannot be construed as having any implications under international law. Frankly, I just do not even want to talk about that.

Although that was bad enough, there are other things that I thought were even worse. Article 6 deals with obtaining the consent of Indigenous Peoples. The original terms of the convention stated that governments had to get the consent of Indigenous Peoples to move them or to carry out any kind of program. Canada supported the removal of the word "consent" in favour of the word "consult" or even "hear". They will "hear" Indigenous Peoples before they do anything. They did not even want to support the term "consult". So, the term "consent" was eliminated and "consult" added. If you look at article 6(2):

> [C]onsultations carried out shall be undertaken in
> good faith, in the form appropriate to the circum-

stances with the objective of achieving agreement
or consent to the proposed measures.

Canada supported a resolution to remove the phrase "with the objective of achieving agreement or consent to the proposed measures". In other words, for Canada, "consult" does not mean trying to reach an agreement. Canada, in the good company of Chile and India, voted for an amendment to remove that phrase. Fortunately, they were defeated by the Nordic countries, New Zealand and even the United States. It was one of the very few times that the United States and Canada voted against each other. This whole process sticks in my mind, and I tell anybody who cares to listen that Canada's definition of consultation does not mean that they wish for agreement or consent. So, beware when you hear the government say, "We're consulting our Native People".

Article 8 is in regards to laws and regulations, and it stipulates that "due regard" be given to customs and customary law. We have laws, we have our own justice system, and we have a way of dealing with our own people that predates European contact. However, according to international law, all Canada is obligated to do is give "due regard" to these laws and customs. What does "due regard" mean? It can mean whatever Canada feels it means. This stipulation has no teeth and gives no support whatsoever to our laws.

Article 9(2) says to take customary laws "into consideration". Article 13 on land is key to why *Convention 107* was initiated: to protect Indigenous Peoples and their land. The new *Convention 169*, although it gives some rights to the land, basically gutted its central purpose. For instance, land is talked about in the present tense, meaning that only the land that you currently occupy can be claimed. They talk about natural resources, but in article 15(2), they take it away, saying that if the right to resources are in the state, if Canada says it owns all of the natural resources in the country, well then, too bad. You are out of luck, because Canada says it owns the natural resources. So, they give you natural resources in one clause, and take it away in another.

They revised *Convention 107* to make *Convention 169* less assimilationist. However, the effect has not turned out that way. All it has done is fiddle with the language so that it does not sound assimilationist, but in reality, it refuses to recognize our laws and customs and allows those who have taken our land and resources to keep everything. This international law justifies the rape and pillage of our land. Yet, this is the document that is supposed to protect us.

What it does do is give us some nice programs in education. They say Indians should be educated in their own language, but this is our right anyway: we do not need a convention to say that. It also says a few nice things about health and treaties. They do say that treaties should be recognized, but we will see how they get around that one. Canada has already said at the UN Commission on Human Rights in 1988, that Canada does not have treaties with Indians, it only has agreements in the form of treaties.

I am not just talking about my personal experience in the ILO, I am talking about the experience of Indigenous Peoples from around the world, from Australia to northern Japan. We went there with our eyes open, but we knew that we would get our rear-ends kicked, because as Indigenous Peoples, we are not recognized as a people or as equals, and we knew it was going to continue this way.

The UN Working Group on Indigenous Populations and the draft *Declaration on Indigenous Rights* are the next steps. *Convention 169* has been passed, but the Mohawk People are not going to sign it. The Working Group on Indigenous Populations and the draft *Declaration on Indigenous Rights* is the next forum.

We are concerned that the ILO process will repeat itself. Although the *Declaration* is an improvement over the ILO convention, it still falls short of self-determination. It still does not recognize our rights to ownership of our land, ownership of natural resources, the right to control of our economy, and to one day take our rightful place in the United Nations. It does not come anywhere close to offering that. I believe, and many people believe, that in a just world, Mohawks have a rightful place in the United Nations.

SIMON McINNES

Simon McInnes was Director of Policy in the Self-Government Sector of the Department of Indian Affairs from 1987 to 1990. Part of his responsibilities was to provide advice to the federal bureaucrats who negotiated community self-government arrangements. Simon McInnes has been working for eleven years in various federal departments. He is currently with Industry Canada. He has worked as an advisor to the Inuit and taught political science at the University of Saskatchewan, York University, McMaster University, and Carleton University.

CANADIAN POLICIES FOR NATIVE SELF-GOVERNMENT

There is no-one in the Government of Canada who would argue that the government has an excellent relationship with its Aboriginal Peoples. Let us face it, the clash of cultures has never been painless, and the way in which my forefathers handled their relationships and encounters with Indians leaves much to be desired. However, Canada is attempting to do something to improve relationships for the future. Whether it is pursuing the right alternatives is for Canadian citizens to judge, but it does openly recognize that the relationship needs repair.

Steps taken by the Government of Canada

One need only look at the *Indian Act*, which any law student should at least read even if they never take a Native law course. I did not appreciate how the *Indian Act* functioned until I was at a meeting a few weeks ago with a high-priced Bay Street lawyer representing an Indian band, and he confessed that the first time he read the *Indian Act*, he took it literally. He was then amazed to find out that what it says is not what it means and that there are an army of professionals who spend their life telling us what the *Indian Act* says. It is a very confusing piece of legislation, completely out of date, drafted in the colonial period, and probably the only piece of legislation in Canada which still harps back to a colonial era. Nonetheless, the government is determined to update the *Indian Act*. The Act was last revised in 1951, and updating the *Indian Act*, assuming it is still worth keeping, will take a considerable amount of consultation with all of the Indian national associations and spokespersons.

The second way in which the Government of Canada is trying to update its relationship with First Nations is by putting more power in the hands of the First Nations. About ten years ago, around 70 % of the expenditures on First Nations were administered directly by the Department of Indian Affairs, and 30 % by the local level of the various First Nations themselves. Today, it is the other way around: 70 % is administered by the First Nations and 30 % by the Department. The Department is shrinking and down-sizing, and the policy of the government is to put more control into the hands of the bands. Eventually, perhaps within our lifetime, the Department of Indian Affairs may, in fact, be a very small central agency. Who knows?

Having control of your expenditures is one thing, but if you still have to jump through hoops laid down by the various program officers based in Ottawa, you are not much further ahead. So, there is another reform called Alternative Financing Arrangements. It is a series of five-year funding agreements which enable bands to spend money on their own priorities. Alternative funding arrangements have only been around for a few years, so, at the moment, we do not have a great number of bands operating under this process.

The federal policy of self-government

I want to spend most of my time talking about self-government. The federal government does have a policy on self-government. However, the self-government policy is not for every First Nation. It is only for those who want to work with the policy. Let me discuss the basis of this policy and the role of the constitutional process. In 1987, there was a First Ministers conference, which was the last of a series of three, and it was designed to create a constitutional amendment on Aboriginal self-government. The conference was not able to reach an agreement, but the Prime Minister made a commitment to push for a return to the process the minute prospects for success appeared sound. You may have read that following a meeting between three cabinet ministers and three or four of the national leaders of Aboriginal associations, there was some possibility of an accord process parallel to the Meech Lake saga. Aboriginal leaders commented that the government appeared ready to add Aboriginal issues to the constitutional process. It may very well be that within the next few years, there will be a return to the constitutional table and, within the Canadian context, the highest level of definition possible is a constitutionally-protected definition.

Self-government arrangements are enacted through parliamentary legislation at the community level when requested by the band. There are ten bands presently that are under their own legislation: the Sechelt Band in British Columbia, eight Cree Bands and one Naskapi Band in Northern Quebec. We are currently negotiating with a number of bands who want to set up their own legislation. The purpose of this legislation is to get them out of the *Indian Act* so that their band or First Nations' government will be accountable to the membership without a minister looking over their shoulder and checking up on every decision that they make. Some bands, such as Six Nations or Kahnawake, even though they are *Indian Act* bands, are different in that they are completely self-sufficient and run all their own affairs very successfully without DIAND. Other smaller communities do not have the resources to deliver services in the way that a large community can.

We are undertaking negotiations with a number of different bands in Alberta, in British Columbia, in northwestern Ontario and in the Yukon. To date, some 130 proposals have been received, and there are sixty-three proposals which are in the so-called developmental stage, which is the stage prior to substantive negotiations.

What do First Nations get through this policy? They get their own legislation with the powers of a contemporary public administration. Think of what governments need to do, and you will find it in the list of powers under self-government. It will also have a constitution amendable by the First Nations, and, once the First Nations are up and running, its own laws passed to run its affairs.

Basically, the guidelines on self-government negotiations say that the federal government can only negotiate those items under its control. If the First Nations want to have self-government in an area which touches on a provincial power or which touches on a shared federal-provincial power, such as environmental management, then the policy states that the province at some point has to be involved in the negotiations because otherwise the legislation cannot stand up in court. Of course, the idea, ultimately, is to come up with something that will pass the test of time.

Another aspect of the policy which bears repeating is that we fully expect that whatever arrangements are arrived at for any of the First Nations, they will be within the context of the *Constitution*. My remarks are quite in contrast to the remarks of the previous speaker. However, this policy really only speaks to those First Nations that want to negotiate an arrangement through the vehicle of parliamentary legislation. For those First Nations who say that they are already self-governing outside the Canadian context, of course, this policy is of no interest to them. While the Government of Canada does not necessarily agree with the perspectives of the previous speaker, we certainly respect their right to disagree with this particular self-government policy.

Self-government is not an imposed policy. It is up to the First Nations and their membership to decide if they want to have a deal outside the *Indian Act.* If they do not want to have a deal outside the *Indian Act,* they will benefit from whatever revisions are made to it. Why is the *Indian Act* necessary? Since section 91(24) of the *Constitution* states: Indians and lands reserved for Indians is a responsibility given to the federal government. The *Indian Act* is the vehicle whereby some of that responsibility is met.

The negotiation process

I would like to conclude by discussing the process of negotiating self-government. Each self-government negotiation is tailor-made to the particular First Nation. When we go as a team to negotiate with First Nations, we do not go there and tell them what they can have; they tell us what they want. The process of negotiation is largely a question of discovery. That is, the First Nations help us to understand where they are coming from and, in many instances, if we are dealing with an area of customary law or with a confederal arrangement involving village councils and different layers of authority, it may take many meetings before we fully understand what is being proposed, and it takes several more meetings to translate this general notion into the technical language that is necessary so that legislation will properly reflect the First Nations' interests. These negotiations are long and complex, but I think that for those that are willing to accept the confines of that policy, it can lead to a more self-sufficient and satisfying arrangement than under the current *Indian Act.*

I would add that since the policy has only been around since 1985, coming after the *Cree-Naskapi Act* and the *Sechelt Act,* we do not yet have any results to demonstrate what the results of this policy will be. Negotiations take many years, because many bands take time to work out their proposals and to determine amongst themselves the content of their demands. It is still too early to say whether self-government in these terms is a success or not. I would agree with those who say that things took a long time to get going. I would say that within another three years, it may be possible to assess the results since by then you may have two or three pieces of legislation put through Parliament involving anywhere from ten to twenty bands. Then we will be in a better position to really see whether the process works and whether, in fact, those self-governing bands are satisfied with the results.

Furthermore, the self-government policy is open to evolving in practice, since it is new for both the federal government and for the First Nations. The policy was originally suggested by the First Nations, although the result is not entirely what they sought. For those that did want something akin to this policy and who are now working within its parameters through negotiations, we are adapting the policy to meet the conditions that they are suggesting. This process of discovery for the federal government will continue to be highly creative over the next few years.

SALLY WEAVER

Professor Sally Weaver was a political anthropologist at the University of Waterloo with a major interest in how federal governments develop policies with and for Aboriginal Peoples in Canada, Australia and Norway. Her career began with research on the health care system at Six Nations and then moved to an interest in the political history of the Six Nations, and from there to Ottawa, where she examined the origin of the 1969 White Paper in a book called "Making Canadian Indian Policy", which was published in 1981. She then focussed on the role of national Aboriginal political organizations as important vehicles for an Aboriginal role in policy-making. Professor Weaver's interest in policy-making was focussed on whether the issue of self-government for First Nations in Canada had made any gains in the last ten years. Unfortunately, Professor Weaver passed away in 1993.

AN ASSESSMENT OF THE FEDERAL SELF-GOVERNMENT POLICY

I want to examine whether, in fact, there have been gains since the mid-70s when self-government was first put by First Nations People on to the national political agenda. I approach this question in a framework that is quite simple. I say there are essentially three policy paradigms existing today. There is the traditional patron-client relationship where we have the *Indian Act*, the Department of Indian Affairs as a special bureaucracy, and historic control and management of Aboriginal People under section 91(24) of the *Constitution*. In short, this is the historic paradigm based on a policy of assimilation.

The second paradigm that emerges in 1969 is the assimilation paradigm. This says we get rid of the whole shooting match, convert Aboriginal People to normal citizens and get on about Canadian business.

The third paradigm is self-government. It is, in fact, not a clearly fleshed out paradigm, but it says real empowerment should occur for Aboriginal People in Canada. I see this as the only constructive paradigm for Canada's future and for Aboriginal People for a few basic reasons. I consider the current situation at Indian Affairs to be undemocratic first and foremost. Governments and their bureaucracies are making decisions for the lives of Aboriginal People that simply are unparalleled elsewhere in our political system. I find the current system inefficient, unproductive, expensive, and, in the long run, guaranteed to keep Aboriginal People in a state of dependency. Therefore, I believe change is necessary.

Has self-government produced changes? I argue it has not. In fact, we have made minimal gains in the past fifteen years, and the 1990s need to see self-government put back on the political agenda in a very different way by Aboriginal People, and put back in certain forms. I will come back to that in my conclusion.

Can I defend my position? I suspect that Ken and Simon, for very different reasons, would say that my logic and empiricism is not factual, and if I had time, I would argue it more fully, so this is a shotgun approach. My first reason for saying that self-government has not made gains is the failure of the First Ministers Conference process. The First Ministers Conference failed to define Aboriginal rights and self-government. Indeed, through interviews I have had within government at various levels and departments, I have found that there is a great deal of disdain within government toward section 35 constitutional rights, whatever they contain. Indeed, I have found in some instances very strong contempt, and I have become concerned about this.

I have been advised by several people involved in the 1982 deliberations that I should not be surprised that the provinces were not participating, since many key units within the government were not involved in shaping section 35 rights. They have no commitment; therefore, I have concluded that these rights are essentially not rights. They simply provide Aboriginal People with a bit of political leverage. To have a right is to have a legitimate claim against the nation-state such that it behaves in certain ways toward Aboriginal People. I do not believe these "rights" have been legitimated by the institutions of Canada. They do give political leverage, but I should not expect benefits to flow from them.

Second, I see the construction of self-government often in terms of services, and there is more to self-governing systems than services. If you look at the service delivery component of a government, you fail to look at how a system becomes legitimated and supported by people.

As a political anthropologist, I question how one establishes the political legitimacy of a governing system within First Nations communities. Therefore, I have considerable concerns about the extent of factionalism in many Aboriginal communities. I do not believe factions are bad or that they ought not to have arisen. Aboriginal People, like all groups in the face of cultural change, develop ideologies about change or no-change and have to address difficult issues. Aboriginal communities are full of these differing deliberations. However, in many cases I have difficulty seeing how systems of self-governance are going to be legitimated. I have no problems with resurrecting notions of Aboriginal justice, but I do have problems in seeing how they would gain legitimacy within the community. So as a political anthropologist, I am not so much concerned with whether the Canadian nation-state has problems with the idea of Iroquois sovereignty as I am with looking within the system and seeing how these systems of self-governance might be legitimated within the community.

Third, the Department of Indian Affairs' programs of nego-tiated self-government that go beyond the *Indian Act* have many problems. Essentially, they exist in a policy vacuum. Despite what Simon says, I do not believe that there is a clear policy in place. Un-like the previous speaker, I do believe there has been enough time to show practical results, and I do find a great deal of frustration within DIAND because of the belief that they lack the support of senior officials. I do see conflicting notions about the limits of ne-gotiation within this program, and I find a lack of credibility within DIAND for the negotiation process. The negotiators face a very difficult role within the Department. I do not think they get the support they need in a lot of ways. I find the process itself colonial. It makes a mockery of notions of self-government by making you go through step 1 and 2 and 3, and then sign X con-tract. However, if you go through step 4 and 5 and 6, we will not sign. My God, I feel déjà-vu taking me back to the colonial Indian agent. I know there are complexities involved here – I am not naive – but that kind of a process is not one that respects a self-steerage in any way, shape or form.

Fourth, I do not see advance in the thinking of the federal government. This may emerge, I hope it does, however, all I see is a confirmation of historic thinking. Indian governments are dele-gated municipal institutions within an existing conception of the nation-state. I do not see creative attempts to carve out units with provincial powers. What capacity is there for First Nations' no-tions of government? I think innovation must come largely from First Nations. This has been clear in the case of the negotiated claims for James Bay and elsewhere. People within government have said to me that innovation will have to come from outside, and then they will market it inside. Therefore, the First Nations will have to, I think, carry a greater degree of the innovative weight than is perhaps apparent.

Fifth, I do not see any progress in their negotiation of financial arrangements. If you are going to act at arm's length in order to create an innovative, reasonably free-standing system of self-governance, you have to package resources accordingly. I again see basic problems. The government's first attempt, in the case of DIAND, to go for block funding failed. DIAND officials sought greater freedom in financial arrangements. The AFA emerged from this process crippled not because of DIAND, but because of the Treasury Board and financial constraints within government. There are bands that were already existing AFA models. DIAND officials have said to me, "Look at the bands that are up and running and already have an AFA scheme; we are just formalising something that exists already." Cassidy and his co-author say in their book that the AFA strangles bands and community governments with their degree of accountability. Come to think of it, we have yet to examine the financial accountability of a minister from Parliament to Indian bands. Therefore, I see the AFA as a minor modification.

Sixth, the Sechelt model, in a nutshell, confirms the historic patron-client relationship moving toward assimilation. This is an old paradigm. Fine, the community wanted it. I have no problems with that. People say to me, "Ah, look at what the Sechelt did." Of course, we look to them. How many models do we have? Very few of us, including academics of my own discipline, produce models that are tangible, touchable and reviewable. However, that does not mean we need to adopt Sechelt on its premises. I do see Sechelt as a negative model for the movement to self-determination.

Seventh, I have problems discerning whether First Nations People, collectively or individually, really do seek self-government. Why do I have these problems? First of all, many of the submissions made to DIAND, passed on the basis of section 63, show that bands do not know the *Indian Act* enough to realize that what they want may be already available within the *Indian Act*. In short, many bands, for a host of legitimate reasons, do not understand the political and legal parameters they are operating in. How can one move to self-government and shape it autonomously when the existing status quo is not clear in the minds of people?

Indian groups themselves do not share common notions of self-government. Some people argue that Aboriginal People distrust each other. They do not want to share their ideas – they want to be first off the mark. When you sit back and ask yourself what people really want, and what is DIAND being told, you realize that everything is secretive. We are told that we cannot find out or share what is taking place within the community, but when you think about it, the only group that can aggregate what Aboriginal People are demanding through this program is DIAND. Down the road, they will say, "Well look, you claim that the bulk of Aboriginal People in Canada want self-government, but our evidence from submission is that only 24 % really want powers and the rest do not." Yet, no-one can prove or disprove this since we do not have an overarching view of the extent Aboriginal People want to move towards self-government. This sequestering of information makes it very difficult for any outsider to deal with the First Nations in terms of intent. There appears to be no sharing, no trusting, no community of experience. That is probably not a very positive factor.

Eighth, I do not see self-government as a personal priority for the current Minister, nor for the last one in the current ministerial program. We are seeing "self-reliance" and other words used which suggest to me we are moving into a review process of the *Indian Act*. God knows the *Indian Act* is outdated and needs to be thought through again. I do not have problems with that. However, it is not a substitute for self-government.

Ninth, comprehensive land claims appear to be an arena in which self-government is not sitting comfortably. Yet, somehow, through it all, self-governing institutions have emerged. I find this raises a mass of contradictions. Obviously, the Cree made significant headway in their land claim. Although one cannot negotiate self-government at the same table, self-governing powers have emerged. My point is we still have a contradictory situation between self-government and comprehensive land claims. If we were serious and genuine about self-government, we should address these issues.

Tenth, if the movement toward self-government were genuine, I think we would have seen more effective *Indian Act* amendments. We have got the Kamloops amendment, however, if Cassidy's recent book is accurate, this did not succeed in its ultimate goal. So, even when we try to say, "Look, if you want to go beyond the Act, negotiate your own piece of legislation into the program or else you fall within the *Indian Act*, and end up passing more bylaws." That route, to date, has obviously not been terribly successful.

The eleventh reason is one of the most telling. If you are serious about self-government, one of the first things you do is move in with training programs. That does not mean you promulgate them for First Nations. What you do is build a facilitating environment where, as powers grow, they are talked through within a training arena. Any serious developmental program in the Third World has training programs or support services attached. I simply do not see that happening here in Canada.

Where am I at? I am at a conclusion that says there have not been many advances for Native People. Were there many incentives? Here I find it even more problematic. If I look at the federal government, I would ask what incentives do I have to run a true self-government program. I believe I would govern less, cut back the number of people in the public service, cut back expenditures, retreat into a role of governance, and alter the federalism of Canada so that it becomes more decentralized. In short, I cannot see any particular reason for launching a strong form of self-government. We know that to make effective change, the start-up cost for new programs will be high. Given the circumstances, what incentives are there for true self-government? Outside of comprehensive land claims, what incentives do First Nations have? First, they get almost no money. Secondly, they do more work. Third, they take on the political risk of dealing with federally designed programs that tolerate only minor modifications. They end up, it seems to me, having to do more work for less money with higher political risk in an uncertain political environment. Unless the *Indian Act* is really chafing in some direct, concrete way, how can there be incentive for these people to move beyond the present structures? All that comes to mind are limited examples of special financial incentives.

Where are we at? I say that the issue of self-government may have been put on the agenda in the mid-70s by the Dene with their talk about the Dene Nation through the Federation of Saskatchewan Indians. Self-government is a state-of-mind. Oren Lyons' address was also key to getting the National Indian Brotherhood on to self-government. It went on the agenda but it did not get any real commitment from the federal government.

The need for First Nations initiative

In 1990, Canada is a very different place than it was in 1980. First Nations People are a very different people for a whole host of reasons. Therefore, I would argue that if self-government is what Aboriginal People want, it has to be put back on the agenda by them. I believe that self-government has to be put on the agenda in a particular way. Public assertion of rights is no longer compelling and, as you listen to the media, you will find that many Canadians, not just in Thunder Bay, are insensitive to cultural differences.

There was a talk-show the other day, and the question was whether we should have a separate system of Aboriginal justice, and I realized they did not have the foggiest notion of what a separate system of justice could be.

The American system, as a potential model, should not be threatening but no-one has bothered to explain it to people. First Nations have to put the American model, as well as others, back on the agenda. They must take on the difficult job of educating the public to see the non-threatening aspects of these kind of changes. Once the public has been pulled on board, the government will follow. There has got to be strong arguments of why special treatment will be functional and helpful, and finally why the financial cost will not, in the long run, be a negative factor.

Efficient, well-run First Nations governments will certainly be of greater advantage to Canada than the current system. However, these arguments simply are not getting shared with the public, and, therefore, I think there has to be a revitalisation of that agenda.

QUESTION PERIOD: PANEL THREE

Question: JACK MILLER
Conflict Resolver, Interlex Group (an ADR firm)

I would like to make a brief comment and ask Professor Weaver to comment or react. In her description of paradigms, she mentioned five characteristics that might be relevant: democracy, efficiency, productivity, expense and dependency.

The issue of dependence and independence, or interdependence, is a crucial consideration to the field of psychology, anthropology and other fields as well. The study of addiction and dependency has extended to include those who live with addicts. This type of relation has come to be known as co-dependency and it is now recognized as an illness.

People who live under the shadow of a dominant power for a long period of time could be in a state of co-dependency, as has been shown by studies of addiction that extend to organizations. There are thus many kinds of addictions; not only chemical addictions, but also work addiction, or love addiction and so on. Have you encountered this phenomenon of co-dependency, and do you think it has any lessons for us in learning how to cease to be co-dependent?

Answer: SALLY WEAVER

The fast answer is "no", I am not familiar with the literature of co-dependence, although I am with the term. I have not actually applied that system to self-government although it may have some validity.

Question: NORA MACDONALD-PLOURDE

In my department, Education, I have found out that we formulate statistics according to what we want to sell. Mr. McInnes, you were saying at one point that once Indian Affairs had all the money, and now it is First Nations who do. I do not think that is true. To all of you on the panel, I have to ask: what did you mean to say?

On the whole, I feel positive with what was said, but why do I get this feeling there is no hope for us Natives? Could it be because many of our leaders have been taught by Indian Affairs, or that those on the opposite side of the negotiating table are people who have worked with us and had the opportunity to discover our weaknesses? I do not really expect an answer, but that is what I feel.

Answer: SIMON McINNES

The statistics first. I was referring to the grants contributions and other transfer payments that the Department makes to the First Nations. About ten years ago, only 30 % of that money was administered by the First Nations themselves, 70 % was administered by the Department through its regional and district offices. Today, the proportion is inverse. 70 % is administered by the First Nations themselves and 30% by the Department. I will leave the rest of your question to somebody else.

Answer: JOSEPH SANDERS

Well, our friend said she did not expect an answer, but she did come to the conclusion that the situation looks gloomy. Speaking from the viewpoint of the United Nations and international law, I have to admit the situation is not very rosy because the United Nations and the people who practise international law there are a club of like-minded people. All of them have internal domestic problems, many with Indigenous or ethnic minorities. So, they are not going to yield too easily.

We are now working at the level of a working group on Indigenous populations, and at that level, relations are pretty friendly. There are five people in the working group and none are representing governments. They are there as experts and are basically very sympathetic. Their recommendations go to the seventeen member Sub-Commission on the Prevention of Discrimination and Protection of Minorities. Again, experts; again, basically sympathetic.

From there, it moves up to the Commission of Human Rights, where there are diplomats and others who represent governments. There are fifty-three people, fifty-three countries, and things get tougher since there are more players. Finally, it goes to the General Assembly where there are 159 players.

When we start off at the bottom of the tree, the atmosphere is quite different from what we end up with at the top. Nonetheless, during my time in the UN, I have seen changes made, for example, in the non-alignment movement. The Americans never liked to use the term "non-aligned movement", but I was there when Dr. Kissinger first did. Further, I have seen Rhodesia become Zimbabwe and Portuguese colonies become Namibia. So, there might be still some hope.

Question: TREVOR SMITH
Student, McGill University

I am a member of a group on campus called "Friends of First Nations" and I would like to make a couple of comments. Our mandate on campus includes bringing about awareness of the issues, so that we can effect change. One of the major issues is the seeming contradiction as the government negotiates on the basis of self-government in some regions while in other regions, it denies the right to self-determination.

Just look around us. We have Canada advertising a eight hundred million dollar NATO base in Labrador, but ten thousand Inuit People live there. The Minister of Indian Affairs has done very little to help them. Look at Algonquin Lake, the people in Temagami, the Lubicon in northern Alberta, the conflicts in British Columbia and many more groups facing similar situations. I have a problem when we hear the Canadian government saying it is moving towards self-government with Native Peoples.

There also seems to be a problem in facilitating this with other government agencies. Is it a question of coordination? Why is government behaving so atrociously in Labrador? In northern Quebec? Why is this happening across Canada? Why is the right to self-determination being denied to all these groups when there is this supposed policy of negotiation for self-government?

Answer: SIMON MCINNES

Let me make a general observation first. The government is not monolithic. It is not a single person: it is a hybrid. You can look at any government in the world, even a government of a country that has no Indigenous Peoples, and you will find examples, time and again, of how one department says this and another department does that. Why is there a contradiction? That is contemporary public administration. Try and see contradictions as noise. The role of government is to try and reduce the noise level to tolerable limits.

If you are saying that the current situation is too noisy and we are beyond the limits of tolerance, I would have to agree with you. The major problem in governments is that each minister has his or her own responsibility and a minister is not going to survive very long if he interferes with the responsibilities of other people. The government has to make certain priorities in dealing with the demands of First Nations, particularly since the First Nations are not a single voice. There are 590 Indian First Nations, all sorts of tribal councils, provincial groups, and we are trying to respond to as many requests as we can.

The point, however, that Sally Weaver made is important. As long as we still have a process anchored in the trappings of nineteenth century paternalism, as long as that superstructure of paternalism is there, despite all of our attempts to get out, we will always be in demand-response mode.

Answer: KEN DEER

From my point of view, that is an excuse, not a reason. The situation of five hundred bands is a creation of the Canadian government, not of Native People, because the Canadian government tries to deal with us on a community basis, dividing us into small groups, instead of dealing with us as nations as we are supposed to be dealt with. I think that it is time that we start looking at things that way.

The education of Native People has brainwashed them into thinking that every single community is a nation. I am not a proponent of that. I am a proponent of Mohawks, all Mohawks, as one nation. The Crees are a little different because there are so many different groups of Crees but they should be able to negotiate as a nation, on a nation-to-nation basis with the government.

The government does not negotiate as a nation, it negotiates as an administrative body. Imagine you want to talk to somebody about self-determination, so, you go to the Minister of Indian Affairs and he says, "I cannot discuss self-determination, go see Justice." You go to Justice and they say, "I cannot talk about that, go see Constitutional Affairs." You go see Constitutional Affairs and they say, "Well, I cannot discuss that, go see Parliament." You go to Parliament and they say, "That is a good question, but go see Ministry of Indian Affairs." And then it starts all over again.

There is no new thinking in the government. It is just the same old bureaucracy that has been rehashed. I think that Sally's suggestion that the initiative has to come from Native Peoples is absolutely correct. Self-determination is asserted. Nobody gives it to you. You do not go ask Canada, "Can I have self-determination?" It does not happen that way. Change has to take place and Native Peoples have to assert that change. Nobody cared about the Innu until they put their tent on a runway. Who cared before that? We have to rattle the cages of the Canadian government so that they will deal on a one-to-one basis.

Another aspect is the relationship: Indian negotiations are extremely paternalistic since the Government of Canada acts as if it were supreme, and as long as the government comes to the negotiating table with that attitude, we will always have problems. We need serious neutral third-party involvement, whether from the UN or from some other international body, that will facilitate meetings and ensure that the Native Peoples and Canada are on equal footing, and can keep Canada in its place.

Answer: SALLY WEAVER

In the event you were referring to my talk as being a situation of no hope, I hope I did not leave that impression. I think that life is for the living and I think that the First Nations have made gains in a lot of ways, although I think the political agenda has been very erratic. When the First Nations were first beginning to say, "We want to get into the Constitutional process", I can remember some of us shaking our heads, saying, "You know, this will never come off." My God, within a few years, there were amendments within the *Constitution*. So, things do occur.

I take Ken's point that the strategy has to be different. If an issue is not put firmly on the agenda, you do need to put up the tents on the runway, but you need to follow-through with Indian political organizations. That is the hope I see. I do not want to leave you with a negative sense. I just think there is a lot to be done and a lot that can be done.

CLOSING THANKSGIVING

TEKARONHIOKEN

Faithkeeper, Kahnawake

Four hundred and ninety-eight years ago, Christopher Columbus arrived on the North American shore and was greeted by the Native People. It has not been the same since, except for One.

However, I know that the young people who are in law are going to make changes and we have a lot of confidence that things are going to change, not only for the Native People but also for Canadians.

I said that it has not been the same since except for One. Our grandfathers stood before the people, they greeted and acknowledged one another and the Great Spirit in much the same words used today whenever they assembled for social, spiritual and political meetings and conferences such as this. Last night, the Thanksgiving address was given in English. I will now give the Thanksgiving address in my language, in Mohawk, to thank and acknowledge the people gathered here today and to thank the Great Spirit.

[address in Mohawk]

At this time, I ask that we greet one another. I am going to ask you to shake someone's hand and greet each other formally.

Now our minds are as one.

The 1991 Conference

LESSONS FROM OKA:
FORGING A BETTER RELATIONSHIP

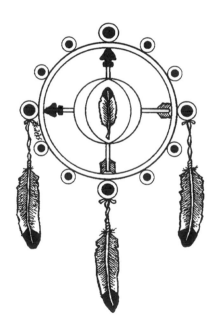

OPENING THANKSGIVING

JOHN CUROTTE

Iroquois Faithkeeper

I will say the ritual for the Creation and Creator in my own language.

[Address in Mohawk]

I am here to say the ritual to honour Creation and the Creator Himself. To ask the Creation and the Creator to give us power, to give us strength, to give us good health while we are here and to give us good words for the people outside.

PANEL ONE

THE PATH TO CRISIS: ORIGINS OF CONFLICT

BRIAN SLATTERY

Brian Slattery is a professor at Osgoode Hall Law School, York University, where he teaches courses in Constitutional Law, Indigenous Rights, and Legal Theory. He holds a Bachelor of Arts degree from Loyola College, Montreal, a Bachelor of Civil Law from McGill University, and a D. Phil. in Law from Oxford University. He has many publications dealing with Aboriginal rights and Constitutional Law.

BRINGING THE CONSTITUTION HOME

Let me begin by quoting a statement from an Aboriginal spokesman:

> What we don't like about the Government is their saying this: "We will give you this much land." How can they give it when it is our own? We cannot understand it. They have never bought it from us or our forefathers. They have never fought and conquered our people and taken the land in that way, and yet they say now that they will give us so much land – our own land ... [O]ur forefathers for generations and generations past had their land here all around us; chiefs have had their own hunting grounds, their salmon streams, and places where they got their berries; it has always been so.

What is remarkable about this statement is, that with some small changes, it could have been made last summer at Oka, or a decade ago, or fifty years ago. In fact, it was made by a spokesman for the Niska Nation of British Columbia in the year 1888, a little over a century ago. If you go back further in history, you will find many similar statements made by Aboriginal representatives in the 17th and 18th centuries. Despite frequent reiterations of this viewpoint over a period of some four hundred years or more, Canadian governments and the legal system as a whole have yet to come to terms with the basic message implicit in these statements:

> We, the Aboriginal Nations of Canada, are sovereign, autonomous peoples with our own laws and lands, our own systems of government. We are the original peoples of this land that we now share with you. You are the newcomers – we are not beholden to you for anything.

Since last summer, of course, it has become more difficult to ignore this viewpoint. The Oka crisis and the Aboriginal role in blocking the Meech Lake Accord have both, in their different ways, called into question our basic attitudes to the Canadian *Constitution* and our understanding of the place of First Peoples in Confederation. Although the events of last summer have given rise to a remarkable amount of political hand-wringing and proposals for reform, I doubt how much of this has been directed at the root of the problem, which lies much deeper, and involves the way in which we have become accustomed to representing the *Constitution* to ourselves.

We have, I think, a defective model of the *Constitution*, one that blocks us from responding to the challenge represented by the Oka crisis, or even from comprehending what it is all about. It is often thought, for example, that the interests of Aboriginal Nations and those of Quebec are opposed and that, with Quebec moving powerfully in the direction of independence, they are on a collision course. At a certain level, of course, there is some truth in this view. However, at a deeper level, the basic constitutional outlooks of Quebec and the First Peoples have more in common than first appears. They are both profoundly at odds with the dominant model of the *Constitution*, which I will call "the Imperial model".

What does this Imperial model entail? In a sentence, it assumes that our fundamental laws and governmental institutions are derived in form and basic substance from the United Kingdom, and further, that the fountainhead of all governmental power in Canada is the Crown: there are no truly indigenous laws or governmental institutions in Canada. Thus, the *Constitution* is embodied in a series of Acts emanating from the Imperial Crown and the British Parliament, ranging from the *Royal Proclamation of 1763*, the *Quebec Act of 1774*, the *Constitutional Act of 1791*, and the *British North America Act of 1867*, to the most recent addition to our constitution, the *Constitution Act, 1982* enacted by the British Parliament at Canada's request. The Imperial model of the *Constitution* also draws comfort from the fact that in the anglophone provinces the basic law is thought to be English common law, as imported by settlers or adopted by local Acts. In Quebec, the basic law is derived originally from France: the *Custom of Paris* as codified in the *Civil Code of Lower Canada*, under the influence of the *Napoleonic Civil Code*. Moreover, the Imperial model explains the survival of French law in Quebec by the provisions of an imperial statute, namely, the *Quebec Act* of 1774.

Exclusion and subordination

It may be noted that this model of the *Constitution* makes good use of two related techniques: exclusion and subordination. The first technique, exclusion, operates to restrict severely the possible sources of our basic laws, confining them, in effect, to a limited range of approved Imperial sources. Excluded are the collective experiences of various national components of the Canadian confederation: most notably the experiences and traditions of First Peoples, but also the distinctive history and status of French Canada, which is downplayed or glossed over. To speak specifically of First Peoples, wherever possible, we lawyers have simply eliminated them from our thinking, swept them off the legal map and treated them as legal non-entities.

For a long time, this simple technique allowed us to treat Canada as if it were legally vacant before the Europeans arrived. From this viewpoint, the Aboriginal Peoples of North America had no rights as independent nations in international law and no territorial rights to the lands they occupied. So, their lands could be claimed by the first European comer and divided up between rival European powers. Since, on this view, there were no indigenous laws or governments when Europeans arrived, it has been thought that our basic legal and constitutional systems were necessarily imported from Europe and that the Aboriginal Nations played no part in the formation of our fundamental law. There are, from this viewpoint, no truly indigenous foundations for Canadian law.

It seems to me that much of this type of thinking still pervades our legal system today. Although there have been some recent dramatic changes in the attitude of the Supreme Court to Aboriginal rights, as we have seen this past summer in the *Sparrow* and *Sioui* cases, I am not confident that we have yet freed ourselves from the basic tenets of the Imperial model. In particular, I do not think that, as lawyers and judges, we have yet to come to terms with the basic fact that the settler peoples do not have a monopoly on the sources of law in this country. We do not have a monopoly on the *Constitution* and on the basic vision of what the country stands for. We do not have a monopoly on the meaning of basic legal concepts such as "sovereignty", "treaties", "rights" and "responsibilities". The First Peoples of Canada have a say in these matters too, even if, for the most part, we have not been prepared to listen. In many respects, Native views have been systematically suppressed or ignored.

However, it has never really been possible to exclude First Peoples from our deliberations altogether. They have a stubborn habit of insisting on their points of view and sometimes of even raising their voices. They have come to court and demanded a hearing. They have sat on roads and railway lines. So, when it no longer seemed feasible simply to pretend that First Peoples did not legally exist, we resourceful lawyers have sometimes called upon a second technique, namely, subordination.

Subordination concedes that Aboriginal Nations may have special legal status and rights but insists that whatever rights they possess must be justified by reference to what we consider "standard legal sources". By standard legal sources we mean, once again, the legal sources recognized by our European-derived legal systems. So, we have assumed that Aboriginal Nations must somehow ground their claims on English common law, English colonial law, French civil law, the *Royal Proclamation*, the *Indian Act*, or the written *Constitution*. We have been slow even to acknowledge Indian treaties as a source of positive legal rights, much less recognize the existence of Aboriginal customary law. More radically, we sometimes treated the questions of Aboriginal sovereignty and rights as if they were dependant on the pleasure of European kings and queens in remote periods of history. In this view, if it appears, for example, that French kings of the 16th and 17th centuries thought that Indian Peoples had no sovereign or territorial rights, then that is an end of the matter. Indian rights are subordinate to

European whims and legal conceptions. They have no legal status in their own right.

Like many others, I find the Imperial model of the *Constitution* wrong in principle and profoundly out of harmony with our collective historical experience. This model is incapable of aiding us to resolve our current constitutional dilemmas. We have yet to come to terms with a basic fact: Canada is not the poor creature of 18th and 19th century British colonial designs, as the Imperial model suggests. The *Constitution* should not be viewed, in effect, as the instrument by which people of largely British descent maintain their authority over nations of Aboriginal, or indeed, French ancestry, – an authority gained by force or intimidation in years past. Canada is an independent, multi-national Confederation with an autonomous *Constitution* rooted in several centuries of collective national experience.

The unwritten law of Canada: living legal traditions

The task before us is to reform our understanding of the sources of the *Constitution* so as to allow these rich bodies of experience to be tapped. We have to replace the Imperial model of the *Constitution* with one grounded in Canadian history and experience. What basic features would this new model possess? Here, I can do no more than paint a picture in broad strokes and refer you, for more detailed treatment, to several of my articles: "The Independence of Canada" published in 1983 in the *Supreme Court Law Review*, and "Understanding Aboriginal Rights" in the 1987 *Canadian Bar Review*.

According to this second model, our most fundamental laws have a local root, grounded in the experiences of the various nations and communities that make up Canada, – a root that may be called, for lack of a better phrase, "the common law of Canada". By that, of course, I do not mean English common law; rather, I mean the unwritten law of Canada.

This body of basic law has two functions: first, it defines certain spheres of autonomy or sovereignty within which the customs, laws, and governmental structures of various national groups may operate; and secondly, it provides the fundamental basis for relationships and interaction among these nations and communities: namely, spheres of commonality. From this viewpoint, Canada is not the artificial creature of British imperialism, it is rather the arena within which various nations meet and interact, to pursue both common and separate purposes. It is an arena defined by our common and separate historical relationships and traditions. Thus, the basic law of Canada relating to Aboriginal Nations is grounded in a body of practice and custom that has evolved in North America over a period of several centuries, involving extensive interaction between First Peoples and incoming European settlers. This distinctive body of custom was neither European nor Aboriginal in composition and origin, but drew on elements of both to produce a unique set of rules which may be described as the law of Aboriginal rights. This body of law, no doubt, was reflected in such British instruments as the *Royal Proclamation*. However, such instruments are not the source of the law in question, neither do they constitute a complete statement of its contents. This body of basic law, I suggest, effectively recognizes the autonomy, territorial rights, political structures and customary laws of Aboriginal Nations within a confederal superstructure linking them to non-Native communities.

This way of looking at the *Constitution* may bring us to a better understanding of the current position of Quebec and the francophone nation within Canada. It seems to me that the long history of relations between francophone and anglophone groups in Canada supports the fundamental principle that, under Canadian common law, Quebec has a special status within Confederation as the homeland of the French nation in Canada. Our written Constitution should be read in light of this fundamental principle. However, a fuller treatment of this important subject must be left to another time.

In closing, let me reiterate my basic point. What we in the legal community have to do is to acknowledge frankly that we have often been blind to the role that First Peoples have played in the formation of Canada, its laws and Constitution. That is, we must be willing to broaden our basic understanding of the sources of law in this country. We must recognize that Aboriginal Nations deserve to be treated as participants in generating the basic laws that govern us, not as peoples on the fringes, not helpless victims, not recipients of constitutional hand-outs from the government or the courts, but as partners in the formation of our Constitution and our most fundamental laws. In short, we have to accept that Aboriginal conceptions of law and rights really count: not as curiosities of another time and place, not as the exotic occupants of some dusty legal pigeon-hole, but as a fundamental part of our living legal traditions. I think that the Supreme Court of Canada has made good initial steps in this direction in the *Sparrow* and *Sioui* cases. However, it is too early to congratulate ourselves: we still have a long way to go, and we have promises to keep.

BRUCE CLARK

Lawyer and History consultant

CONSTITUTIONAL ALTERNATIVES: IN DEFENCE OF THE IMPERIAL MODEL

In my view, Dr. Slattery's statement is not the solution – it is the problem. The Imperial model is the solution, not the enemy, for Aboriginal Peoples in this country. I suggest, with all due respect to Dr. Slattery, that he does not understand the Imperial model and that he is throwing out the very best allies the Indians could possibly have.

The reason is that when the Imperial model, for legal purposes, came into existence, Aboriginal Peoples were powerful, militarily and numerically. Up until the time of the *Royal Proclamation*, the basic relationship between Indians and the Crown was expressed in the *Two Row Wampum* belt: co-existence in a relationship of peace, friendship and respect, as two sovereign societies moving down the stream of life. The *Royal Proclamation* essentially enacted the *Two Row Wampum* into law.

In that context, colonial governments were sovereign over themselves, and the Indians were sovereign over themselves. It has never been repealed, but what has happened in the interval from 1763 to the present time is that population and military dynamics have radically shifted in favour of the non-Natives. So, what we find over the years is that Canadian society has forgotten its legal roots. Practice and law have taken different paths. What we are attempting to do now is consistent with politics, but out-of-sync with the law; that is, out-of-sync with the Imperial model.

Nothing the Indians can negotiate today will put them in as strong a bargaining position as they were in three hundred years ago, nor will they drive such effective bargains. In the *Royal Proclamation*, what they achieved can be seen by examining the *Royal Proclamation's* words: several nations, or tribes, of Indians should not be molested or disturbed. You cannot get much clearer than that in legal language. The *Proclamation* says that several nations or tribes, meaning collective political entities not individuals, should not be molested or disturbed. By whom should it not be molested or disturbed? Well, the *Royal Proclamation* provides the answer to that, too.

If you have studied any Aboriginal rights, you will know by heart Part IV of the *Royal Proclamation*, which is the Indian part. Unfortunately, if you have been educated in a Canadian law school, you probably do not even know that a Part II of the *Royal Proclamation* exists. Part II of the *Royal Proclamation* is the part which constituted the colonial government. The first colonial government set up the basic format for all subsequent constitutional governments in Canada. Part II of the *Royal Proclamation* did two things: it gave the colonial government power to set up courts and to grant lands. This is the process that breathed life into the constitutional governments. That breath of life was counterbalanced by Part IV of the *Royal Proclamation* which said that the several nations or tribes should not be molested or disturbed. When you understand the very existence and creation of colonial governments, you realize that from the outset their existence hinged upon the sovereignty of Indian Nations and their right not to be molested or disturbed. That is the Imperial model.

Over the past three hundred years, the colonial governments have changed the balance of power. Imagine two separate spheres: in terms of law, both spheres are equal, but in terms of power, the white sphere is huge. Practically speaking, the power of the whites have overwhelmed the Indian's sphere.

This is where the rule of law (and for law students, this is absolutely everything) comes so much into play. In order to defend the Indians, we must turn to the rule of law. That is what makes their power position equal to the colonial government's power position, even though militarily and in population they are so dramatically weaker. Therefore, when I hear Dr. Slattery say that the Imperial model is the problem, my blood runs cold and I think, "My God, you fool! My friend for 15 years, how can you say this?"

What we essentially have in Canada is the old story about the king that wore no clothes. We have an academy of tailors, call them law professors, and the king has no clothes on, and he is walking down the street, led by my friend, Dr. Slattery and the other law professors in this country, and they are remarking on the fine cut of his suit and they are talking about the design. I am the guy in the back saying, "Guys, the king has no clothes on." What I am telling law students today is to reject this garbage about the Imperial model being the problem. The Imperial model is the Indians' only hope, their only defense. The rule of law is there for them because they fought and died three hundred years ago to get the *Royal Proclamation* into force. For goodness' sake, do not let these law professors flush it down the toilet.

LAWRENCE COURTOREILLE

Vice-Chief, Assembly of First Nations

THE LEGAL ORIGINS AND DEVELOPMENT OF ABORIGINAL AND TREATY RIGHTS

We First Nations have always had our own legal systems. Of course, our legal systems are quite different from the European models because they reflect a totally different set of spiritual, cultural and social values. While our approach to making laws is different from yours, it is nonetheless valid. Perhaps when you consider the state of the country today in terms of crime, wars and damage to our environment, you might even begin to agree that our approach to these matters may be more appropriate and sustainable in the long run.

The major thrust of European law is property, and, for the most part, their laws regulate how property is held, traded and shared by states and persons. Areas of law like contracts, banking, taxation and business are all centred on property. As a result, Native law, as it is evolving within Canadian jurisprudence, has quite a lot to do with property, and is expressed in terms of Aboriginal title and treaty rights: hunting, fishing and gathering rights are included because of their connection to land. However, this "Native law" is not the same thing as "First Nations law" because "Native law" has to do with conflicts between Canadian laws and First Nations rights. First Nations laws, on the other hand, are expressions of our own values and needs. These laws flow from our inherent jurisdiction as First Nations.

The European civil and common law systems, as I mentioned, deal mainly with land-holding. This is a significant point, because the First Nations' approach has to do with responsibility towards the earth and sharing of the land and its resources. Simple possession of the land is not enough on its own, because there is always the potential for abuse of the earth and its resources. We can see this quite clearly today when we look at what is happening to our environment. Of course, two hundred years ago, when it was being decided that First Nations legal systems and rights were to be ignored by the colonial societies in North America, nobody except the First Nations realized that there were serious problems with the European approach to the earth. Now we are in a position to see the results of that approach. We live in a polluted environment where many different types of wild animals are either totally extinct or can only be found in zoos and wildlife refuges.

International doctrines concerning First Nations rights

During the 16th century, there was a lot of discussion in Europe about whether or not North American Indians were really human. A theologian named Francisco de Vittoria argued that Indians were human and that we had souls, and therefore, we had legally enforceable property rights to our land. On the other side of the debate was Bartolome de Las Casas, who argued that Indians were not human but human-like. This being the case, de Las Casas said that we did not have souls and could not be considered to have any legal rights to land or liberty. Vittoria's views won, and in 1537, Pope Paul III issued an edict to all Christian nations. This Papal edict, entitled "Sublimis Deus", directed that:

> Indians are truly men. They may and should,
> freely and legitimately, enjoy their liberty and the
> **possession** of their property; nor should they be
> in any way enslaved; should the contrary happen,
> it shall be null and of no effect.

These principles were later written about by such international legal theorists as Grotius and Vattel.

It is undeniable that the Spanish monarchy was notorious for disregarding these rules in their oppression of the various First Nations they came into contact with. It is also true that the principles espoused by Francisco de Vittoria, and later by Grotius and Vattel, are part of the foundations of modern-day law in relation to First Nations rights.

Recognition of First Nations sovereignty in the *Royal Proclamation*

The *Royal Proclamation* made provision for the protection of Indian lands. The famed British jurist, Lord Blackstone, wrote about the distinction between lands which were occupied and cultivated and lands which were "deserted and uncultivated". Those lands which were occupied and cultivated, he wrote, could only be gained through conquest or by treaty. In the 1770s, a major conflict was brewing between the Ojibway First Nations and the colonists. The reason for this conflict was that the population of the colonies were growing rapidly and there was a serious need for more land

and resources for the settlers. Many people were beginning to move out into First Nations lands looking for fur, farmlands, lumber, and precious metals. This outraged many First Nations because the Crown had always promised that this would not happen without their permission or the benefit of a treaty. In the 1750s, an Odawa Chief named Pontiac began to gather the various First Nations together to wage a war to drive the British out of what is now known as Ohio, western Ontario and Michigan, and western New York State. They successfully defeated the British throughout those areas and closed down a number of British forts.

The First Nations only ceased fighting because the British promised that they would no longer allow any of their people to buy, sell, or occupy Indian land without the consent of the First Nations. This promise was embodied in the *Royal Proclamation* which, of course, is still law in Canada today and is also referred to in the *Constitution Act, 1982*. This is the historical background of the *Royal Proclamation* and it shows how the treaty process became an integral part of the founding of Canada. It makes clear that the First Nations are founding partners in the building of this country and that we are not conquered or subjugated peoples. We are and always have been nations.

When the British Crown entered into treaties with the First Nations, they did so on a nation-to-nation basis. Treaties are political contracts between two or more nations. Our First Nations were represented throughout the whole process by our chiefs, or "national leaders". The British Crown recognized that we were nations and that we had our own laws which would enable our chiefs to agree to the terms of treaties on our behalf. We, as First Nations citizens, would then be bound to observe our treaty obligations because our own laws said that we must do so.

A federal policy of termination, avoidance and denial

While there are treaties in existence throughout much of Canada, the major portion of lands in this country have not been dealt with through the treaty-making process. Those First Nations which have entered into treaties have found it extremely difficult to exercise their rights under treaty or to protect their traditional lands from third-party development and environmental damage. Successive Canadian governments have attempted to marginalize and even to unilaterally extinguish our treaties. The federal *White Paper* of 1969 and the recommendations produced in a report by the Conservative government's task force, chaired by Mr. Eric Neilson

in 1985, *The Buffalo Jump* report, are both clear examples of this ter-
mination policy.

On one hand, the federal government desperately wants to
terminate the treaties made with the First Nations. It does not seem
to matter to the government that it is bound by law to respect and
to live up to these agreements. It appears that some people at the
highest levels of government believe that they are "above the law"
when it comes to our rights. On the other hand, if the government
cannot succeed in terminating our rights, the next best thing is for
them to avoid doing anything about them. So, they do not want to
talk about our rights; they do not want to resolve any of the outstanding problems that have been lingering around for so many
years and making people frustrated and angry. Their desire is to
simply avoid the issues as much as possible, and to do nothing
about grievances and unfulfilled entitlements. The objective of
this policy is to minimize the First Nations' expectations in terms
of treaty-based rights and benefits. It also serves to lessen awareness of the reality and scope of our treaty rights and confuse people about the importance of Canada and the First Nations.

We saw this approach at the First Ministers Conference on
the *Constitution*: all of the Premiers, along with the Prime Minister,
simply sat around and pretended that they did not know anything
about our Aboriginal and treaty rights. The excuse they offered us
for doing nothing at that time was that they did not know what
our rights were, so they could not deal with these issues. Up to
then, we had only been successful in defending our Aboriginal and
treaty rights in a few legal challenges. This situation has changed
quite a lot since then.

Some recent legal victories

In recent years, the First Nations have begun to resort more
heavily to the Canadian legal system in order to secure the recognition and protection of our rights under treaty. We have done so because the Crown, as represented by the federal government, is un-
willing to conduct itself according to the sacred promises which it
made when it asked us to sign the treaties. Furthermore, the provincial governments have been doing all that they can to diminish
our rights and interests in the lands and resources of Canada. The
provinces, by the way, promised to respect and provide for our
rights in the constitutional agreements which they entered into
with the federal government when they were formed as provinces.
In any event, both the federal and provincial governments are le-

gally bound by the *Royal Proclamation*, as well as by the *Constitution*. However, neither level of government has ever shown us that they are willing to live up to their obligations.

As a result, we have had to take these issues to court – and we have won. In cases such as *Sioui, Sparrow, Guerin, Flett, Simon,* and *Nowegijick,* we have been able to show the courts that our rights have substance and are protected by law. The courts have repeatedly instructed the federal and provincial governments to respect our rights and not simply override them through legislation or policy. However, both levels of Canadian government have thus far chosen to simply ignore the courts and continue to oppress us through their out-dated, misguided and illegal policies.

When we ask them to change their policies they refuse. When we point out to them that their policies have no legal basis and are, in fact, contrary to the laws of Canada, they pretend that they cannot understand what we are saying or that there is nothing that they can do because the policies are already in place and cannot be tampered with.

Since when are governmental policies superior to laws in Canada? We know that the government is bound to obey its own laws in all of its activities. It seems, however, that the present federal government believes that it is above the law. Our lands and resources are being stolen from us illegally. Our rights are being denied to us illegally. Our environment and our way of life are being destroyed, once again, illegally. The government has a clear and strict fiduciary duty to protect our rights and interests according to the law. Yet, we see that the government has many treaty obligations which it has failed to live up to and is still failing to live up to.

ROBERT VENABLES

Robert Venables is Senior Lecturer in the American Indian Program at Cornell University. He was formerly the Curator of American Indian History at the Museum of the American Indian in New York City. He has also acted as an expert witness in a recent Canadian case concerning Mohawks.

INDIAN POLICY IN THE UNITED STATES

Any policy or plan designed by white people will serve white people whether they speak French or English. In contrast, the *Two Row Wampum* model of the Haudenosaunee is an Indian model not an Imperial one. However, white people like to think that what Native Americans want is, after all, what they want too – and by the way, we will use your language to describe it, if it makes you feel comfortable. The fact of the matter is no white-designed model has ever done anything but serve white interests, whether you call it an Imperial model or not.

Let me tell you a story. In 1763, Pontiac led a rebellion in Ottawa in rebellion against that Imperial model. It failed, and he surrendered in 1766. Three years later, it seemed possible that he was organizing another war – and a war would be bad for business. Business in the 1760s was the fur trade, and in the city of brotherly love, Philadelphia, the merchants decided that another war would damage business. In 1769, Pontiac was assassinated by someone hired by the merchants of Philadelphia. The assassin was a Peoria Indian. The people that hired him were from a Christian firm of merchants and a Jewish firm of merchants. What you learn from that little story is that Indian policy is going to be determined ecumenically. It will involve French, English, Jews, Christians, Buddhists and Indians, but it will be some Indian or other who assassinates – an Indian who cooperates with the white model.

In addition to being ecumenical, it will be economical. Do not kid yourselves and think that it all fits into legal theory. You are talking about economics, and economics is extremely self-serving. Finally, when it is all over, you will find that history has been edited. We will conveniently forget all the ecumenical and economic realities of the crisis.

There have been two major policies that have dominated Native American affairs in the United States and that exemplify what I am saying. The *Dawes Act of 1887* promised Native Americans that if they divided up their land and lived on that land as individuals, they would be able to adapt into the mainstream. By 1934, only three percent of the land distributed by the United States government under that policy was still in Indian hands. So much for the Dawes Act.

In 1934, the *Indian Reorganization Act* came along attempting to reverse the *Dawes Act*. Now, one would assume that an act whose avowed purpose was the reversal of the *Dawes Act* would lead to a different result. However, under the *Indian Reorganization Act*, Native Americans lost three times as much land as was returned to them under the announced government policy of returning land to Native America. In the past, wherever the fur trade or deerskin trade had become less important, wars initiated by the whites were fought to seize land. After the American Revolution, debts had to be paid. Who paid them? Not the enfeebled government of George Washington – it was Native Americans. Land was seized by the Washington government at .008 cents per acre and sold at a $ 1.00 an acre so that Alexander Hamilton's treasury could come up out of the red.

In 1862, there was another wonderful white policy called the *Homestead Act*, backed by the "Free Soilers". Ever hear of a free lunch anywhere? Whose soil was free? Native Americans'. Whose government took it? Abraham Lincoln's. Lincoln was fighting a civil war and he needed money to win it. Where did he get the money? From gold on the land stolen from Native Peoples in a series of wars which continued after the Lincoln government.

Today the issues are more complex: oil and uranium. Here is a little mathematical problem for you. The Navajos in New Mexico were sitting on top of ten million pounds of uranium. This is in the 1970s. The State of New Mexico was sitting on six million pounds of uranium. The State of New Mexico signs a piece of paper with a uranium company that allows the uranium company to come in and strip out the uranium. The State of New Mexico, just for signing a piece of paper, got eight million dollars for the rights to six million pounds of uranium. The Navajos are sitting on top of ten million pounds of uranium. The United States government set up the B.I.A., the Bureau of Indian Affairs, to make sure that Native Americans do not get cheated. Right, an Imperial model. So, the white guys got eight million bucks for six million pounds of uranium. What do you think the Navajos got under my government? I bring this example up because the Government of the

United States to this day will not admit that a fraud has been committed. Listen very carefully: twenty-four thousand dollars.

It does not matter whether it is land in the 18th century, gold in the 19th century, or uranium in the 20th century. Any policy designed by non-Indians has only served non-Indians. There is a marvellous phrase in American law called "treaty substitutes". Treaty substitutes are executive orders, congressional acts, or supreme court decisions. The United States finds that most of its Indian policy is now being determined by these so-called treaty substitutes. I would suggest to you that treaty substitutes are a little like sugar substitutes: too much of them will cause cancer. The bottom line is that nowhere in the history of Indian/white relations have Native American rights been mutually recognized as equal. Unless history changes, the white model will continue to serve the non-Indians, and Indians will continue to pay the cost.

QUESTION PERIOD: PANEL ONE

Comment: BRIAN SLATTERY

Dr. Clark and I actually go back a long way. I do not think we disagree as much as Dr. Clark suggests we do.

The point that I want to make is not that we should throw out instruments like the *Proclamation* or section 35 of the *Constitution Act, 1982* which recognizes and affirms Aboriginal and treaty rights. Both of these instruments are clearly fundamental to a proper understanding of the position of First Nations within our Confederation.

However, we cannot stop there. These documents are only partial, imperfect reflections of a larger historical and legal reality. That larger reality is found in the history of relations between First Nations and incoming groups of settlers from the 17th century onwards. We have to open ourselves to that body of history, which is far better understood and preserved among First Nations in Canada than among non-Indian communities. Essentially, we have to enlarge our understanding of the *Constitution*.

So, I am not suggesting that we throw out anything; rather, we should put things like the *Proclamation* in their proper setting and see them as part of a larger historical and constitutional reality.

Comment: BRUCE CLARK

I would like to respond to two points made. Mr. Courtoreille, like Mr. Slattery, mentioned the *Sparrow* case and the *Sioui* case as great victories. They are not victories. They are the worst damn thing that could have happened at this time in Canada.

Point one: in the *Sparrow* case, the lawyers acting for the Indians conceded one point essentially without arguing it. They conceded jurisdiction. So, premise number one: federal and provincial governments have jurisdiction. Premise number two: when the governments exercise that jurisdiction, Indians ought to have a helping hand up because of section 35(1) of the *Constitution*. So, the court ended up saying white conservation law, *prima facie*, applies to Indians.

Point two: when this law applies, Indians have to have special treatment. They have to be able to show, for example, that in the drafting of the conservation law, the legislators intended that even if white guys could only take six fish, Indians could take twelve. You pat the Indians on the head. That apparent victory damns Indian sovereignty by giving up a key point, jurisdiction, without a fight.

I am currently fighting a sovereignty case for the Delisle Water Mount Currie Indians before the Supreme Court of British Colombia, and every time we mention Indian sovereignty, Crown lawyers and timber company lawyers just smile and cite *Sparrow*. They cite *Sparrow* since the court says that whites are sovereign, and the court can say that because the Indians did not fight the sovereignty issue. The reason the Indians did not fight that issue is because their damn lawyers did not fight it. Do not buy the arguments of lawyers and professors who regard cases like *Sparrow* as victories. They are not; they are the problem not the solution.

Moving on to Dr. Venables' speech, which was the best I have heard in nineteen years, there are dramatic and crucial differences between the United States and Canada. Dr. Venables is right to say that the United States has a concept of treaty substitutes that allows state policy to govern. The Indians, without constitutional protection of their rights, are screwed. Without making a treaty, without Indian consent, the government can get rid of their rights.

Therefore, the Imperial model is still crucial in Canada. Canada did not join the American Revolution. Canada remained under the *Royal Proclamation* without developing the concept of treaty substitutes. The *Royal Proclamation*, a simple document, says: several nations or tribes should not be molested or disturbed; secondly, if the whites want land, they ought to buy it. "Purchase" is the verb. In law, to express one thing is to exclude others, so, the sole mode of acquisition of Indian land is purchase, and this is still law in Canada. This approach was first and most clearly expounded by Dr. Brian Slattery in his doctoral thesis in 1979. I ask Dr. Slattery to go back to his pioneering research and remember that the Imperial model is the solution for Canadians, even if not for Americans.

Comment: LAWRENCE COURTOREILLE

The point I would like to make is that regardless of what law they use, regardless of whether they are Supreme Court decisions, they are unenforceable if the Government of Canada chooses to ignore them. I do not know how Mr. Clark became the Indian expert, but if we had ten white lawyers here, you would have ten different arguments telling you how these things are right and those things are wrong. By the way, when the other lawyers are wrong, it is big business. However, the reality is that even if the Prime Minister specifically says that the rule of law applies and Indian Peoples abide by it, even if we win cases like *Sioui* and *Sparrow*, the government can ignore the rule of law.

Last year in Alberta, a new law came in saying, "wear a seat belt". Well, you can be damn sure you would be charged if you were not wearing a seat belt the next day. However, when it comes to Indian decisions, nobody wants to enforce or apply them. In Nova Scotia, a Micmac won his right to hunt in spite of provincial hunting laws. The Supreme Court found that he was under treaty and therefore not subject to provincial laws. The provincial government just said, "Well, that's for Mr. Paul. Yet, if the other Micmacs want to exercise their treaty rights, each and everyone of them is going to have to go to court." So, they are still charging Indians for hunting in Nova Scotia. Even if we win a decision in the Supreme Court of Canada, who can force the Canadian government to respect that law?

Question: TRACY JACKSON
Law student, McGill University

During your speech, Professor Slattery, you mentioned that judges and lawyers need to acknowledge our blindness to Aboriginal viewpoints, that we, as judges and lawyers, must broaden our understanding of other sources of law, and that we must learn respect for Aboriginal legal thinking. What role do you think law schools play in assuring that these viewpoints are heard. More specifically, coming from McGill, a law school where there is no annual course offered in Aboriginal law, do you feel that McGill is fulfilling its role?

Answer: BRIAN SLATTERY

Let me speak generally, and since I am not familiar with McGill's current curriculum, perhaps people can draw whatever conclusions are appropriate. Law schools are very important in this process. Law will not be the only factor, or even the most important one, but law will continue to be important in this area – constitutional law in particular. When I went through McGill Law School, I believe there were no Native rights courses in Canada. In the courses that I took, I cannot actually remember a single occasion when First Nations were mentioned. I myself did a research paper for Professor John Brierly on the position of First Nations in Quebec under the French regime – an interest of mine which later developed. However, there was no real opportunity to see how First Nations might relate to the *Constitution* and legal system.

Now, imagine lawyers and judges who have had an education of that kind and then are confronted in court with an Aboriginal claim to land, sovereignty, or treaty rights. To them, it must seem that these claims come out of a legal "nowhere". Considering their education and background, this is an understandable reaction. To the extent that our courts have been able to grasp any of this, it is because counsel has pointed them in the right direction and they have been able to re-educate themselves.

It is important that our law schools play a leading role in this educational process through courses on Aboriginal rights. Nevertheless, I think it would be a mistake to confine the matter to specialized courses, because that again would suggest that Aboriginal rights are on the fringes of the law or that they are an "optional" subject like international criminal law. Aboriginal rights should be discussed in basic courses like constitutional law and property. That would bring about the kind of awareness we should be aiming for.

Answer: ROBERT VENABLES

I would like to clarify something. In the United States, courses are offered in "Native law", but they do not teach Native law at all. They teach laws written by non-Indians for and about Indians. True Native law comes from within the communities and nations that have survived the last five hundred years. Any study of Native law therefore must include and incorporate legal concepts from those nations. Do not mistake Aboriginal rights for the law that comes from within the community.

Question: DR. GORDON
from New York

It is very clear, Dr. Clark, from our history that the land at Oka was placed in the settlers' hands by white people, by the Sulpicians, not by the true owners of the land. The Indians of Kanesatake knew that the golf course was their land because they had never sold it. The Quebec police went in by force, as we can see in videos and in the marks on trees that show that thousands of rounds of ammunition had been fired on Indians. Other Indians then gathered and set up blockades. All that is history now.

Now the government has brought criminal charges on more than fifty individuals, and they will go to trial before the Superior Court. The usual process of a pre-trial hearing, where preliminary evidence is heard, has been circumvented by the Attorney General granting a preferred indictment. When these people go to court the prison doors will be yawning wide open. I ask you, Bruce Clark, how would you defend them?

Answer: BRUCE CLARK

I am so delighted to be asked this question. I would object to the jurisdiction of the Court, on the basis of Indian sovereignty. As far as I am concerned it is an air-tight defense. So far, the courts have heard no mention of Indian sovereignty. Yet, those Indian Peoples were prepared to die for it.

Like Professor Venables says: as soon as it gets into the system the lawyers start yakking about whether the concessions were voluntary. In a criminal trial, they talk about the crisis in terms of *mens rea* and other criminal defences. These are terms that the white society enjoys. What the Indians and their lawyers should say — well, I should not put sovereignty words in Indian mouths especially when Sugar Bear and Patricia Montour are here. But why the hell don't you raise sovereignty and tell the court it does not have jurisdiction?

Part II of the *Royal Proclamation*, paragraph 1, breathes court jurisdiction into colonial governments. When jurisdiction was given to colonial governments, it was counter-balanced by the recognition that the several nations or tribes of Indians should not be molested or disturbed. White courts did not have jurisdiction in Indian territory over Indian Nations.

In 1803 and 1821, Imperial legislation was passed with respect to crimes like murder, and it was said that the same criminal law applies to everybody in this country. Although by virtue of Imperially enacted legislation there is an argument that criminal law does apply to Indians, no such argument can be made in regards to civil law. Indians continue to be self-governing and beyond the jurisdiction of Canadian courts for the purpose of civil law.

At Oka, Indians were legitimately defending their civil rights. They drew a line and said, "White society: don't cross that line." White society crossed that line and in doing so, committed criminal acts contrary to sections 424 and 431 of the *Canadian Criminal Code*. Those two sections say that it is a crime for Canadian peace officers to threaten, or to assault internationally protected persons. Without a doubt, Mohawks are internationally protected persons. The *Royal Proclamation* is tantamount to a treaty, and we also can refer to the *International Covenant on Civil and Political Rights*, as well as the *International Covenant on Social, Cultural and Economic Rights*. Specific sections of these conventions make clear that collectivities, such as the Mohawks, are internationally protected.

Even in the terms of the criminal law, Natives have the right to self-defence against crimes committed against them. Furthermore, there is a basic legal principle that you cannot be both judge and party to a case. Yet, that is what is happening. White courts have an interest in the outcome of a trial judging another nation and race of people. That is not only inappropriate, it is also illegal. The way to prove it is illegal is to object to the jurisdiction of the courts on technical legal grounds.

Question: MARTIN JENSEN
McGill law student

What optimism do you have, Dr. Clark, for the continued existence of the constitutionally-binding *Royal Proclamation* in an independent Quebec? Why should the province of Quebec, as an independent nation, retain such an inconvenient instrument in its constitution-to-be?

Answer: BRUCE CLARK

It would heave the *Royal Proclamation* out the window lickety-split. Therefore, my answer is: get behind the Indians. They are the only people with the guts to defend their constitutional rights and prevent this monstrous human rights abuse from happening. Boy, I do not know if it is true, but we heard in British Columbia that the Quebec police are getting three tanks. Why the hell does a police force need tanks? Because the Mohawks have the guts to defend their constitutional rights and the rule of law.

Mr. Courtoreille asked, "What will we do when we win in court?" That is: what do we do? It is the same thing that President Jackson said about Chief Justice Marshall's decision in the States. "Chief Justice Marshall has made his decision, now let him enforce it. I've got the guns and power." That is the problem Mr. Courtoreille faced, and that we all face. Say the Indians do go to the Supreme Court of Canada, and it is shown that the law is on their side. They turn around with their piece of paper and they say, "See? We not only have the *Royal Proclamation* in our hand, we have a court order saying: yup, the *Royal Proclamation* is right. What do you think will happen with those three tanks or with the Canadian army? The rule of law is breaking down in this country because the Attorney General is a criminal.

Question: ALFRED ZIMMERMAN
Lawyer

Until recently, I knew nothing about Indian affairs, but now I am trying to learn. The origin of my interest was the crisis at Oka. Here was a dispute over a piece of land, and the Indians at Oka were saying the land was theirs and that they had religious and emotional ties to it. What a mistake they made – all they had to do originally was put a fence around it and set up a registry office in their Long House, inscribe it in the register and then no one would be able to attack it. That is exactly what happened when the English defeated the French in French Canada. However, no farmer lost his land, because they had put fences around it.

I think the issue brought up by what I just said about Oka is really an issue which applies to the whole controversy. Land rights or property is not being discussed. The problem is that when the Aboriginal Peoples in Canada or even the United States were given the right to be left unmolested, no Indians marked out the boundary of the territory within which they lived. That is the crux of the problem. They had no fence and no registry office.

Here was a clash between Europeans, who knew property only as places bounded by fences or international lines registered somewhere, and the Indians who, because of their culture and background, did not perceive property that particular way. Indians have been shoved further and further back as other people displace them and put fences around their properties.

Answer: BRUCE CLARK

There is a fence, there is a fence Mr. Lawyer. Mr. Lawyer, I am right here.

Question: ALFRED ZIMMERMAN

If there is a fence, I have never seen it.

Answer: BRUCE CLARK

No, you are never going to see it because it is conceptual and legal. The fence is the *Royal Proclamation* which said: all land not purchased from the Indians with their consent is Indian territory. You start with a fence around the whole continent. So, when it is not Indian territory, according to the *Royal Proclamation*, it must have been purchased.

I know where you are coming from when you talk about territoriality. The reason I know is because nineteen years ago I asked myself that same question, and I pissed away fifteen years going after territoriality and land claims. At the time, Indian Elders were saying to me, "We're sovereign. We never gave it up." However, my lawyer-brain would say, "Sovereign is a big word. What you really mean is you have some kind of proprietary right." For lawyers, God is a property owner. They have to translate everything into property. So, I spent fifteen years pushing land claims when Elders were saying sovereignty. And by golly, we could have proved it in law already if we had listened to them in the beginning.

Answer: BRIAN SLATTERY

First Nations' perspectives, outlooks, traditions, and ways of understanding have not been properly represented in our legal system or, indeed, elsewhere in our culture. That situation has to be changed, not by non-Indian lawyers, but by Indian lawyers and spokespeople. There has to be a great deal of listening on the non-Indian side, and a relationship built up between Aboriginal and non-Aboriginal perspectives. We have had too much of one dominating the other. Good fences make good neighbours, but you still have to talk over the fences to your neighbours. You have to understand what they are saying.

Question:

For years, I believed that my Indian land was in the boundaries of my reserve. That was the thinking forced upon us by Indian Affairs. When I look at my treaties now, I look at it as sharing the land and allowing you people to live on it. We have never given up title, so, regardless of how many fences you put, we do not believe it is yours. However, we as Indian Peoples also believed that it is not our land, since we are just caretakers. We do not have any words in my language for ownership of land.

The Oka crisis brought out the same questions as Meech Lake, like who are these Indian Peoples any way? Throughout our history, the government has deliberately excluded Indian history from educational books. People in Calgary, for one thing, did not even know who the Sarcee Indian were, when they were living just outside of the city. Canadians do not know who the Cree or Mohawk are, or any of the different nations.

The reason for that ignorance is a deliberate lack of respect for Aboriginal Peoples. Take the war in the Gulf. From watching television, a little white kid in downtown Montreal thinks an Apache is a bloody war machine. What does he know about a tomahawk? It is a bomb. What does he know about the Huron? It is a war ship. That is the kind of education non-Indians are getting. That is all they know about Indians: the Cherokee plane and Pontiac car. Why don't they call their killing machines the Irish or the French?

I am not disagreeing with you, just saying that we have to sit down and not listen to leaders like Brian Mulroney. It scares me to think that I have to ask non-Indian Peoples for public support. You guys can't even protect your own rights. Look at the GST, and all the other things happening across the country. How the hell can we expect you guys to protect our rights?

Question: MARIE-CHRISTINE KIROUAK
Law student

Our federal government has made official apologies to Canadians of Japanese decent for what it did to them in the Second World War, namely taking their property away and interning them. As far as I am concerned, our government has been doing the same thing to Natives for over two centuries. Is it not about time we stop trying to justify the Imperialist system which has brought apartheid against Natives? Wanting to enforce the *Royal Proclamation* is one thing, but defending imperialism is quite another.

Answer: BRIAN SLATTERY

I agree with the questioner, if I understood properly. What was done to Japanese Canadians in the 1940s is, on a small scale, a hint of what has been done and continues to be done to many First Nations in Canada. That is a shocking reality that we have to somehow come to terms with, both in our historical understanding and in our image of the future. However, it will be a difficult and often painful process.

Answer: BRUCE CLARK

There is a fundamental difference between the Japanese Canadian situation and the Indian situation. The Indians were here first.

Imagine reality as a circle. Now the Europeans, who are few at first, arrive. They conform to that circle, but have their own way of going about things. A legal translation of that social reality was expressed by the Indian society in the *Two Row Wampum* belt. The *Two Row Wampum* belt defines a relationship of societies co-existing in peace, friendship and respect. The *Royal Proclamation* enacts into constitutional law the *Two Row Wampum* based on co-existence, peace, friendship and respect and two sovereign societies. That is the foundation of this country. No other group or race is in a similar position. So, while I appreciate your point, I want you to be careful. It prejudices the Indian cause to group all minorities together. Natives, as Madame Justice Wilson said in 1989, are *sui generis*, and constitutionally unique.

Before I close, I would like to develop the idea of circles further. If you take those circles to the modern time-frame, moving from 1763 up to the present, we find that the first circle, Indian reality, is in the same place. Skip to the third circle, *Two Row Wampum* Indian law, and it is in the same place. The fourth circle, the *Royal Proclamation*/constitutional white law, is also in the same place. The only thing that is out of sync is the second circle: white society's attitude, which has shifted out of place. The problem is not the law – the problem is how white society's attitude is out of sync with the law, yet enforced by the power it holds. We have to bring this circle back in place to remind our society of the law and to come back to that law.

That is why I keep harping on the rule of law, and why I see Oka as a time when Mohawks stood at the far point of the circle, and said: we have gone far enough. The course of history must turn back now.

Oka was a genuine historic turning point for this society, and a wonderful event for that reason.

Answer: LAWRENCE COURTOREILLE

I did not know until recently that Ukrainians, Italians, and Japanese were all interned during World War II. Who was not interned during World War II? The English and the French. No person should be interned or have their rights taken away. So, I can understand what the Japanese, Italians and Ukrainians went through – but unfortunately they have forgotten what we went through. They are free now and they forget that they were once interned because they got rid of those shackles.

I think what is happening today is scary. It is scary when you have a white guy like George Bush with little Brian running behind him talking about the new world order, especially when you see what is happening in places like Panama. Canada stood by while massive graves were filled with kids. What have they done to Indigenous Peoples in Grenada, throughout South and Central America? It scares me to think about the new world order that this guy is establishing, regardless of what laws you turn to, whether American or Canadian or international. I had the chance to go to the Hague in Europe with Chief Joe Norton, and when I walked into the World Court, I saw the statue presented by Argentina and I thought of all the human rights infractions they have inflicted on their own people. Yet, there is the statue that they donated to the World Court. It may be that Aboriginal rights are again going to be the price for the new world order.

Answer: PROFESSOR VENABLES

I would like to return to a point I made earlier, although I am sorry to pick on Professor Clark, in regards to *Two Row Wampum*. The *Two Row Wampum* belt symbolizes the ability and the intention of Indigenous Peoples to come to their own conclusions exclusively. The first and second rows do not interfere in the other's constitutional determination. Unfortunately, Professor Clark keeps suggesting that somehow the *Two Row Wampum* belt and the *Royal Proclamation* can be synthesised or worked out together. The only way *Two Row Wampum* is effectively implemented is when decisions for Indigenous Peoples are being made one hundred percent by those Indigenous Peoples.

Please do not tell me that the *Royal Proclamation* is such a marvellous protection. That is like a fundamentalist Christian or marxist who says, "Don't judge us by how it has come out." Let us face reality: where did the *Royal Proclamation* get us? We are not talking about political theory, we are talking about real choices that allow Indigenous Peoples to develop entirely on their own, with no interference from historians or lawyers that are not members of that particular Indian Nation.

It has been suggested that Natives have a different concept of property. They have a different concept of virtually everything. So, if you want to resolve a situation working together, there are only two ways. You can think like they do, which is impossible, or you can let them do it entirely by themselves. I am not being facetious when I say the proof will be when an American Indian Nation north of the United States has full membership in the United Nations. Lithuania has twenty-five thousand square miles – the Navaho Nation has twenty-five thousand square miles. It seems to me that we regard rights of Indigenous Peoples much differently.

PANEL TWO

THE CURRENT PICTURE: PROGRESS OR IMPASSE ?

OREN LYONS

Oren Lyons is a Six Nations Iroquois Confederacy spokesperson and faith keeper for the Onondaga Nation. The Mohawk Nation is one of the six that make up the Iroquois Confederacy, the traditional government of the "Longhouse" People, whose central fire is at Onondaga.

SOVEREIGNTY AND THE NATURAL WORLD ECONOMY

Sovereignty is a term that we hear being used all the time and particularly in relation to Indians. It is a term that should be applied to Indians. However, I have noticed in the past ten years or so a certain change in terminology. Nationally and internationally, the term "sovereignty" is often being replaced by the term "autonomy". I have noticed this in relation to the Nicaraguan conflict and the Mesquitoe Indians.

What is the difference between the two terms? What is sovereignty? We have always taken a rather simplistic view. We said that sovereignty is the act thereof. You are as sovereign as you are able to be. Generally, sovereignty is applied to nations and today, to nation-states. Indians have always perceived themselves to be nations, sovereign and independent. Further, we apply sovereignty even further than nations. We apply it to individuals in the form of respect. Indian People, of all people, understand the concept of freedom and being born free with rights.

Columbus landed here five hundred years ago. Across America and the world there was a tremendous preparation for 1992. I know that the President of the United States set aside some eight-two million dollars for this "celebration" as they call it, and Spain has spent even more than that. All of the world has become involved: the Catholic Church, for obvious reasons, Italy, the United States, as well as Latin America. Everybody is pointing to the year 1992.

Why? Since 1992 is a year of assessment, where we stand back and look at five hundred years of activity in the western hemisphere and assess what condition we are in. It can be a year of atonement for what happened to the Indigenous Peoples who caught the brunt of this invasion, or it can be a year of commitment to see that the next five hundred years are going to be better than the last five hundred.

This process of reflection will have to involve Indian nations. We have to make our own assessment of our condition. We have to present a position to challenge this idea of a celebration, to challenge this idea of a discovery. Discovery is a very arrogant perception; we were "discovered", sort of like the flora and fauna of North America. In truth, there were free nations here with a real understanding of government and community, of the process and great principles of life. In fact, on the landfall of Christopher Columbus, freedom was rampant in North, Central and South America. Everybody was free and living in a natural world economy where they had economic security in perpetuity. They had adjusted themselves to working with the land, and understood that every year that the land renewed itself.

Now, coming across the water were peoples with a different perception about economy. As a matter of fact, up to the present day, the Governments of Canada and the United States have spent their time trying to get our people involved in this economy. They have spent a lot of time trying to tell us about the importance of private property as opposed to community property. We hear terms like development, progressive development, sustainable development, but our perception is that if you do not operate around the real laws of the universe, you are challenging fundamental cycles that you depend on for life.

So, there was obviously a conflict between Christopher Columbus' perception, and the people that he met. All of the writing says the First Peoples were healthy, happy and well-fed, and not overly inclined to warfare. Yet, the process of domination began immediately. He said: these would make good slaves. That was his first message back to the Queen: we can make slaves of these people since they are easily subjugated, and they do not know much about warfare. Any ten of my men can take over this island with the technology and weapons we have brought over.

The basic conflict relates to economy because Indian Nations operated on the basis of a natural world economy. They had Thanksgiving ceremonies that went around the clock and around the calendar year. Something was always coming up so there was always Thanksgiving in a land-based economy. It was part of the structure of a community. It was an instruction to respect what was growing. This was true across the Americas. Yet, our white brother kept telling us there was a better way: get rich. Our people had a hard time with that. They said, "No, our land is held in common, everyone owns the land. Water is free, air is free, everything you need for life sustenance is free." And he said, "I would like to buy your land." They said, "What do you mean by buying?" Now we have people "buying" his argument. We have people, our own people, who are now willing to "sell" long-term sovereignty for short-term personal gain.

As we sit back and assess these last five hundred years, let us look at what has happened to our people. How have the Indian Nations fared? How have our children? How are our institutions? Are they holding up? How are our principles? Are they holding up? We have to look at ourselves because as tough as these last five hundred years have been, the next five hundred or even fifty years are going to be tougher.

There is a fundamental issue here that we have to look at because human beings are displacing life around the world. Huge populations are displacing life whether it is trees, the elephants in Africa, the tigers in India or the buffalo in this country. They are not here anymore. Yet, there are more and more people. There is a displacement going on here of things a fundamental economy needs. The Indians understood one thing: they understood that the law of flesh, blood and bones is common to all living beings. We are under one common law here. We are animals, but we are animals with intellect. Intellect is what makes us dangerous because we have the foreknowledge of death. Animals know when death is coming, and they prepare for it. Yet, we know from a very young age that we are going to die. This is a tremendous knowledge, but how do you use that knowledge? How do you work with it?

When one speaks of generations the way the Indians speak of them, we must see that the next generations, those faces coming from the earth, have the same good that we have and can enjoy the same law that we do. Well, in assessing five hundred years in this country, we see that the next seven generations are not going to enjoy that. Every day, at least six species of life become extinct. So, when you talk about the philosophy of sovereignty, you must talk of longevity and the future. This is the common sense that comes from the long experience of Indian Nations being in one place: if you do not work with the laws that surround you, you will not survive. It is quite simple. We know that there is no mercy in the natural law whatsoever. It will exact retribution in direct ratio to violation. You cannot discuss this – there are no lawyers, only the retribution. The problem here is that we visit this retribution on our children and on our grandchildren. We leave them the problem of our excesses. What do we say to greedy individuals that say sovereignty is money?

I never believed the white man when he said his way was better. I never believed it. I always believed that our way was better, maybe just because I knew more about it. The truth is, if we sit back and really look at it, there is some hard news here for all of us no matter who we are.

When we speak of sovereignty, we have to have a large conceptualization of what it is we are talking about. With Indian Nations, it is not just a political term, it is also a spiritual term. It may be even be more spiritual than political. One of our people once said that spirituality is the highest form of politics. So, let us keep the parameters of what we are talking about clear.

The parameters are beyond the oceans that surround us, and they are beyond our time here on earth. The parameters we are discussing reverberate into the future. If your economy does not function within those parameters then you are shortchanging those future generations we talked about. Maybe it is only the Indians that talk about the seventh generation. I do not know. Since we have talked about it a lot, I have heard it again and again. I hear it from strangers, I hear it from strange places. Why not? It seems to us common law and common sense. So, let us say that sovereign is common sense in its most basic fundamental form: common sense and respect for all life.

Land is the issue, land has always been the issue. We cannot trade our jurisdiction over lands and territories for money. Our lands and our right to govern ourselves are all we have. If we gamble our lands for money, jurisdiction and taxation, we will lose because that is the white man's game.

MATTHEW COON-COME

Matthew Coon-Come is the Grand Chief of the Quebec Grand Council of the Crees.

DIFFERENT LAWS FOR DIFFERENT PEOPLES

Quebec has invented the concept of an English Canada, and English Canada has accepted the myth of an English and French Canada. Meech Lake described a Canada based on a falsehood: the racist notion of two founding peoples. The debate once again attempts to push the real founding peoples, the First Peoples, entirely aside. I understand the reason for this. Canada has an unsavoury history in its relations with my people. While the French and English are arguing about which of them came first, they both know that their arguments fail when they are forced to confront the truth. May I ask a question? Have I become your enemy because I tell you the truth? Indigenous Peoples lived in Canada and governed themselves for thousands of years before the spoilers of this land came here and began squabbling among themselves. It is ironic that these people do not want to recognize our existence and rights now because our presence spoils their arguments. That is why Canada prefers to make this a debate between the French and the English.

Prime Minister Mulroney could never bring himself to acknowledge the role that Elijah Harper had in stopping Meech Lake. There is a reluctance to concede that the First Peoples, the original peoples of this land, should have an interest in shaping its future. Elijah Harper made it clear that we are interested. We do not want to be pushed aside or shut out. The Mohawks showed Canada in the summer of 1990 that they will not be left out. We are looking for solutions and the question is always asked: what about the treaties, what about the *James Bay Northern Quebec Agreement?* Is that a solution? Is that a model that can be followed? The answer is "No".

Neither Canada nor Quebec really wishes to acknowledge the right of the Indigenous Peoples to participate in decision making. We, as Indigenous Peoples, are excluded from the process of government. Nothing makes this more obvious than James Bay I and the history of the *James Bay and Northern Quebec Agreement.* The decision to build the complex around 1975 was made in Premier Bourassa's office. Little acknowledgement or consideration was ever given to the presence or the rights of the Cree that live in James Bay.

Archaeologists have shown that we existed and lived there for five thousand years. No one from the Government of Canada even thought it necessary to come to the Cree committee to discuss the proposal to build what was then the largest hydro-electric project in the world in the middle of our communities, in our own backyard and on top of our graves and hunting grounds. As far as Quebec was concerned, we did not exist.

Now let us look at the position that the Government of Canada took. I do not need to remind you that the federal government has the constitutional responsibility for Indians. It is required to protect our interests. Well, when the James Bay project was announced, Canada did nothing. Canada, as I think you know, has the well-earned reputation for doing nothing when Indian rights are threatened. James Bay was the biggest land-grab in Canadian history and the Government of Canada was entirely silent. Canada did later lend the Grand Council of the Crees of Quebec money to cover some of the costs of the court cases. Nevertheless, the fact is that Canada took no initiative on its own. Quebec ran over our lands and our rights. They did as they damn well pleased with no consideration for the people that lived there. In every way, the construction of the James Bay project reflected the unilateral behaviour of the governments toward Indigenous Peoples, and when we did object, when we did raise our voices in protest, Quebec said our actions were against the law. We were told that in the eyes of the law we had no title to the land. According to their law, we were squatters. I ask: what kind of law is it that makes squatters out of people who have been living in a territory for thousands of years?

There are certain laws that are unfair. Look at the laws that Hitler's regime developed against the Jews. In Africa, they developed laws against the black people. Just because something is law, does not mean that it is just or fair. You may be surprised to learn the James Bay project, James Bay I, was never subject to environmental impact assessment. It was just built, in spite of our objections and in spite of the objections of environmentalists and human rights activists. Why is it that every time you build projects, whether they are mega-projects, whether they are forestry, mining, or tourism projects, they are built on Indigenous lands? James Bay is not a good model. It has not set a precedent. It simply follows the old tradition of the government when it comes to Indigenous rights, do exactly what you want to do. That is the reality. Different laws for different people.

Another aspect of James Bay I that calls for examination is the treaty making process itself. At the start of construction of the *James Bay and Northern Quebec Agreement*, the Government of Quebec took the position that it was under no obligation to talk to the Crees. As I mentioned a moment ago, we were considered squatters. It was only after numerous failed attempts to get a hearing from Quebec and only after the Indians of Quebec Association failed in its efforts to stop the project, that the Crees were able to bring the issue before the courts. Construction proceeded during the nine months we were in court. When finally Judge Maluk decided in the Cree's favour, recognizing Quebec's failure to respect the *Quebec Boundaries Extension Act of 1912*, the construction of the project was blocked forty-four days before Quebec succeeded in having the decision overturned. Again, their law applied. By that time, most of the damage had already been done and there was little that the court could do except award financial compensation for damage. However, money could never compensate the Crees for the loss of their way of life and for what was done to the forest, to the rivers, to the animals and the Cree People.

Quebec, however, continued to be concerned that the Crees might succeed in going before the Supreme Court and having the previous judgment vindicated. It was only this fear that led Quebec to negotiate a treaty with the Crees. Once again, Canada hid in the background, refusing to take part in the negotiations until almost the very end. The *James Bay Northern Quebec Agreement* is a treaty negotiated at a gun point. The Crees had lost in court on appeal and the project was being built. The *James Bay Agreement* was a last ditch effort to have some benefit out of a disaster. The Crees used the opportunity to make some enormous gain and negotiated for control over our education, and the creation of Cree school boards. We took control of health services for our people. We understood that we could implement an environmental regime that was intended to protect the territory from any future development and any attempt to unilaterally build any other projects. In the future, we said, we would gain control. James Bay could never happen again.

I think we all know what has happened to the *James Bay Northern Quebec Agreement*. The governments of Canada and Quebec have used the implementation process to minimize government obligations to the Crees. They pick and choose which provisions they are going to interpret and what is going to be in their interest to build. They even attempted to force the Crees to make one final settlement for all the agreement benefits by holding up their explicit obligations and instituting an elaborate media campaign to create a false public perception that the Crees had received more than their due.

As for the agreement itself, the Crees negotiated for rights to which we should have been entitled whether the James Bay project was built or not. Why should Indian Peoples have to sign a land claims agreement to gain control over the education of our children? These are the things we negotiated for. For most other Indigenous Peoples in Canada, the level of control we have achieved in the *James Bay Agreement* has still not been reached. The *Agreement* contained the basis for Cree self-government, the first, and still the only constitutionally-based Indian self-government in Canada. Cree self-government was affirmed as a constitutional right. This has not yet been achieved by any other Indigenous Peoples in Canada. Yet, these rights have never made much of a difference to Canada. Even though the Cree are no longer under the *Indian Act*, the government still insists that we come under the control of the Department of Indian Affairs and Northern Development.

Is there really a solution? In British Columbia, the Gitskans, like all the other Indigenous Peoples in Canada, want the basic democratic right to govern their own people. There appears to be some fear in the non-Native community that the Indians might win their case. It has led to speculation on the dire consequences that could follow. Some have complained that the Indians would impose their own rules on non-Natives. What is wrong with that? Some people in British Columbia went crazy when a lawyer for the Gitskans suggested that the Indians would constitute a third order of government. I think we have to recognize that the Indians already are a third order of government, but that the government under which the Indians live is a dictatorship.

The Federal Minister of Indian Affairs exercises arbitrary power over the lives of Indian Peoples. He determines who is an Indian. He controls the right to education, Indian land, Indian resources, health services. He even has the power to invalidate the last will and testimony of any Indian. He does not provide any rationale. Maybe we should have special legislation for Greeks, Italians, Jews. Why Indians? I think Canadians need to realize that Indian Peoples live under a dictatorship. We are beneficiaries of a trusteeship which has been terribly abused. Further, under the law, we have little power to refute our trustee. Look at Oka; look at

James Bay. What good is a treaty that is broken, over and over and over again. No, I do not see any good models that we can follow.

If we are to succeed, we need to do something entirely new. Not confine ourselves to Quebec. We have to go farther than that. We need to stop lying about the history of Canada. We need to end the racism and deceit that denies us our basic rights. Canada claims us as subjects. Quebec claims that it, too, will treat us as subjects if it separates from Canada. We were nations long before Canada or Quebec came into being, and we will not agree to subjugation, no matter how it is legally construed. There comes a time when people cannot take any more abuse. The time has come. Enough is enough.

PETER W. HUTCHINS

Peter Hutchins obtained his Bachelor of Laws degree from Laval University in 1969 and his Master of Laws from the London School of Economics and Political Science in 1971. He has conducted a private practice specializing in Aboriginal law since 1972, particularly land and resource issues, Aboriginal self-government and treaty implementation. He has been involved in negotiations and implementation of the James Bay and Northern Quebec Agreement since 1972. He acted for First Nations in constitutional negotiations and the First Ministers' Conference process during the 1980s and has been a special adviser to the Minister of Indian Affairs on Indian self-government. He has acted as counsel for First Nations before the courts in a number of jurisdictions as well as the Supreme Court of Canada. He is also a lecturer in Aboriginal law at McGill University's Faculty of Law.

This presentation reflects the author's thoughts on the state of the law in 1991. There, of course, have been developments in the law since that date. These developments, however, have not dissuaded the author from the views expressed below.

A PRACTICAL ASSESSMENT OF LITIGATION FOR NATIVE PEOPLES

The thesis I would like to put forward is that while the courts have been less than effective as dispute resolution mechanisms when judged in terms of specific problems, they have been important agents of law reform from a long-term perspective. There are signs that they are contributing to a new understanding of the relationship between First Nations and non-Aboriginal peoples. The courts themselves have moved from, and have moved government away from, a Euro-Canadian or Eurocentric view. They have moved from a colonial view of the relationship between Aboriginal and non-Aboriginal Peoples towards a greater understanding of a nation-to-nation relationship based on mutual rights and responsibilities.

While Aboriginal litigants have been frustrated by cases arising out of immediate problems or confrontations, from a long-term perspective, litigation has played a significant role in, to use the title of this conference, "Forging a Better Understanding".

Just to kick off my thesis by examples of the courts re-examining their approach, I can do no better than to refer you back to Chief Justice Dickson of the Supreme Court of Canada, and the 1985 Nova Scotia Micmac treaty case where the Chief Justice was very critical of an earlier decision. In 1929, Justice Patterson described the treaty process and First Nations as follows:

> Treaties are unconstrained acts of independent powers. But the Indians were never regarded as an independent power. A civilized nation first discovering a country of uncivilized people or savages held such country as its own until such time as by treaty it was transferred to some other civilized nation. The savages' rights of sovereignty even of ownership were never recognized.

Chief Justice Dickson remarked:

> It should be noted that the language used by Patterson J., illustrated in this passage, reflects the biases and prejudices of another era in our history. Such language is no longer acceptable in Canadian law and indeed is inconsistent with a growing sensitivity to Native rights in Canada.

Of course, there is a yawning gulf between the theory of law being proposed by the Supreme Court of Canada and the reality of government activity. Of course there is. However, I do maintain that the courts, the appellate courts and more particularly the Supreme Court of Canada, are attempting to redress the balance by rapping fingers and directing government to behave itself, to respect its obligations and to better understand the history which gave rise to the relationship between Aboriginals and non-Aboriginals.

Reluctance to interfere

Nonetheless, we face many problems in Aboriginal rights. One problem is that the courts tend to be reluctant to interfere or to settle issues between parties. To pick an example, First Nations' attempts to defend territory and jurisdiction in the face of large-scale development, whether resource development or military operations, have been highly problematic.

Matthew Coon-Come referred to the entire James Bay experience starting in 1973. While the James Bay Crees achieved a major victory in obtaining temporary injunctive relief against the original James Bay project through the judgment of Mr. Justice Malouf of the Quebec Superior Court, maintaining the interlocutory injunction before the Court system proved impossible. The Quebec Court of Appeal first suspended the injunction and subsequently reversed Mr. Justice Malouf. The suspension was based entirely on a balance of convenience rational: six million Quebecers versus ten thousand Crees and Inuit. The judgment dismissed the interlocutory injunction while purporting to analyze the *prima facie* case for Indian title in Northern Quebec. The courts again found in favour of a development project on the grounds of balance of convenience.

As Matthew indicated, however, the injunction issued by Mr. Justice Malouf was enough to force governments to the negotiation table starting a process that ultimately resulted in the signing of the *James Bay and Northern Quebec Agreement*. However flawed, this Agreement has provided certain benefits and now forms one of the bases for the development of the Cree Nation. The combination of a Superior Court injunction and the possibility of a decision in the Supreme Court in favour of the Aboriginal Peoples was enough to induce government to negotiate.

Across the country examples abound. It is remarkable how the difficulty in obtaining injunctive relief is directly proportional to hydroelectric capacity, oil and gas potential, or jobs in the forestry industry. The Lubicon Nation in Alberta has learned this lesson with respect to oil and gas reserves. The Algonquins of Barrier Lake have encountered the court's reluctance to interfere in forestry activity. The Superior Court was moved to declare in the latter case that the "theory of Aboriginal and treaty rights" had no application within Quebec:

> [A]u Québec, la situation juridique des Autochtones est différente de celle de la Common Law et de la situation en Colombie Britannique, basés sur la Common Law et des traités, alors qu'au Québec, la *Proclamation Royale de 1763* et l'absence de traité a empêché la création de tels droits. La théorie des droits ancestraux quant aux terres comprises à l'intérieur du territoire du Québec n'a pas été acceptée par la jurisprudence prépondérante.

A later judgment from the Court of Appeal appears to agree with this point of view, albeit in an *obiter dictum*. An Application for Leave to Appeal has been filed with the Supreme Court of Canada.

British Columbia, notwithstanding certain interlocutory victories in the area of forestry, have shown the limits of its judicial
tolerance. Any suggestion that injunctive relief for First Nations
might have a cumulative or wide-spread effect appears to be
enough to convince courts not to intervene.

Finally, there is the disturbing case of low altitude flights im-
pacting on the Innu of Labrador. Citing economic impact on non-
Aboriginal communities, the Federal Court held that the project
should not be stopped during environmental and social impact assessment of the project itself.

There is also considerable evidence that courts are not prepared to step into the shoes of parties in confrontation. The courts
are increasingly directing complex resource or jurisdictional issues
towards the negotiation table and away from the courts. The British Columbia Court of Appeal in *MacMillan Bloedel Ltd.* v. *Mullin*
was quite explicit:

> I think it fair to say that, in the end, the public an-
> ticipates that the claims will be resolved by ne-
> gotiation and by settlement. This judicial pro-
> ceeding is but a small part of the whole of a
> process which will ultimately find its solution in a
> reasonable exchange between governments and
> the Indian Nations.

Procedural problems

A further problem is that litigants seeking to resolve disputes
through the courts must traverse procedural mine fields which,
even when not fatal, impede progress.

Current attempts by the James Bay Crees to deal with James
Bay II have resulted in three legal proceedings. All are bogged
down in procedural preliminaries. Proceedings were filed almost
two years ago before the Federal Court of Canada to ensure federal
environmental and social impact assessment of the proposed James
Bay II project. Motions for particulars by Canada have been
pleaded twice and are the subject of two decisions. Yet, we are nowhere near a hearing on the merits of the case.

In the case of injunction proceedings filed in the Quebec Superior Court, in addition to motions for particulars, declinatory objections by Canada claiming to have no interest in the proceedings
resulted in a three day hearing before the Quebec Superior Court, a

decision against Canada, an appeal to Quebec Court of Appeal, a two day hearing before the Quebec Court of Appeal with judgment pending. The Court of Appeal has since confirmed the judgment of the Superior Court against Canada. Application for leave to appeal to the Supreme Court remains a possibility. Again, we can see that a trial on the merits of the case is a distant prospect. Keep in mind that the injunction proceedings were meant to halt an imminent project.

The courts as agents of change

While these examples show the frustration experienced by specific litigants dealing with specific conflicts, there is little doubt that much has been accomplished through litigation in the past twenty years. Change has come about by way of constitutional reform as well as other levels of legal and political restructuring involving First Nations.

Litigation has certainly forced changes in government policy over the years. One important example is the decision by the federal government following *Calder* to pursue a treaty-making process based on unextinguished Aboriginal rights and titles. In the words of the 1986 revised federal policy on comprehensive land claims:

> In the aftermath of the 1973 Supreme Court of Canada decision in the case of *Calder* v. *the Attorney General of British Columbia*, the tradition of treaty-making was renewed in the form of a comprehensive land claims policy.

The Supreme Court in *Sparrow* confirmed the significant effect of *Calder*:

> In the light of its reassessment of Indian claims following Calder, the federal government on August 8, 1973 issued "a statement of policy" regarding Indian lands. By it, it sought to signify the Government's *recognition and acceptance* of its continuing responsibility under the *British North America Act* for Indians and lands reserved for Indians, which it regarded "as an historic evolution dating back to the *Royal Proclamation of 1763*, which, whatever differences there may be about its judicial interpretation, stands as a basic declaration of

the Indian People's interests in land in this country.

Change in the law

Examples of changes made to statutes or prevailing interpretation of statutes forced by successful litigation are also available. I will provide two. With respect to income tax exemptions provided to Indians under section 87 of the *Indian Act*, after years of dispute and litigation, the Supreme Court of Canada in *Nowegijick* established the appropriate principle of interpretation and clarified possible exemptions:

> It is legal lore that, to be valid, exemptions to tax laws should be clearly expressed. It seems to me, however, that treaties and statutes relating to Indians should be liberally construed and doubtful expressions resolved in favour of the Indian. If the statute contains language which can reasonably be construed to confer tax exemption that construction, in my view, is to be favoured over a more technical construction which might be available to deny exemption.

In 1985, long-awaited but only partially adequate amendments were brought to the *Indian Act* reinstating Indian women and children who had lost Indian status through the operation of discriminatory provisions in that Act. Pressure to deal with the blatant sexual discrimination in the *Indian Act* originated in cases such as *Lavell* and particularly Sandra Lovelace's proceedings before the United Nations Human Rights Committee under the *International Covenant on Civil and Political Rights*. The latter case contributed in prompting Canada into action.

Constitutional change

There is no doubt that litigation by Aboriginal Peoples in the period leading up to 1982 contributed significantly to the inclusion of sections 25 and 35 in the *Constitution Act, 1982. Calder* and *Kanatewat* are concrete examples. As the Supreme Court acknowledged in *Sparrow*:

> It is clear, then, that section 35(1) of the *Constitution Act, 1982* represents the culmination of a long and difficult struggle in both the political forum and

the courts for the constitutional recognition of Aboriginal rights.

Change in the relationship with Aboriginal Peoples

It is only fair to recognize that the courts, in particular the courts of Appeal and the Supreme Court of Canada, have contributed to a substantial change in the relationship between Aboriginal and non-Aboriginal Peoples in Canada.

Even if governments are not ready to listen, decisions by the Supreme Court in *Sioui* and *Sparrow* are leading to a legal redefinition of this relationship. Perhaps I am speaking as a professor of law rather than as a practitioner when I say that the judgments in *Sioui* and *Sparrow* (which I gather were maligned during the first panel) are significant. I would try to defend their importance.

In my course on Aboriginal Peoples and the Law here at McGill University, I always draw attention to the speech given by former Prime Minister Trudeau in Vancouver, August 1969. The very existence of Aboriginal rights was denied and the treaty relationship belittled. The Prime Minister stated:

> [W]ell, one of the things the Indian bands often refer to are their Aboriginal rights and in our policy, the way we propose it, we say we won't recognize Aboriginal rights. We will recognize treaty rights. We will recognize forms of contract which have been made with the Indian People by the Crown and we will try to bring justice in that area and this will mean that perhaps the treaties shouldn't go on forever. It's inconceivable, I think, that in a given society one section of the society have a treaty with the other section of the society. We must be all equal under the laws and we must not sign treaties amongst ourselves and many of these treaties, indeed, would have less and less significance in the future ...

These observations are quite interesting given the present constitutional context. It would be hard to justify a position saying that nothing has changed since Trudeau's 1969 speech. It has changed significantly, even though there is still a long way to go. Much has been done and that to a large extent is a result of efforts in and by the courts.

In 1991, Aboriginal and treaty rights are not only recognized, they are constitutionally protected. A renewed treaty process is underway notwithstanding all its flaws. The most recalcitrant of provincial governments, British Columbia, has relented and is now presumably ready to negotiate Aboriginal rights.

Consider the words of the Supreme Court in *Sparrow*:

> This Court found that the Crown owed a fiduci-
> ary obligation to the Indians with respect to the
> lands. The *sui generis* nature of Indian title, and the
> historic powers and responsibility assumed by the
> Crown constituted the source of such a fiduciary
> obligation. In our opinion, *Guerin*, together with *R.*
> v. *Taylor and Williams* (1981), 34 O.R. (2d) 360,
> ground a general guiding principle for section
> 35(1). That is, the Government has the responsi-
> bility to act in a fiduciary capacity with respect to
> Aboriginal Peoples. The relationship between the
> Government and Aboriginals is trust-like, rather
> than adversarial, and contemporary recognition
> and affirmation of Aboriginal rights must be de-
> fined in light of this historic relationship.

Indeed, much has changed and it has been the result of a cumulative impact of judicial *dicta* in cases such as *White and Bob*, *Taylor and Williams*, *Guerin*, and *Nowegijick*.

The Courts have assisted in developing an understanding of treaties

I would like to deal with the treaties and the treaty process as an example of how the courts have been redefining the relation-ship. Litigation has virtually revolutionized the treaty process and our understanding of treaty instruments in Canada. The courts have encouraged, if not forced, parties into, or back into, a treaty process. The result of *Kanatewat* was the eventual signing of the *James Bay and Northern Quebec Agreement*. The British Columbia Court of Appeal in *McMillan Bloedel Ltd.* v. *Mullin* gave instructions to the parties to negotiate, as referred to earlier.

First, what is a treaty? Previously, there was a set concept that it had to deal with surrender or cession of land and that it had to be signed by various people. There was a form that had to be re-spected.

This set concept has gone and the courts have opened up the parameters of what can be considered a treaty. The classic case illustrating this point is the decision of Mr. Justice Norris in *White and Bob* cited with approval by the Supreme Court in *Simon* and again in *Sioui*:

> In the section [88] "Treaty" is not a word of art and in my respectful opinion, it embraces all such engagements made by persons in authority as may be brought within the term "the word of the white man" the sanctity of which was, at the time of British exploration and settlement, the most important means of obtaining the goodwill and co-operation of the Native tribes and ensuring that the colonists would be protected from death and destruction. On such assurance the Indians relied.

Twenty years ago, no treaties were believed to have been executed in the Maritimes or in Quebec. Again, it was believed that treaties had to deal with the specific surrendering of lands or of an interest in land.

The courts have disposed of this narrow doctrine. *Simon* held that a treaty of peace and friendship concluded with the Micmacs in 1752 was a valid and binding treaty. Recently the Supreme Court in *Sioui* concluded that an instrument signed by General Murray in favour of the Huron Nation in September 1760, prior to the fall of Montreal, was a treaty of peace. *Sioui* contains explicit language stating that land cession was not necessary for a treaty. *Sioui* confirmed *Simon* in this respect and concluded that a section 88 treaty includes agreements on such matters as political or social rights.

The important feature of the *Sioui* judgment is the significance given to oral negotiations between General Murray and the Huron Chiefs. The document was not signed by the Hurons. We put before the Court documents recounting the negotiations between the parties, documents such as Murray's own journal and reports of subsequent conferences at which the parties made reference to the peace agreements concluded. The Court considered the context and concluded that first, it showed that the British wanted the Hurons as allies against the French and second, that a treaty of peace had been made. The judicial reasoning in *Sioui* represents a significant step towards judicial recognition of the oral component of treaties. Negotiations during the treaty process were more important to Indian Nations than the actual written documents since Indian Nations had oral cultures. The courts are now recognizing this fact.

Construction of treaties and the protection of treaty rights

Over the years the courts have developed a clear doctrine on "large and liberal construction of treaties" beginning again with *White and Bob*, through *Nowegijick*, to the Supreme Court in *Simon* and *Sioui*.

In conjunction with this, the courts have gradually developed a clear position on the importance of the historical context of treaties as well as the binding nature of the oral portions of treaties. In *Taylor and Williams* we read the following:

> Cases on Indian or Aboriginal rights can never be determined in a vacuum. It is of importance to consider the history and oral traditions of the tribes concerned, and the surroundings circumstances at the time of the treaty, relied on by both parties, in determining the treaties effect.

In *R. v. Horse*, Mr. Justice Estey analyzed Treaties No. 6 and 7 in light of the treaty negotiations surrounding those instruments. Mr. Justice Lamer in *Sioui* dealt extensively with the importance of the historical context prior to, during and subsequent to the signing of the treaty.

Consequently, protection of treaty rights has undergone considerable progress. In 1960, *Sikyea* and *George* held that, notwithstanding the regret expressed by certain justices, Parliament could override treaty promises. Persistent litigation, particularly since 1982, has altered the situation.

The courts have developed important *dicta* through cases involving alleged infractions under the *Migratory Birds Convention Act and Regulations*. Prior to 1982, a breach of treaty rights was possible, and no remedy existed. With the coming of the *Constitution Act, 1982* and in particular sections 35 and 52 of the *Constitution*, a remedy now exists to terminate the continuing breach. Rights are now recognized as having continued unextinguished and may now be exercised (*R. v. Arcand; R. v. Flett; R. v. Stevenson*).

While Chief Justice Dickson in *Simon* was somewhat ambiguous as to whether treaty rights could be extinguished legally, Mr.

Justice Lamer in *Sioui* comes down clearly against unilateral extinguishment of treaty rights:

> It would be contrary to the general principles of law for an agreement concluded between the English and the French to extinguish a treaty concluded between the English and the Hurons. It must be remembered that a treaty is a solemn agreement between the Crown and the Indians, an agreement the nature of which is sacred: *Simon* at p. 410, and *White and Bob* at p. 649. The very definition of a treaty thus makes it impossible to avoid the conclusion that a treaty cannot be extinguished without the consent of the Indians concerned. Since the Hurons had the capacity to enter into a treaty with the British, therefore, they must be the only ones who could give the necessary consent to its extinguishment.

This is very strong language. The Court did not even refer to the constitutional protection of treaty rights under section 35 of the *Constitution Act, 1982*. It refers to the inherent nature of treaties. A treaty is made nation-to-nation and it cannot be suggested that one party to the treaty can extinguish the rights of the other party unilaterally. We have come a long way from *Syliboy* and Mr. Justice Patterson's statements made in 1929.

Conclusion

My thesis has been that, notwithstanding all the frustrations for litigants as they proceed through the courts, if one stands back and considers the developments over the last twenty to thirty years, there are promising signs that the courts are encouraging an equitable, sensible, fair and just relationship between First Nations and non-Aboriginal Peoples. I believe that they should be encouraged in this. I think that it is important for lawyers working in this area to contribute to the development of this approach.

I leave you with one last idea in regards to developments in litigation. I would hope and expect that the next development in this area would be increasing reference to and use of international law, norms and principles. These are being pleaded before the courts. However, the courts have been somewhat reluctant to incorporate expressly these norms, although there are indications, as in the judgment of Chief Justice Dickson in *Simon*, that it may be useful to analogize principles of international law. This is a very interesting development which should be explored by litigators.

MARK STEVENSON

B.A., M.A., LL.B.

THE INHERENT RIGHT TO SELF-GOVERNMENT

We have all heard the term "inherent right" tossed around quite a bit, as of late. Recently, in Ontario, the inherent right to self-government was referred to by Premier Bob Rae at a conference co-sponsored by the Assembly of First Nations and the University of Toronto (October 2, 1990). The Premier stated that Ontario recognized that First Nations have inherent jurisdiction, or the inherent right to self-government, and is prepared to deal with First Nations on a government-to-government basis. The concept of inherent right is extremely important for First Nations and for governments.

Some of you may remember that the constitutional process from 1982 to 1987 focussed on whether or not the right to self-government is inherent, and already recognized in section 35 of the *Constitution Act, 1982*. Section 35 recognizes and affirms Aboriginal and treaty rights.

In addition, section 37 set up a process to define the rights referred to in section 35. The section 37 process involved a series of constitutional conferences in which Aboriginal leadership and governments put forward their positions.

It is important to understand that a number of provinces and the federal government put forth a constitutional amendment that would recognize the right to self-government. That notion of self-government was rejected by Aboriginal leadership because the proposed right was only enforceable at the end of a negotiation process. It was not really a right at all – it was a "contingent right".

What Aboriginal leaders said at that time was that they would be prepared to accept a proposal recognizing their inherent jurisdiction. What they meant by that, as I understand it, was that their right to self-government had never been ceded. This right comes through a special relationship with the land and continues to exist, regardless of whether or not it is recognized by a constitution. Recognition of the inherent right would mean a recognition that the source of the right comes from original Aboriginal occupation of the land, in organized societies. The content was to be negotiated, but the source must be recognized.

The precedents set by Chief Justice Marshall of the United States Supreme Court

Earlier today we heard references the Marshall judgments and the model of tribal sovereignty in the United States. There have been some criticisms of the American model as well as some praise. Regardless, it is important to understand the American example because it gives us an analytical and practical framework to approach the right to self-government.

The Marshall judgments, or the Marshall trilogy, are a series of decisions by Chief Justice Marshall of the Supreme Court of the United States, rendered in the early 1800s. In his decisions, Chief Justice Marshall articulated a number of key propositions or principles related to original tribal sovereignty. First, a discovering nation acquires the right to deal exclusively with the Indian People, and the Indians can only alienate their lands to the discovering nation. Second, the legislative body of the discovering nation, now the United States Congress, has something called "plenary powers" to carve away at Indian jurisdiction. Third, Indian jurisdiction can be diminished only by the discovering nation, and until such jurisdiction is diminished by the discovering nation, Indian Nations retain full sovereignty. According to the Marshall judgments, therefore, Indians have full and inherent sovereignty until that sovereignty is minimized by the exercise of the plenary powers of Congress.

There are three important cases which articulate the above theory of tribal sovereignty. The first was *Johnson* and *MacIntosh* (1823). In this case, Johnson purchased land directly from an Indian tribe, and the same lands were subsequently surrendered through treaty. MacIntosh then purchased them from the government of the day. The court had to determine who had valid title. They found that since the Indians' sovereignty was diminished, they could only deal with or alienate their lands to the discovering nation. They no longer had the right to sell their land to private individuals. They only had the right to sell their land to the United States, and MacIntosh therefore had valid title. In other words, Johnson lost.

The second case I would like to refer to is called *Cherokee Nation v. the State of Georgia* (1831). In this matter, the State of Georgia tried to enact a series of laws that would diminish the sovereignty of the Cherokee Nation. The Cherokee Nation then sued Georgia under a specific clause in the American Constitution only available to sovereign nations and states. The Supreme Court of the United States said, essentially, that they understood the position of the Cherokee but the specific provisions were not available to the Cherokee because they, in the courts view, were not a sovereign nation, but were a "domestic dependant nation".

The third case I would like to refer to is *Worcester* v. *Georgia* (1832). The State of Georgia enacted a law providing that nobody could go into Indian country unless they had permission from the State. Samuel Worcester, a missionary, was accused of violating the laws of the State because he entered Indian country to do his missionary work. He was sent to four years of hard labour for having gone into Indian country without permission. He challenged the laws of the State. Marshall found that a state has no jurisdiction over Indian territory and that only the discovering nation had jurisdiction.

As a result of the Marshall decisions, a theory of tribal sovereignty emerged in the United States which saw tribes exercising original jurisdiction, based upon their inherent right to self-government. States had no ability to interfere with tribal matters, and only the plenary powers of congress could diminish the exercise of tribal jurisdiction.

The theory of tribal sovereignty as articulated by Chief Justice Marshall was first tested in *Ex Parte Crow Dog* (1868). In this matter, an Indian killed another Indian, in Indian country. The accused was found guilty under Indian law, and dealt with accordingly. However, the matter was also pursued in the non-Indian courts. The matter went to the Supreme Court of the United States. In the Supreme Court, it was found that the United States had not exercised its plenary powers over criminal matters, the individual was dealt with under traditional Indian law, and therefore the general provisions of American criminal law could not be applied.

This decision was followed by a movement in the United States which led to the diminishment of the power and jurisdiction of tribal nations. The United States enacted something called the *Major Crimes Act* which listed those crimes or matters over which Indian tribal courts of tribal governments would not have jurisdiction. Later, *Public Law 280* was enacted, and this law gave a number of states jurisdiction over certain civil matters.

So, that is a rather brief and somewhat simplistic overview of the theory of tribal sovereignty and how it works in the United States. Of this, it is important to remember that Indian Nations in the United States are recognized as having original sovereignty. Sovereignty can be diminished by the exercise of the plenary powers of congress, and until such powers are exercised by congress, the inherent right to self-government, or tribal sovereignty, continues to thrive undiminished. While the courts and congress have diminished tribal powers, the principles remain unblemished.

The development of Canadian caselaw

Now, what is the situation in Canada? Peter Hutchins has stated that there remains a lot of scope, within Canadian law, for the exercise of self-governing powers, and I agree. I think there is a lot of scope for doing things within the existing legal framework in Canada because the courts have become fairly sympathetic to Indian litigants.

On the issue of sovereignty, many lawyers and jurists might be inclined to say that Indians are not sovereign. The fact is, it has never been dealt with by the courts – there is just no law. Canadian courts have been preoccupied with the notion of Indian title. In some instances, they have borrowed language from the Marshall judgments in developing a Canadian theory of Aboriginal or Indian title, but they have not discussed sovereignty.

Yes, there are a couple of cases from the early 60s which talk about whether or not an Indian band is a sovereign nation. Well, every school kid knows that an Indian band is an administrative body under the *Indian Act*, so it is not a great deal for a court to say, "No, an Indian band is not a sovereign nation."

Therefore, Indian Bands are not expressions of tribal sovereignty. However, there are many district Indian Nations in Canada with their own laws, languages, customs and traditions, and these nations exist independently of the *Indian Act*. In British Columbia, I think of the Nisga'a, the Gitksan, and the Wet'suwet'en Peoples. These are not Indian bands. These peoples are nations.

Nonetheless, the courts have never really looked at the issue of Indian sovereignty and whether an Indian Nation itself has sovereign powers. They have danced with the issue in *Calder* (1973). I believe it was Justice Hall who said that when Europeans arrived, Aboriginal communities were here governing themselves according to their own laws and their own traditions. *Calder* established the notion in Canada that the source of Aboriginal rights comes from the original occupation of lands, and that when the Europeans arrived, Aboriginal Peoples were here governing themselves according to their own laws and traditions.

Recent court decisions on the issue of sovereignty

Until very recently, there was very little upon the subject of sovereignty outside of *Calder*. However, there are two very important cases that have recently touched on the notion of sovereignty. The first was the *Sioui* decision which talks about the legal capacity of Indian Nations in 1860 to enter into treaties. The Supreme Court of Canada discussed whether First Nations were independent nations. The Court said, and I quote:

> The mother countries did everything in their power to secure the alliance of each Indian Nation, and to encourage nations allied with the enemy to change sides. When these efforts met with success, their understanding were incorporated into treaties of alliance or neutrality.

This statement clearly indicates that the Indian Nations were regarded by European nations, at least during this period, as independent nations.

We also have the recent decision of *Sparrow*. *Sparrow* only talks about Aboriginal rights to fish for food. The content of the rights that *Sparrow* talks about may not be viewed by some as significant. However, *Sparrow* provides a Canadian analytical framework to judge the content of an Aboriginal right and whether it continues to exist. In *Sparrow*, the court states that section 35 of the *Constitution Act, 1982* protects those rights existing when Aboriginal Peoples first made contact with Europeans as independent nations. Once a right is established, and there has been an infringement, the onus shifts to the government to justify the infringement, always keeping in mind the fiduciary obligation on governments to protect section 35 rights.

Much of the debate around the application of the *Sparrow* test is over the concept of extinguishment. How do you, or rather, how does a court determine if a right has been extinguished? *Sparrow* tells us that the statute proposing to extinguish must do so in clear and plain language. After all, extinguishment of a right or a group of rights, without consent or compensation, is not something that the courts treat lightly.

However, with respect to clear and plain language, all we really have is the *Indian Act* setting up a regime which governs basically every aspect of Indian life. However, it does not extinguish rights. *Sparrow* also tells us that the regulation of a right presupposes the existence of that right, so that by regulating the right to self-government, the *Indian Act* actually presupposes the existence of that right. So, with *Sparrow*, we have at least the beginning of a "made in Canada" analytical framework to determine whether or not Indian Nations can continue to exercise full sovereignty. Of course, we really do not know where the courts are going to go in the future, but I think there is an opening to sovereignty now. In British Columbia, the *Delgamuukw* case is making its way through the system, and will likely address, head on, a number of these issues.

In Ontario, we have accepted the *Sparrow* framework and now need further direction. To tell you the truth, we are not certain; we know that we are supposed to negotiate the inherent right to self-government with First Nations, but there are a number of ways to go about this. We could re-institute the national Aboriginal constitutional process – we all know how successful that would be. We are currently looking at section 43 of the *Constitution* which allows for bilateral constitutional amendments between the federal and provincial governments. We are also contemplating a new trilateral treaty process whereby Canada and Ontario would give up jurisdiction and enter into treaties based on Indian sovereignty. This process would allow original Indian sovereignty to flourish once again, after federal and provincial jurisdiction is withdrawn. This process would have to rely upon federal participation, in addition to the participation of Ontario and the First Nations, creating a trilateral treaty process. I suppose that if Canada did not wish to participate, the Province could argue that, under the Royal Prerogative, the Province can indeed enter into treaties within its own areas of jurisdiction. All of these matters are proceeding on an exploratory basis, but we are looking for creative solutions to some of the problems that have been created by the imposition of federal and provincial laws over Indian jurisdiction.

I would like to conclude by saying that the recognition or entrenchment of the inherent sovereignty of First Nations is inevitable in any new constitutional relationship, with or without Quebec. It is inevitable, not because of people like myself or other lawyers, but because of the type of Indian political leadership today – leaders such as Matthew Coon-Come, Lawrence and also

Oren Lyons, who tell us that Indian leadership thinks beyond the next election when making decisions. The Elders, as well as new leaders, tell us that Indian leadership must think to the seventh generation. For that reason, they will be successful.

QUESTION PERIOD: PANEL TWO

Question:

This question is directed to Mr. Lyons. I want to quote to you a statement you made earlier today. You referred to spirituality as being the highest form of sovereignty and I agree with you.

I face imprisonment because of my actions this past summer. Many of the Haudenosaunee have condemned my actions. They have called me criminal. I have met Six Nations People like Harvey Longboat who told me that my actions were illegal. The procedures of protocol were not followed. In the Syracuse press, a fellow brother by the name of Leon Shenandoah, Tatoharho from Onondaga Nation criminalized me and now I have to go before the courts with no attorney.

As a child, I was told that I had the responsibility to carry the burden of peace. In my understanding, in order to have that peace, you have to have justice. In order to have true justice, you have to have truth and honesty. You have to have the freedom to determine what you want to be. If that is not there, then it is our responsibility as young men, as men here on this earth, to liberate those forces.

My question, Mr. Lyons: was I a criminal in my actions this summer, for trying to protect the seventh generation. To protect human existence, to protect our Mother Earth, to protect our brothers, the trees. Was I a criminal?

Answer: OREN LYONS

When you said Leon Shenandoah, was he talking about you in person? Did he use your name?

Question:

I am referring to the people that were confined within that medical centre in Kanesatake.

Answer: OREN LYONS

I can answer a little bit of that broad question. I was part of a negotiating team called in. What we discovered was that, of course, there were many individuals defending precisely what you said. However, there were some involved that were not. They had other agendas, and so, the original issue of Oka was lost.

So, in answer to your question, we recognize that there were people there acting in truth and right. As a matter of fact, we said to Canada that not dealing with land claims is what brought this about. That was our initial response and still is. Canada does not deal with its problems and especially with land claims. However, there were also people who were thinking not of Oka but of commerce. That created a further problem. So, it is a mixture.

Question:

Was I a criminal, Mr. Lyons?

Answer: OREN LYONS

I do not think so.

Question:

Thank you.

Comment:

I would like to make a comment on sovereignty. In 1975, the Commonwealth was attempting to put into operation a new economic, social, moral and political world order. The incoming Secretary General of the Commonwealth, the former Justice Minister of Guyana stated this:

> A world order determined by concepts of sovereignty and founded on adversarial systems is irrelevant and inimical to contemporary human needs and must be dismantled ... consultation, cooperation, conciliation, conservation and communication around the world is the only viable strategy for human survival.

In this planetary bargain, there are no losers. If there are no losers, then everybody wins. Everybody can learn, as the speakers have said, to live together, to work together, to pray together, to play together in perpetual peace, prosperity and progress with justice, joy and jobs for all. Is that a good statement of sovereignty? If it is, then it eliminates the paradigm of an adversarial system.

Question: Mr. CURADE
from Queens Law School

What would the strategic legal ramifications be for an accused from Kanesatake who fails to fully raise and defend the *Two Row Wampum* Treaty and specifically their rights arising from it?

Answer: PETER HUTCHINS

I think it would be a mistake not to raise any possible defence and I think that a defence based on the *Two Row Wampum* Treaty can be legitimately raised. It is important for the defendants to raise all defences that they feel are available to them. That is their right. Not to do so might be prejudicial in the future.

Answer: MARK STEVENSON

I would agree with that statement. I think it is important to understand that it is probably easier to raise those issues in a criminal proceeding than in a civil one because of differing tests. Nonetheless, each strategy depends on the circumstances and the particular facts, although in general, I think these types of arguments should be raised.

Question: Mr. CURADE

I meant the ramifications in regards to Native sovereignty in the long-term rather than for an accused individual.

Answer: PETER HUTCHINS

That is a different question. I think that it is dangerous to assume that Aboriginal sovereignty depends upon one individual's actions before courts or in negotiations. I have trouble seeing how Aboriginal sovereignty, whether Mohawk, Cree, or otherwise, should be prejudiced by the actions of individuals developing a personal defence in their individual case. The individual is distinct from the community, therefore individual actions should not prejudice the position of the community and the nation.

Question: TRISH FRAGNITO

My question is directed to Matthew Coon-Come. I have seen you on television making your cause known to the public. I think it is great that you are letting us know in advance about growing problems. The problems in Oka were not known by the public in advance of the crisis. No one knew what was going on, even though there have always been problems and there has always been the issue of land claims. Now the problems have come violently to the forefront. Although you are informing the Canadian public in advance, there seems to be continued frustration with the government and their policy of avoidance. Is there going to be another crisis such as the one in Kanesatake and at James Bay?

Answer: MATTHEW COON-COME

Oka was not planned. Oka was part of a response to strangers coming on to the land with no respect for the rights of the people there. Oka was a response to the abuse of a process. Mohawks have negotiated in good faith for over one hundred years and then somebody from the community of Oka passed an injunction right in the middle of that process. There was an emphasis on law and order with no concern for the principles of justice, fairness, and equity. Everybody assumed that just because it was law that it was fair.

We cannot avoid major confrontations. We certainly can learn from the Oka crisis. Certainly the government should know by now that Oka has elevated and heightened the awareness of issues to be addressed by the federal and provincial governments. This awareness is one of the strategies of Aboriginal Peoples in Canada. We would like to participate in some form of a political process. We would like to use jurisprudence and the judicial process like any other Canadian, like any other Quebecer.

One of the reasons I carry out a public awareness campaign is to simply raise awareness of what is at stake. We cannot rely on the information that is given by Hydro- Québec. They are in conflict of interest regarding James Bay II. We cannot rely on them to evaluate, to act as the assessors, as well as the trial and jury. We need an independent body to really analyze, to raise the debate here in Quebec about energy needs. What are the Native Peoples really talking about?

People do not realize that a lot can be done if we really come to terms on Aboriginal issues, whether in relation to health, education, or land. It helps surrounding communities, Native and non-Native, to settle once and for all the question of ownership and jurisdiction over land so we can get on with developing sound relationships with the people around us.

Why talk about sovereignty when it is the Indian who has the worst education, the highest rate of suicide, the highest rate of unemployment and the worst living conditions. At the grass root level, who cares about the concept of sovereignty? We care about the right to education, the right to health, the right to manage and be master of our own destiny. If these issues are not dealt with, it is very difficult to get any meaning out of "sovereignty". In Cree, we do not even have a word for sovereignty. Those are your words. Maybe my lawyer-friend here developed them. I do not know. We, the Cree, also have no words for self-determination, self-government, or lawyers.

We do have one word. That word, when it is translated, is "care". Care for the land, care for the people, care for morals and values which this society does not have.

Question: LORAN THOMPSON

In your response, Mr. Lyons, you said that the issues at Oka were obscured by other issues on the agenda. In particular, you suggested that commercial issues were on the agenda. Should it not be on the agenda that members of the Confederacy of Haudenosaunee have the right to conduct their commercial affairs, as well as other affairs, according to their own law? Should not it be on the agenda that within the framework of agreements that have been reached with outside parties, such as the British Crown, these members have the legal capacity to pursue commercial enterprises under their own law?

Answer: OREN LYONS

Yes, it is probably fundamental if we were talking about economics. In any discussion of economics. One of the principles that goes with nationhood is that law on Indian territory is Indian law. However, in Iroquois law, the first law of our nation is that whatever action might affect the welfare of the nation must have the agreement of the people before taken. That is the number one law. It is up to the people to decide what should occur.

Answer: LORAN THOMPSON

Okay, if you believe that it is up to the people, I would like to ask you how you feel about the agreement that was reached with Ontario/Quebec and New York State authorities for outside policing at Akwasasne?

Answer: OREN LYONS

Well, that was an agreement that did not involve us. We did not have anything to say about that. I do not believe that Indians should be policed by any outside authority. Nevertheless, that is what happened.

Question: LORAN THOMPSON

Do you believe that members of the Haudenosaunee have the right to defend their land from outside interference, and outside authorities?

Answer: OREN LYONS

Well yes, definitely.

Question: LORAN THOMPSON

In 1984, we were sitting in a meeting at Onondaga where the different nations were sitting except for the Tuscarora. We decided in that council that we would not use the term "land claims" because we were not claiming the land. We said we were going to use the term "land rights". I would just like to correct you on that.

You also said that you are not in favour of accepting the idea that the white man has a better way. Yet, our teaching says: one day you will see many footprints go into a church and very few come back out; and one day you will see many footprints go into a school and very few come back. If you share this teaching, then why do you compromise your position and work in a white school system teaching our children when our teaching says do not participate.

Answer: OREN LYONS

It does not say that and now I will correct you. What it says is that you have to learn the white man's ways to get along. That is what it says.

Question: LORAN THOMPSON

It says that, but it does not say to participate in his ways, because if you do, very few people come back. There are two ways of looking at the situation. However, I just cannot understand why you prefer to teach in a system that is oppressing our people and teaching them something other than what we really are, rather than finding a way to create an education system of our own children right up to college students.

Answer: OREN LYONS

When you talked about the twelve, the chiefs said: we can send twelve people into your system and we will be lucky to get one back. That is what was said.

Question: LORAN THOMPSON

And it is true. I agree they are lucky to get one back. I agree.

Answer: OREN LYONS

What I do in this system is talk to Indians whenever they come in. I talk to them about a lot of things. In fact, our system at the University of Buffalo is that you have to go back into your community and do a project that is going to help the community itself in order to do our masters program. That drives the youth back into the community. Further, I teach American history to white people. They need to know the same history.

Question: RICHARD JANDA
Professor, Faculty of Law, McGill University

My question is for Mark Stevenson. A lot of people in Canada were quite relieved to see that Premier Rae had taken leadership on the issue of Aboriginal rights when we have had a vacuum of leadership elsewhere. In light of the preliminary experience of Ontario, I would like to ask two questions: first, who is to exercise inherent sovereignty in the eyes of the Government of Ontario, and second, what role is there for the federal government in the process launched by Ontario?

Answer: MARK STEVENSON

On the first question, I think the statements of the Premier were fairly clear. He said that we now recognize the inherent right of First Nations, so you will have to assume that he is talking about First Nations exercising inherent jurisdiction.

On the second question, I went through about four or five different mechanisms which could be used to constitutionalize this notion of inherent right. It could be done through a national constitutional process but I have very serious doubts about that type of process. I think there may be potential in the use of section 43, however this would again require federal participation. We are also looking at the capacity of a province, through the exercise of the Crown prerogative, to enter into treaties with First Nations within the areas of provincial jurisdiction. Further, we are looking at trilateral treaties. So, there are a number of different ways.

Question: HARRIETTE BOUTSOME

I would like to speak to Matthew Coon-Come. I have seen him on television and with his father fighting for James Bay. Since Oka happened, I have gone home and decided the children need some education. I have started teaching the little ones. Matthew Coon-Come inspires a lot of people. Our people have had many orators like Matthew, and we are going to have many Native People across Canada speaking like Matthew did today. I hope I am going to still be alive to see my children speak that way.

I will give you an answer to "Why shouldn't there be any lawyers speaking for the Native People?" We have the Confederacy, we have laws, and that Confederacy tells us how we should live, how we should conduct ourselves everywhere. No matter who is around. We already have that Constitution – all we need to do is to get together.

Matthew. I want your card. I am getting your address. I have some children that need to see exactly what is going on in this country. The beautiful things that are going on in this country. I am tired of hearing who did what yesterday. I want to hear who is doing something for the children and seven generations. That is why I am wearing these clothes. I want everybody to know – everybody here is beautiful in their own way. All they have to remember is that we all have to live together, but leave us in peace. We bring up our children to be good. We do not bring them up to fight each other. Please, we are mothers, we do not want our children to die. We do not want them to kill each other. We do not want them to kill anybody. We do not teach that way.

Question:

I too would like to thank Mr. Coon-Come for carrying the ball for our people. I have a question for Mr. Lyons. This summer a lot of things happened and the Confederacy did move in certain directions. Why did the Confederacy choose not to go to the Mohawks first to see what the problem was rather than to Bourassa? And secondly, what process was used to send delegates to Bourassa's office?

Answer: OREN LYONS

I think the Confederacy wanted to hear what Bourassa had to say. A meeting held at Onondaga on the 25th of August. They decided that four people would be sent, although that number was not limited. "Who is willing to go there?" That is how it was decided. We were willing to be assigned and so we went.

Question:

How could a Grand Council pass a decision to do such a thing when the Mohawk and Cree chiefs were not sitting there in full numbers?

Answer: OREN LYONS

The Mohawks were there as our Constitution says they must be. And you know that there are not a lot of [word unclear] chiefs.

Question:

Yes, and that is why I am asking how that process could take place when those chiefs were not sitting there.

Answer: OREN LYONS

The same way it is been happening over the past thirty to forty years.

Question:

So the Confederacy was there legally?

Answer: OREN LYONS

Of course they were.

Question:

I have heard reference from Mr. Hutchins of a court case in 1929 called *Syliboy*. I am the grandson of Gabriel Syliboy. I would like to ask Mr. Hutchins why it took sixty years for that decision to be made known to the Micmac People?

Answer: PETER HUTCHINS

I am afraid that I do not have a definitive answer except perhaps to refer back to what Chief Justice Dickson said about both the attitudes of Mr. Justice Patterson. I think the same comments can be applied to the justice system generally. The Chief Justice of the Supreme Court of Canada, was condemning not only one judge and what one judge said in one judgment. I think he was condemning a system of jurisprudence, a thought-pattern among judges, lawyers and jurists of the day. He was saying, "This is no longer appropriate." Not only is the language of Patterson no longer appropriate, but the situation that you have just described is no longer appropriate or indeed tolerable.

All I can say is, yes, there were considerable problems in the past and part of my intention today was to at least suggest that there has been an improvement. There is an effort in the judiciary and part of the legal community to make radically changes. I think the system is beginning to change.

PANEL THREE

WAYS FORWARD: THE SEARCH FOR JUST SOLUTIONS

Patricia Monture

Professor, Common Law, University of Ottawa. Please note that this text is a shorter version than the original presentation.

NOTES ON SOVEREIGNTY

The fighting and dissension that my nation lives with breaks my heart. I have been thinking about how to talk about it and I would like to begin with a teaching that was given to me several years ago while I was involved in a political organization in Ontario. It was an Indian organization and we were thrashing each other a lot and I was very upset by what was happening. I spoke to a teacher about this, and he said, "What you have to understand is that when you open your mouth to speak, you can talk about somebody else if you want to. But you really only have the right to talk about one person. Yourself."

When I open my mouth to speak, I am telling you who I am. I cannot really tell you anything about anyone else. I can only speak to you about who I am, the way I walk. So, when I was preparing to speak to you, I decided to speak to you from my heart, in the tradition of my people. I decided to speak to you as a Mohawk woman and a mother, not as a law professor.

I have spent a large part of my life being angry, which is why the anger in my nation hurts me so much. I was sexually abused as a child and beaten by a husband. It took me more than twenty years to understand that I did not have to live in anger and violence, and to learn how to feel.

I am frightened by the violence that we saw this summer at Kanesatake. In twenty years time, I do not want to turn on the television set and see one of my two boys standing there holding a gun. That is not what I want for their future.

I heard Ellen Gabrielle speak in Toronto and she said, "Think about our little ones in Kanesatake: if you think this generation is a problem now, well, the young ones growing up now have no respect for authority, either Mohawk or Canadian." So, where do we go from here? I think the answer is sovereignty.

Sovereignty means taking responsibility and living in a self-disciplined way. It means speaking the truth, and that truth comes from speaking what is inside. I know that the truth is not in books. The Creator put each and everyone of us down here complete, and the truth is inside of us, in our hearts. Your instincts tell you what is fair and just, not law books.

When I speak about what is inside of me, although you do not have to agree with me, you must respect me for speaking what I understand to be the truth. Within the Mohawk nation, we need to remember how to respect each other, and talk in a good way to each other, or we cannot do anything. That respect is the first step to self-discipline. It is the seed out of which sovereignty grows.

I do not deny that territory, land claims and a relationship to the land is important to sovereignty, but the sum of the problem is much more than territory. Until you respect the truth of others, and understand your relationship with yourself through self-discipline, you cannot understand what it means to be sovereign as nations.

Without self-disciplined individuals, families are broken and women are left alone to raise the children. Without those families, we cannot have clans. Without clans, we cannot have nations. Without nations, we are not sovereign.

However, it is clear that the problem is not just within our nations. Coming here on the plane from Halifax, I picked up *The Chronical Herald*, and read the headline, "The Prime Minister Makes an Impassioned Plea For National Unity". I read through the long, front-page article, and the Prime Minister did not say one word about Aboriginal Peoples. Not a word.

The Canadian government does not understand what we mean by sovereignty, because they do not understand what it means to be responsible. Canadians are beginning to realize that they must make sure their government shows respect to Aboriginal Peoples, but Oka is not over. You have seen the pain in this room today. It is not over.

We know that the lawyers are not going to help us out there in the bush when we have no food, no water, no shelter. In the natural world there is no mercy. However, we have to understand that law no longer has a heart in it. Any plea for mercy before Canadian courts will be met by the "objective" Canadian law, which does not allow you to feel. That is the law of Canada. The law has taken the heart out of the relations between Aboriginal Peoples and Canada.

In searching for just solutions, I think we have to continue as citizens of the Mohawk Nation to walk in the way that was given us: to walk in respect, to speak the truth, to speak what is in our hearts, to live by natural law. By doing that, the other nations will learn from us.

My prayer for my people and for my sons is that we start living in that good way taught by our Elders, with respect for all creation around us, and with regard for all our relations.

JULIO C. TRESIERRA

Julio Tresierra is an Associate Professor of Sociology at Concordia University and has been Coordinator of their Latin American Program Development since 1990. He has acted as advisor to a number of Indigenous communities and organizations at national, regional and international levels; in particular to the Presidency of the World Council of Indigenous Peoples (1987-1991). He has also acted as consultant for international organizations such as the UNDP, UNICEF, and the OAS. His areas of expertise include economic development, globalization (NAFTA), Indigenous Peoples, and higher education.

SYSTEMIC APPROACHES TO A CHANGING WORLD

Efforts to generate long-lasting solutions to the conflict between Indigenous Peoples and the governments of nation-states have met with failure. One of the reasons for this failure is that we have been preoccupied with discussing issues in a fragmented manner rather than analyzing comprehensive structures that encompass far more than a particular event. Such an approach isolates conflicts in Nicaragua, for example, from events in Oka, placing each in a historical vacuum where conflicts remain unconnected and disjointed.

Dominant, eurocentric paradigms have promoted, overtly and covertly, a subjective, partial view of the Indigenous question. It is necessary to recognize that issues involving Indigenous Peoples are inherent in the political/economic system of which they are a part. Solutions have been sought from a system that is in itself a problem, leading to perceptions of victory where there is defeat. Thus, while theoretical discussions on Indigenous self-determination and sovereignty multiply, the dominant system exterminates Native Peoples and their cultures. At the same time, this reality is camouflaged under ideological and economic manipulations.

At each juncture of history, dominant systems take up new ideological themes, one of which is today's concern with the environment. There are radical ecologists, biologists, environmentalists, and Marxists all discussing the environment. Their views tend to ignore the fact that the market-oriented economy has an immense capacity to turn any disaster into a profit-making opportunity. Thus, the system generates ways of making profit while appearing ecologically responsible. Through so-called productive activities, they will continue to pollute the rivers, the air, and the oceans, as long as a magic filter can be installed in everyone's home for a profit.

These opportunists invent a language for the new fashion; they talk about "sustainable development" and "environmental management". Their words are reminiscent of the terms "just war" used when the United States military invaded Iraq. Each was an ideological attempt to cover up the immorality of killing and destruction with a veil of justice.

Political powers coordinate worldwide fora, at a cost of millions of dollars, such as the upcoming United Nations Environmental Summit in Rio, which will be hosted by the Brazilian Government. Indigenous representatives and/or issues have been excluded from the agenda. This conference was originally based on the well-known Bruntland report, *Our Common Future*. However, the United States Government promptly gathered resources, as only the United States Government can do, and hired prominent consultants to compose an alternative document. *Our Common Future* was relegated to a secondary position on the conference agenda.

As it is known, the Indigenous world view is highly critical of private property, however, the prevalent agenda for discussing ecology and development assumes private property as a given. This dominant view pays attention to movements like "Save the Trees" or "Save the Dolphin". However, even though some of the most important ecological areas in the world are populated by Indigenous Peoples, and their very existence is in serious danger, any movement to "Save the Indian" is ignored. Such a movement does not fit into the priorities of the dominant world system.

Subjective reactions, such as anger, triumph, or defeatism, have only limited effectiveness. A rational comprehension of the system as a whole, and how it operates, is mandatory. Current structural changes must be perceived and analyzed in the context of the movement for globalization. Economic and political actions are becoming truly global, and within this context, the nation-state is withering away as geopolitical borders are being redefined. At the same time, new sources of political identity are being created.

The true nature of the problem confronting Indigenous Peoples is rooted in an economic system where growth has no boundaries, and profit is never enough to satisfy its inherent greed. Awareness of this problem and personal sacrifices are not enough to bring about the systemic changes needed to promote real solutions to the problem. Eliminating plastics and nuclear weapons is not going to make a significant difference as long as we do not change the socioeconomic nature of contemporary international relations, at the root of which lies the need for such commodities. In so far as the knowledge to produce these commodities exists, and the need for them persists, all "solutions" are insufficient and of temporary value. We need to generate an answer that is as structural and comprehensive as the system which we are attempting to change.

Opportunities for change in the new world system

Contemporary Indigenous Peoples face a unique opportunity as the traditional nation-state paradigm weakens. As the system changes, new spaces for action are created. Native Peoples, their leaders, and their organizations must rationally define where they fit in this "reorganized" world, where they fit in the context of emerging political configurations, and what real opportunities they have to develop in their own terms.

The emerging world system is organized around regional blocks, integrating formerly diverse political entities. Our structural views must also be comprehensive, integrating the realities of people from Oka, Nicaragua, Bolivia, Mexico, and other dominated peoples. Even when we look at so-called ecological movements, we must uncover their inherent structural dimensions. Such an approach is necessary to link efforts of Indigenous Peoples around the world. Otherwise, their isolated efforts cannot succeed. We have already witnessed how attempts of Indigenous Peoples in Mexico, Panama, Guatamala, and Nicaragua, among others, to establish control over their natural resources have been crushed.

A revolution in thought

Indigenous Peoples should draw on their world view of nature, which is based on unity. They have always defined themselves as guardians rather than owners of nature. This highly rational world view is based upon the harmonious interaction of all forms of life that is neither romantic or utopic. This type of rationality is needed to save our planet.

We need a revolution in thought that will open the minds of those who have never perceived this relationship between humankind and nature; that will lead us to change the current legal system; that will not glorify the private property of natural resources, but abolish it; that will allow us to see the rights of the collectivity that, in turn, confirms the right of the individual.

The Indian world view, their cosmic vision, contains the elements necessary to generate this revolutionary movement. It is up to us, to all of us, to eliminate the barriers that have prevented this movement from becoming a reality.

DIOM ROMEO SAGANASH

Vice-Chairman of the Cree Regional Authority and Executive Chief of the Grand Council of the Crees of Quebec.

JAMES BAY II: A CALL TO ACTION

The pattern of history has been clear to Indians: whatever the white man wants, the white man gets. Whatever the government wants, the government gets. This is our experience with the Canadian government. The same pattern has been repeated over and over again since foreign government was imposed upon us. The government wants something that we have. There is conflict over the violation of our rights, whether it be over land, over the right to hunt, or even just to be left in peace. The government checks its laws, and it always turns out that the Indigenous Peoples are wrong and the government is right. The government uses its power to force the Indian to concede. So, claims are followed by conflicts, which are followed by concessions. It is always the Indian that makes the concession. On and on it goes. That is our unfortunate history.

The historical reason for this relationship is that the law we live under is not our law. *A priori*, the way law is conceptualized condemns us to lose. For the law presumes that this land is not ours. It holds that the theft of our lands was no theft at all, but was in fact a valid legal claim. So, for Indigenous Peoples, the law is racist and fundamentally flawed since it legitimizes the theft of our lands and denies our fundamental rights. Canada has stated that there is no legal basis for Indian claims to land. I must agree. There is no legal basis *under Canadian law*. Canadian law says that our land was never ours, so how can there be a legal claim?

Canada does admit that it is morally obligated to settle Native land claims. So, I ask: how does this obligation arise? Why should there be a moral obligation but no legal obligation? Canada knows that this entire country was stolen from Indigenous Peoples, and everyone knows that it is reprehensible morally. Yet, the law does not allow us to submit a claim for theft as it should.

Although the law does not recognize our claim of theft, it twists and turns and struggles to avoid the obvious and the inevitable conclusion it can never admit. So, Canada, the thief that stole our land, can never reconcile its laws with the fundamental ethical and moral principles of justice. Something, it is felt, must be done to resolve this dilemma. So arises the moral obligation to settle Indigenous land claims: a moral obligation having its basis in principles of natural justice that stand in direct conflict with the law of Canada.

International principles of natural justice

However, when Canada states that there is no legal basis for our claims, it is dead wrong. In international law, the principals of natural justice give rise to an entire edifice containing international instruments which affirm our basic rights and fundamental freedoms, and recognize our rights to our lands and resources, and our right to determine how we will live and govern ourselves.

The Canadian government would prefer to characterize its obligations to the Indigenous Peoples as moral rather than legal. They know, however, that these obligations are both moral and legal; hence, the realization that the land claims must be settled before the international community begins to take undue notice of what the Canadian government prefers to consider as a purely domestic matter.

We keep coming back to that nasty question: how did Canada really begin? Quebecers are forcing Canada to take a look. Can you found a nation on a lie? Meech Lake spoke of two founding nations, the English and the French. In terms of laws, maybe that was correct; but, as I have shown, that law is flawed. Who the hell gave the English and the French dominion over my people? In Canadian law, that question is taboo. That is why Elijah Harper acted as he did; that is why Oka is still unresolved.

Canada likes to fall back on the principle that this is a country that respects the rule of law. I began with the explanation that the rule of law has always forced Indigenous Peoples to concede their lands and rights. I, too, would praise the rule of law if it meant that every conflict would be resolved in my favour, for that is its effect whenever there is a conflict between Indians and Canadian governments.

It appears to me that the government can do nearly everything that it wishes and claim that it respects the rule of law. Dam the Old Man River, flood the Cree in Manitoba, relocate an Inuit village, deforest the Gitskan hunting grounds, or build James Bay I; there is always some way to do it under the rule of law. Every time, no matter what, the Indians lose.

When I was a kid, a big concession was made: the signing of the *James Bay and Northern Quebec Agreement*. The James Bay project was being built. The Crees objected and went to court, but the construction went on. After nine months, the Crees won the historic Malouf judgment, but the rule of law only favoured my people for four days. A "balance of convenience" judgment: ten thousand Crees and Inuits versus six million Quebecers. The Appeal Court judges stated that they did not believe that hunting and fishing were as important as the Cree claimed. The Hydro-Québec lawyers had gained an admission from one Cree that he occasionally ate pizza. A fatal admission – a little pizza.

The project was allowed to continue: no environmental impact assessment, no Cree permission, no concern for our lives and traditions. The work continued. So, the Crees tried to negotiate, although I do not know if it really should have been characterized as negotiation. However, it does reflect the meaning of negotiation with Indians since Confederation. The Crees felt that the dam was going to happen anyway, so they tried to make the best of it. Under these circumstances, and Matthew will be glad to hear this, maybe I too would have signed the *James Bay Northern Quebec Agreement*.

The potential for conflict

Now Mr. Bourassa has announced James Bay II and everybody wonders, "Will there be conflict?" You bet. There is conflict already. There has been no environmental impact assessment for James Bay II. Quebec already has the highest per capita consumption of electricity in the world. Every major environmental group in North America has condemned James Bay II. Yet, the Government of Quebec proceeds, oblivious to this criticism. What have we learned about the environment? Do we, in fact, treat the environment any differently than we always have? What about the Indigenous Peoples whose rights are enshrined in the *Constitution*? Has anything changed? Is Canada exercising its fiduciary responsibility, as instructed by the Supreme Court, and defended Indians from the incursions on their land? Has the Government of Canada become an advocate of Indian rights?

The region potentially affected by James Bay II is the Amazon of the North, the last refuge for many species of fish and animals. It is one of the principal feeding grounds of the Atlantic flyway for waterfowl. All of the reasons have been given: the massive mercury contamination; the destruction of freshwater seals; the destruction of a people who have lived in James Bay for thousands of years. However, it is clear that reason does not play a large part in this debate. Once again, the rule of law will provide justification for a project that is universally condemned as a travesty against the environment.

So the question remains: will the Crees make another concession? Will the project be built over Cree objections? Has Oka changed anything? I see no evidence that government thinking has changed. Government, as usual, is considering force, as shown by the recent purchase of three tanks by the Quebec police. The age-old use of violence against the Indigenous Peoples who will not make concessions will again be used.

Lessons from Oka

However, Oka has changed the way Indians think, or rather Oka represents the realization that Indians could no longer continue to concede and continue to live. Oka was a kind of ultimate provocation – the blatant application of law to justify the use of force against the Indians. Meech Lake signalled the indifference of Canada and Quebec towards Indigenous Peoples in this country. Elijah Harper stood his ground against the threats and abuse and refused to concede. He said, "No more concessions." Again, when Quebec tried stealing another piece of Indian land at gunpoint, the Mohawks of Kanesatake decided that the line had to be drawn. No more concessions could be made of Indian land.

So, the situation has changed. The Crees have stated that they oppose James Bay II, and this time our survival as a people is clearly threatened. Our objection is more than a complaint, more than a plea for reason. It is a call for action. The Crees will not permit James Bay II to be built. We do not want it. If, in spite of all reason and logic, Quebec tries to build it, we will do everything in our power to stop it. Read my lips: no more concessions.

I conclude that perhaps the rule of law will now have to accommodate Indians because they insist on justice. In the meantime, our Great North remains silent, just waiting for the contest.

QUESTION PERIOD: PANEL THREE

Comment:

I am a Mohawk woman and a mother of two. I am also a wife of a veteran of the treatment centre in Kanesatake.

When we talk about law, there are two kinds: one for Natives and another for non-Natives. For example, we have two kinds of protesters. We have people that protest at abortion clinics. They blockade the entrance, and when the police are called in, they handcuff people and drag them off to jail. Then we have the Natives. We protest that we will not give up an inch of our land to build a golf course. We blockade the entrance. The police come. Do they handcuff us? No. Do they drag us off to jail? No. They get the order to go in the area and open fire on the protesters.

Question:

I would like to thank the speakers, particularly Julio Tresierra for his call to be aware and conscious of structural relationships, and the continental changes that are occurring.

I was wondering if Mr. Tresierra or perhaps Diom Saganash would also like to touch on the continental waterways and how the current movement towards the mega-project, the hydro-electric project, the damming of waters in northern Canada might be related to the current drought occurring in the southern United States.

Answer: JULIO TRESIERRA

Most of these projects do contain the rationale of the system: the need for constant sources of energy. As we move toward globalization, for instance, through the Free Trade Agreement extending to Mexico, Central America and eventually to South America, there is the need to establish sources of energy that are compatible with the kind of economy being generated. If anything, in the next twenty years we are going to see the multiplication of mega-projects. The extent to which we are prepared to respond to these kind of initiatives is a question mark. I am not aware of any Indigenous organizations which at this moment are, within law or outside, capable of actually stopping the multiplication of these projects. This is particularly true in so-called Latin America.

Answer: DIOM ROMEO SAGANASH

Speaking of massive projects, there are many environmental and social questions raised by these massive development projects and that is the reason why we are calling for a large and an independent public inquiry. They have not been done for the James Bay I project and it seems they will not be for this one either. That is why we are calling for a large public and independent inquiry into these projects.

The Grand Canal project is still in the works. People, especially Quebecers, really have to start questioning themselves with respect to Robert Bourassa because with the Grand Canal project he wants to export fresh water from James Bay to the Americans. We know that the James Bay project is specifically for the benefit of Americans. I mean, who elected this guy, Quebecers or Americans? Yes, we are calling for serious public inquiry into these projects and I hope we can get them soon.

Question:

I have a question for Mr. Saganash. Even if you do have groups like the Coalition for James Bay asking for an in-depth public debate, and even if you have an independent environmental assessment, what if the Government decides to go ahead anyway? Personally, I do not care if the majority of people in Quebec decide for the James Bay project – I am absolutely opposed to it because if I submit to this, thousands and thousands of square miles will be

raped again. Are you thinking about what some of the consequences will be if your present tactics do not work? What next?

Answer: DIOM ROMEO SAGANASH

First of all, I think there is a distinction to be made between
the environmental impact assessment of James Bay and whether or
not the Quebec government has the right to build these projects.
Two distinct things: one, we want an environmental impact assessment of all these projects, and two, we are in court contesting the
right of the Government of Quebec and Hydro-Quebec to build
this project without our consent.

We are arguing in court that these lands belong to the Crees.
We are sovereign. We have full control and authority over these
lands, our traditional lands. That should be the case. There is also
wide public support for the Crees' position on an environmental
basis. However, no matter what, I know damned well that they
will try to build those projects anyway. In Quebec and also in the
rest of this country, we do not have a democracy. An elected dictatorship, that is what we have. So, the Crees cannot count on the
will of the majority. Nonetheless, like I said, we will not make
concessions.

Comment:

I just want to respond to Patricia, on behalf of the young men
running around with guns, and as a young man that was fortunate
enough to walk out of Oka. Maybe I can take away some of the
worry that she has.

We never used the guns that we had. It was not our intent to
use them, all we were saying was: enough is enough. People were
forced to choose. Our role as men is not just to pick up a gun, but
we must defend the life of our people. Guns were a last resort because of the stuff that happened. The people of Oka went to every
community within the Six Nations and asked for assistance. We
started asking way before July 12, 1990. The People of Kanesatake
asked everybody for assistance. Any assistance was welcome, but
we were the only ones that came. Now you have people like Oren
saying that we were wrong in the actions that we took.

What other choice did we have? Our women were being shot
at. There were kids in there. We did not go out into their communities and start shooting. We stood where we were and we de-

fended what we had. Some people say there must be another reason why we were there, because they will not give up their life for trees and land. There has to be money involved. So, our own people criminalized us.

That is where the anger comes from: our own people believing things like that. There was no money involved; I will vouch for everybody that was there. You do not give up your life for bingo, or a dollar, or even ten million dollars. That was not why we were willing to give up everything. I have little children at home too. I was speaking to them when I was there.

Question:

My question is for Julio, regarding resources and Indigenous Peoples. Canada is going to go ahead again without the consent of the people to Central America and eventually South America. Canada is entering into a process with the United States to do business in Mexico for more profit and gain. In your opinion, how is that going to affect Indigenous Peoples from Central and South America?

Answer: JULIO TRESIERRA

We have to consider first of all that Canada, economically, in the process of globalization, is in a very precarious situation. Eastern Europe has already been earmarked by the European Economic Community. Therefore the active participation of the United States or Canada is limited. Canada has never had any close links with so-called Latin America because the United States had established dominant relationships and has actually prevented Canada from entering into the area. Canada has also managed to alienate itself from South African Nations. So, that is why some of the representatives of the Canadian Government are urging Canada to move into this trade with Mexico. They are trying to somehow corner a part of the world market.

There are some Native People in North America that prefer to deal with Canada rather than the United States. They believe that by salvaging trade relationships with the Government of Canada, they are going to be better off than with the Government of the United States. Like I said, there is still this naive perception with no basis whatsoever.

Native People in South and Central America have already been oppressed; "oppressed" is such a meaningless term in the context of one of the greatest genocides witnessed in Central and South America. This is precisely why we need to establish links amongst Native Peoples of North, Central or South America. It is only through those kinds of links that we can generate common fronts. The enemies won and we know exactly the nature of the tools and techniques they are using to destroy Native Peoples. For as long as we remain ignorant, we are going to attempt isolated answers that will be incapable of stopping the formidable enemy, which is this kind of economic system.

Comment: JOE NORTON
Chief of the Kahnawake Mohawk Band Council

I would like to welcome you all to Mohawk Territory, although we might get an argument from our brothers the Algonquins, but that is an internal historical argument that we will settle one of these days.

Basically, we have heard throughout the day about the issue of sovereignty and the reality of what happened in the past. The difficulties that we have been dealing with in the past are the reality of today.

We heard, from the people I mentioned, about the various things that are happening on a global level; in South America, Canada, and North America in general. We have heard about the way our rights are being trampled on and the difficulty of standing up and taking pride in who we are. It used to be that saying you were Mohawk was like saying a dirty word. That does not prevent us from getting up, talking about who we are, pushing for who we are. Sooner or later the message will again be received by the people in this area, and sooner or later people will understand that they are going to have to live in a co-existing relationship with us.

We are going through decolonisation. Let us face it – it is going to take place in one way or another. The colonizers are not going to leave this country, so we are going to have to live side-by-side as our ancestors did, hopefully peacefully. I was not here for some of the emotional stuff that went on, but I can imagine what was said and why it was said. Throughout the summer I had the fortune, or at times the misfortune, of being involved in one way or another. Either I was a hero or I was the devil. One way or the other, depending on who I was talking to and depending on where the criticism or the congratulations were coming from. Throughout this time period, from before July 11th up to today, we had contacts with all the various groups and nations that supported us from within Quebec, outside of Quebec, from North America down into South America.

We had visitors from all over South America, including Brooklyn Riveria from Nicaragua who said, "Joe, the last time I was here I had to sneak out of my country under the threat of being shot by the army. What of you? I come here and you were such a free person, and now the army is here. Somewhat of a humorous situation. But in any event, we lend our support, we lend our support to Mohawk People, People of Kahnawake, to all the various people who supported us."

We heard from Mr. Saganash about what is going on in James Bay. I am somewhat hesitant about saying we support you one hundred percent, because somebody is going to turn around and say: they are ready to block the bridge again. However, we do support you. Make no mistake about it because your people have done whatever they could to support us throughout our situation and, basically, we send you all our regards and our support.

A couple of years back, you will recall, we did sign an agreement or arrangement between several nations from across this country that during times of crisis we will support one another. It is still there and we are going to, regardless of the situation, because your fight is our fight. And our fight is your fight. I believe that just the mere exchange between Mohawk People and Cree People will alert the federal and provincial governments that we are indeed allies, we are indeed friends and no matter what they say about us or how they attempt to drive a wedge between us, they are not going to be successful.

Hopefully, they understand that we are going to support one another during times of need and that we are not going to believe their propaganda. If it is an issue of law and order, again I think it was made very clear by everybody here what type of law and order we have. We saw examples of that. Look at last week when those people, who had literally stoned our people, I call them the white terrorists, were given minor fines and were let off scot-free. Yet, this week we found out that some people in this very room have been put on a fast track system, to get rid of them in jail. Sounds sort of like South Africa, where they can do whatever they want to black people and get away with it.

In closing, there was somebody after the first panel, I believe it was a Mr. Zimmerman, who said what you Indian People should do is put fences around yourselves to define your boundaries. Well, we tried to do that this summer and they sent the army in to take them down.

Question:

I work for the Cree Committee Health Team, and I would like to ask a question of the gentleman who asked Diom Saganash, "What will you do if this way of stopping James Bay II does not work?"

I would like to ask what will you do, what will we do, those of us here, because there is a lot at stake for us. It is not just our environment, it is our conscience. It is also our future. What is being done with our money? That money is not just funding James Bay II, but also propaganda. So, what are we going to do?

I have had the privilege of spending time in the James Bay communities because of my work, and I have seen firsthand what James Bay I has done. The devastation on many levels: social, health. It is all intertwined. I have seen the destruction of what Diom calls the traditional way of life. When people talk about losing their traditional way of life, we do not know what that means. However, I have seen it, and it is the destruction of who you are. It is as if somebody said to me I could never again be a health care worker. That is what people there have been told by losing the area for their trap lines. They cannot be who they are any more. So, what do you think it would do to you if you knew you could never do again what you have always done? How would your children feel about you? What kind of role model could you be?

It is incredible what it does to the communities. Therefore, the question for us is: what are we going to do down here? That is the important question and we do not have to ask Diom that. We have to ask ourselves: how do we organize?

Answer: DIOM ROMEO SAGANASH

Someone told me before that in every challenge there is an opportunity. The next challenge, not only for us Crees, but for Quebecers is James Bay II. There is an opportunity now for Native Peoples there to show solidarity amongst themselves. There is also an opportunity for the Quebecers to say to their government, once and for all, enough is enough. I hope – I do not want to get into a conflict here – but I dearly hope that you will do that as Quebecers.

Question:

My question is for Julio Tresierra. However, first, I think it is necessary to give a little bit of background.

There is a principle in the law that says *hear the other side*. I am not a lawyer and I do not want to be a lawyer. I am an organizer and co-founder of the Green Coalition which is an umbrella group of forty-four environmental groups. We have been successful in saving over two hundred million dollars worth of green space in the greater Montreal Urban Community region, and have launched major projects nationally and internationally. We have also had the pleasure of working for the creation of Canada's future forest alliance which represents 110 environmental groups and over one million Canadians. Recently I was invited to a session as an observer for the Canadian Environmental Network, which represents 1,800 environmental groups across Canada.

The reason I am telling you this is because as I understood from something that you said, Julio, that there were environmentalists and ecologists out with a primary objective to save trees. I do not know if I heard you correctly, but I would like to state our position. Our position is that we would like to preserve, protect and conserve the planet. The reason why we want to save the planet is because we would like to save the human race.

With respect to the upcoming Brazil conference, the Ministry of Forestry called together a number of volunteers and also paid persons to put together the National Forest Congress for Canada before the Brazil conference. Coming out of that will be what is called the National Forest Sector Strategy. At the meeting, there were no Indigenous Peoples although certain people had been invited to attend. In another steering committee, two representatives from Indigenous groups were present and will either play a role in it or decide what role they wish to play.

The reason I am bringing this up is that it seems to me there are a number of divisions between the Native and the non-Native Peoples. Those who are for James Bay II and those who are against it. I wonder if what you were saying suggests that it is beneficial for us to go on criticizing each other, Native or non-Native, and environmental groups versus Indigenous groups. Dare we take the

risk of shooting each other in the foot. It seems to me there is no
"us and them" here, there is only us and the planet.

Answer: JULIO TRESIERRA

History is retrospective prophecy. Looking at the evolution of
our planet, we cannot ignore the immense truth of the systematic
destruction of Native Peoples. I think it is commendable to speak
about the human race, but when one speaks of such an abstraction,
one tends to become short-sighted as to the inequities that prevail
in human society. By doing so, one tends to forget the victims that
have fallen as a consequence of that kind of a short sighted vision.

"Save the planet", as logical as it must seem, cannot lead to
any kind of long-lasting solution if we keep ignoring the basic element which is the human component involved in this struggle. As
long as we do not see, or fail to see, the role of Indigenous Peoples
in maintaining this ecological balance, and as long as we intend to
solve the problem by ignoring Indigenous Peoples we are not going
to actually resolve anything.

As I said, the market economy has an immense capacity to
turn tragedies into profit. The Amazon is a good example of this.
James Bay is another example. I believe that your movement, and
the thousands of people you may represent within your movement, could do a lot if you simply allocated resources so that the
Indigenous voice could be heard throughout the world. The best
lesson could be learned from them.

Question:

My name is Rhanatata. I am a Mohawk man from Mohawk
Territory. The reason why I can say this is because I was born under the Clan of the Turtles. I have a right to speak as a Mohawk
person. I have been sitting here listening to people talk about the
law, but I have been waiting to hear the one law that belongs to our
people: The Great Law of Peace. I have not heard it as of yet. You
are sitting here looking for solutions. Well, I bring you the solution
now.

Come back all caretakers of the land. Come back home to
where you belong. As Indians we have the right to retrace the
roots, the roots of peace. We have the right to retrace and seek
shelter underneath the Great Tree of Peace. I see a lot of white people here, or non-Natives, because they call us Natives. They are

looking for the solution. They are tired of their governmental system. It does not seem to want to work. The Creator gave Indians a law to follow, but he did not give it just to us. He gave it to everyone. Everyone has that right to come and seek shelter under that Tree of Peace: if you are willing to give up your birthright, your political ways, your religion, your customs and retrace those roots back, back home where you belong.

The reason why I am saying this is because people seem to be tired with their system of law and their system of government. Not only is it unjust to our people, but also to you. If you cannot find justice and peace of mind in your way of life, then jump in your canoe, go behind your birth right, go behind your laws and your religion.

This is the solution that I would like to tell to the people; remember, it is not you that we do not like. It is not non-Native or Native Peoples that we dislike. It is your ways.

The way to seek justice is come back home to where you belong.

Comment:

I am not a lawyer, my field is theology, but an aspect of theology is divine law. I had the privilege, with a group of other people, over the last six days, to be up in Great Whale River, and two nights ago I sat in the home of a sixty-four year old woman, Agnes Natasquawan, and she spoke very beautifully about divine law, and I would just like to share a few of her words. They came to me through translation because I have not yet learned Cree. She said:

> The Cree People are very strong and want to take a strong position to protect the land. They get their strength from a certain power. I know that you will understand. We see how beautiful the land is that God created for us and we cannot reject the things that the Creator has created for us: the trees, the rocks, the sand, the waters. God created lakes and rivers and put them where he wanted them: big ones, little ones. He created everything according to his will and we must protect that creation. If God had wanted to build bigger lakes or rivers he would have done so. We know

that for sure. God created all these things for our use and the Cree People are trying to protect God's creation. As Cree People, we see no need for things to be changed. We must look after the land as a part of obedience to God's will.

It is a pity that Hydro-Québec does not have this way of thinking. As Hydro-Québec works every day on this project, we will see the destruction and the disrespect for God's law. Every day we will see them destroy more and more of God's creation. As each day passes and we see Hydro-Québec at work we will see its destruction of something so precious, a gift we have been given to enjoy.

As Hydro-Québec destroys the beauty of the land it will be hurting us in our hearts because it is destroying something we love. Hydro-Québec will be accountable for its actions at some time. So, we do not want the land destroyed, and we are trying to save the land as the will of the Creator. My husband is getting old and I have medical problems and when the level of the water is raised at our campground and will come close to our hunting area, it will be as if in our old age hell was coming towards us to destroy us.

I am very glad that I had this opportunity to share this with you. The source of wisdom in my view of creation comes from a powerful source. Please share with others my feelings and views concerning the Hydro project.

KEYNOTE SPEAKER

Elijah Harper

Elijah Harper was born at Red Sucker Lake in north-eastern Manitoba. He studied at the University of Manitoba, and later worked as a community development worker and researcher for the Manitoba Indian Brotherhood, and as a program analyst for the Manitoba Department of Northern Affairs.

In 1978, at the age of 29, he was elected as Chief of the Red Sucker Lake Indian Band (now Red Sucker Lake First Nations). In 1981 he was elected as M.L.A. for the Rupertsland Constituency, a position which he held for the next eleven years. In 1986 he was appointed to cabinet as Minister Without Portfolio Responsible for Native Affairs, and in 1987 he was appointed as Manitoba's Minister of Northern Affairs.

In 1990, while sitting as an Opposition Member in the Manitoba Legislature, he was instrumental in blocking passage of the Meech Lake Constitutional Accord, which had proceeded without adequate participation by Canada's Aboriginal Peoples.

In April of 1993, Mr. Harper was nominated as Liberal Candidate for the federal riding of Churchill in northern Manitoba. On October 25, 1993 he was elected as Member of Parliament for Churchill.

A TIME TO SAY NO

Meech Lake represented many things. It became a symbol for why we opposed the Accord. It represented hundred of years of frustration. Hundred of years of disappointment. It represented the lack of fulfilment of government promises and the lack of government will to deal with Aboriginal Peoples in this country. If we had supported the Accord, we may have locked ourselves into a process for decades. It would have been the same thing over again. We were simply saying "no" to that process. We were saying "no" to the continuation of the present policies of the government. However, we were saying "yes" to a new relationship between the Governments of Canada and Aboriginal Peoples.

Of course, we know that in the *Constitution*, the only two founding nations recognized are the French and the English. This lie must be recognized and rectified directly. So, one of the main reasons we objected to the Accord was the lack of recognition of the founding role of Aboriginal Peoples in this country. We have played a very important role in how this country was developed. We established relationships with the newcomers that came to these shores. We welcomed them and we helped them. We respected them and treated them equally. We shared knowledge, land and resources with these peoples. We made treaties and signed agreements. It was never envisioned by our forefathers that we would be dominated by the settler people, but rather that we would live side-by-side with respect for each other.

Presently, we are totally dominated by the Canadian government, particularly by the federal government. The *Indian Act* dominates us on a daily basis. A few weeks ago on "The Journal", there was a show on the *Indian Act*'s tremendous impact on us as Aboriginal Peoples. In this program, we saw one of the richest reserves in this country with millions of dollars. My home town is poor money-wise, but rich in culture and surroundings. Yet, we have the same problem: any decision that we make has to be approved by the Minister of Indian Affairs. That had to change, and that is why we said "no" to the Meech Lake Accord.

We want to be recognized as the distinct people that we know we are. We will be recognized in the future. I know for a fact that the time will come when we will take our place as the First Peoples in this country. That recognition will come about in the near future. I know there is great discussion about unity, and we have commissions talking about it right across the country. Considering the events of this summer at Oka, they have not really learned what the issue is about. Nothing has really changed. I find it amazing, incredible that nothing has happened. I guess I should not be too surprised.

Even the Prime Minister stood up before Christmas to say that Aboriginal issues would be dealt with and Aboriginal land claims would be accelerated. However, all he has done is set up a special Commission to deal with the question of unity. As a matter of fact, we heard Senator Murray say that Aboriginal issues would not be dealt with until the Commission had completed its task. Once again, Aboriginal Peoples have been betrayed by the Prime Minister and the government. History shows that we have been promised so many things time after time, and these promises have been broken.

That is why it was so important to say "no". Enough is enough: it is time for action. There had to come a time, and that is what happened this summer. The Prime Minister used all his influence and authority to try and convince the Chiefs to support the Meech Lake Accord. He sent in his heavy hitters, like Senator Murray, to meet with the Chiefs and win their support so that we would pass the Accord. Mulroney made about six proposals. One of them was that Aboriginal Peoples would sit on yet another committee to study the so-called "Canada Clause" to determine whether we were a distinct society. Why study that? We know that we are distinct, and yet this is what he offered us along with the Royal Commission. The Chiefs said, "Well, if you really are concerned about Native issues why offer another round of talking during a constitutional crisis. You can do that any time as a government. Why offer it now?" Of course, the federal government did not listen, and their actions reminds us that they cannot be trusted. The promises they made to us were nothing more than promises.

It is time for action. We have studies already, for heaven's sake, piled up in Ottawa. We have spent a lot of dollars already on Indian self-government reports, land claims reports, criminal justice reports. Nothing has happened. We have to get the governments to do something. There is a lot of political will to deal with us but the efforts are being frustrated. I find it more frustrating than ever. Aboriginal People have been the most accommodating people, the most patient people, but that patience is wearing thin.

Did you see Prime Minister talking about how great this country is? How united we should be? Yet, one thing he forgets to mention is Aboriginal Peoples. The government has to deal with the Aboriginal Peoples first – it should be the first order of business. We deserve it. As an Aboriginal, it is personally frustrating for me, and now all across the country, we all say: enough is enough.

Now is the time for action. We can act alone but we want allies to help us to resolve the outstanding issues. We must realize that if the land claims issues, the sovereignty issues and other issues are not resolved in this country, there is going to be a greater price to pay. Not resolving these questions will cost more in the end.

As I travel from province to province, many Canadians are asking why their government has not resolved these issues. So, there is a greater awareness or understanding and a desire for more information. We do not need sympathy, we need action. We need support to force the government to deal with us. There are many issues to be dealt with.

Aboriginal Peoples went through a lot of emotions in Winnipeg in terms of who we are. We have been assaulted as Aboriginal Peoples. We were not treated as equals under the *Indian Act,* we were not even recognized as a people. That is how we were treated.

In the House of Parliament, I said that Canada's policies have been based on racism, assimilation, integration and genocide. It still exists today. Nothing has really changed in the last hundred years. We are still controlled by governments. They still dictate to us and legislate who we are. They are tinkering with a lot of things through *Bill C-31* – another class of Indians to screw up. The government has done a miserable job but we can do better. It is our right, our inherent right to govern ourselves.

When I talk about assimilation and genocide, a classic example is the old residential school system. I went through the residential school system. I saw beatings taking place – small children being put on a table and strapped over a hundred times without their underwear. Screaming, they were screaming because they were strapped until they were black and blue and could no longer stand up. We were forced to stand in attention while this beating went on. Another example I can give you is a young woman about thirteen years old who was made an example of in front of all the other students because she wrote to her parents in Cree. I also wished I could have written in that same language to my parents, but she was made an example of. They told us, "You are here to learn English and not to learn anything else." The government removed children from their parents and families, supposedly to educate and civilize them. They used deliberate policies to eliminate our culture and our language.

Worst of all, the government in this country passes laws to outlaw our ceremonies, outlaw sundances, outlaw the Potlatch ceremonies, deny our religion, our spirituality. You might as well just turn into a robot, if you run a country with no heart and soul. We need to have that love and that understanding amongst people if we are to enjoy peace. And government has outlawed that too. The policies of the government and its laws deliberately wipe us out, wipe out our heart and soul as Aboriginal Peoples.

Aboriginal Peoples have been very strong and withstood all those injustices – it has made us stronger. When I talk to the young people across this country, I always tell them stories of our great nation. I tell them we are a great people. I tell them it is not what you acquire materially that makes you a great person. What makes you a great person is what you are able to give and what you are able to share. Aboriginal Peoples across this country have demonstrated generosity and how do we get treated? We are not even recognized as the First Peoples in the supreme law of this country, the *Constitution*. That has to change. And it will come about, maybe not in my time, but it will.

I talk about the inherent right to self-government which has to be recognized. We were never conquered people. It is not as if the first Europeans found Aboriginal societies running with no structure or order. We had our communities. We had our social structures. We had our political structures. There was trade between Indian Nations. We had been sovereign thousands of years prior to the arrival of any Europeans.

People ask me, what do you mean by self-government or sovereignty, and I try to put it as simply as I can. Basically, it is the ability to determine our own lives and to manage our own affairs. It is not so hard to understand, but I know that when I go through these constitutional conferences – and I have attended every single one of them along with Trudeau and Mulroney and all the First Ministers – I know what the real game is. It is about power and control. I know that. They do not want to share and that is why they keep asking us, "Will you define what you mean by self-government?" They want to know exactly what they are losing.

The kind of recognition we want is not the kind of self-government being advocated by the Department of Indian Affairs. They think, "Oh, we are giving you self-government. We will give you a contribution agreement here, a financial arrangement there and gee, you have self-government." Managing your own affairs is more than that. It is something that cannot be legislated. Will-power comes from people. You cannot legislate dignity. You cannot legislate respect. It is the confidence in our people that lets us act as nations. We will act like sovereign people. However, we have been so devastated for far too long. That is why it took so long for us to speak up: because of all the injustices, the oppression that has been inflicted on us. I talk to many of the people who have gone through the Canadian systems and they are carrying a lot of hurt inside.

Today, Oka along with the Meech Lake Accord and other events have led to an awakening of Aboriginal Peoples spiritually and politically. I know there is solidarity and unity. Many people have expressed support for the Mohawk People at Oka. However, the government tries to divide and conquer us. They say we have the Warriors, we have peaceful people, we have elected people, we have traditional leaders and they play on these differences to the hilt and say that we are not together. Yet, I have seen them fighting in the Senate, in the House of Commons. They are wild animals. We are no different than anybody else: we fight amongst ourselves. The government should have the respect to let the Mohawk People or any other people determine themselves how to resolve these issues. We do not tell other people what to do. I know that the Minister of Indian Affairs says that he wants to negotiate, but then he tries to decide who will do the negotiating for our people. That should be none of his business. He should let our people decide. In our land claims, I know that the federal government is piece feeding land claims and other arrangements. That is how eventually they divide us. We as Aboriginal Peoples have to be more conscious and aware of government strategy and we have to be more determined and united than ever before.

We are all in the same boat, although some issues may be a little different. We are trying to achieve the same goals for our People whether as Mohawk, Ojibway, Cree or Haida. Now is the opportune time for us and those who support us to be more aggressive, more determined than ever before because the events of this summer have awakened the consciousness of the Canadian people. The result is that there is a lot of support for Aboriginal issues.

The international community is also questioning the relationship between Aboriginal Peoples and the Government of Canada. Last fall, Joe Norton and some other people travelled to Europe to talk to their Parliament about Aboriginal issues and to encourage them to come to Canada to look into the situation. I know that there is a human rights commission along with Amnesty International questioning whether human rights violations took place in Oka. Of course, Canada denied that any fundamental human rights were violated. The international community's awareness of Aboriginal issues has never been so great as now.

At the same time I sense that Aboriginal Peoples are more united and able to support each other than ever before. I go into communities and talk to the young men and women – they are less patient, they want things to happen quickly. They are aware of what is happening – even the Elders in those communities are aware. Even the small children know something has happened in this country. Are they going to be future leaders? They are growing up with a new sense of awareness of the community.

Now what do we do with all these things happening? Where do we go from here? How do we pressure the governments to deal with us more honestly and sincerely? If they will not deal with us, where do we turn? How do we go about getting our issues dealt with?

I know that here in Quebec you must also deal with Quebec's aspirations of sovereignty, and how this affects its relationship with the Aboriginal Peoples. One thing I want to make clear is that we were not saying "no" to Quebec at all. As a matter of fact, Aboriginal Peoples have never denied anyone in this country the right to who they are, to their identity, to their religion. It has never been part of our history. We welcomed many of the people who came to the shores of this country we call Canada, and it is these new settlers that set up governments and made Canada what it is today.

What would have happened to the people in Quebec, especially the James Bay Cree, if we had passed the Meech Lake Accord? Quebec would have achieved its distinct status whereas the James Bay Cree would not have. There will be a lot of support for the James Bay Cree because what they are going to be fighting for is the same thing that we are fighting for across this country. That support for the Cree I can guarantee you.

The federal government has a constitutional obligation and also a moral obligation to uphold the rights of the Aboriginal Peoples in the province of Quebec. Often times they do not. The *Musqueam* Supreme Court decision told them that they have to uphold the rights of the Aboriginal Peoples over and above anything else.

We also have the *Sparrow* and *Sioui* decisions. The federal government, instead of changing its policies, tries to interpret these decisions to suit their own purpose instead of enhancing the right of the Aboriginal Peoples. That has always been the case. Our well-being has never been a priority for this government.

Fundamental rights are being violated, and the law enforcement agencies who are supposed to uphold the law are not doing anything. We have been mistreated throughout our relationship. We are still being treated as second class citizens when the Mohawk People are invaded by the army. We called for Parliament to reconvene because we felt that any use of armed forces against the First Peoples in this country should be approved by Parliament. Parliament should have dealt with it. However, it was more concerned with the Gulf War in the Middle East than its own "golf war" back home. It makes me sort of sad and furious at the same time because of the way we have been treated. It has to change. How?

Basically, what I have been doing is going across the country collecting information and speaking to many groups. I try to facilitate understanding and write down information, because knowledge is very important. Knowledge is power. Knowledge is understanding. People can be informed about issues and develop a greater understanding of who we are. They do not need to be scared about us taking control of our lives. I mean, the government has done a miserable job anyway.

We as Aboriginal Peoples have to take control of our lives. I know that there is no other way. We have to do it. I know that we have a fight on our hands and we have to fight every inch of the way even if we do not have the resources. Government cannot tell us we are not sovereign if we do not have an economic base. Money is not a prerequisite for self-government. We need to educate ourselves, to develop our economies and to be self-sufficient as much as we can.

Self-government does not take away anybody's rights or respect. What we hope for is the ability to live, to co-exist with each other, to have justice and equality, to have a good life and to have respect. We are not asking for anything more or anything less. All we ever asked for is the honour and respect denied to us, and for the government to live up its promises and to recognize that as the First Peoples of this country, we do have an inherent right to sovereignty.

CLOSING THANKSGIVING

JOHN CUROTTE

Iroquois Faithkeeper

All the speakers spoke well and the people here understood many things. Understood the good and the bad. We understood what the Indian People want. We understood what the government is doing now. We can now say a prayer for this before we depart.

The first thing to do is to give thanks to the Creation and to the Creator Himself. In the opening prayer this morning, I talked about the Creation. I thanked our Mother Earth, and asked her to come amongst us, to stay with us the whole day. I asked the Creation to be amongst us. I asked the waters to be here. I asked the fishes and the animals. I asked the trees and the birds and the other people to be here to help us so that good words would come out from the people on the panel. The good words tell us what should be said amongst our people, amongst other people too.

So I thank the Creation again, the animals, the trees, our Mother Earth. We thank them for the things that they gave us – for the meat and things like that. We thank them. I thank the little people who stay with the Indian Peoples; they take care of the mothers, they take care and give us strength and power. I thank them for what they do.

Now I go up to the Sun and the Moon. First, I talk to my Brother the Sun, and ask him to shine amongst us to show us the road where we are going, to let us see when we are looking for medicine, when we look for each other. So, I thank our Brother the Sun.

Now our Brother the Sun goes down, and our Grandmother the Moon comes up. Our Grandmother does many things. If our Grandmother the Moon did not do these things, we would not be able to see each other over here. Our Grandmother takes care of what the Creator made in this world. Whatever He put here, She takes care of. She takes care of us too because She works with the women. We give thanks to our Mother Earth and we give thanks to our Grandmother the Moon.

When you look up in the air you see the stars sparkling and the old people used to say:

> *When you look up in the air, you see your ancestors watching over you so that you will not get hurt. So, nothing happens to you. Watching over you with the love from their hearts, the ones that passed away.*

Some of them say:

> *You see stars jumping up and down, those are the little ones that passed away. They play up in the Creator's world. They jump here and there so that we will see our little children up there looking after us too.*

We go to the Creator when we leave this world. The Creator said:

> *You will not seen my face any more, you cannot look at me but I will send Someone to look after you.*

He comes down and walks amongst the people of the nation. He walks so that he can help the people in any way that he can, in any way that they ask for. He is the only one to go back into the Creator's world. When he left he said:

> *Do not be in a hurry to leave this world, because I made everything on the earth for you, my people. When you go up there, the only different thing is that you have no worries and no sickness.*

So we give thanks to One that was sent.

Now we look up into the Creator's world to the Creator himself. He put us here and watches over us at all times. He watches the way we move. He watches the way we talk, the way we do everything. Like they always say in the Great Law: he is the only one that can judge the people. Today we do the same as Him. We judge people, but it is different.

So, now I ask the Creator Himself and our Mother Earth to watch over us on our way home so nothing will happen. To watch so that we get back home and see our loved ones: that we have smiles and we have the land and we have talks with the little children, our grandmothers, our mothers and our cousins. So, we take from our hearts thanks to the Creation and to the Creator Himself.

The 1992 Conference

JUSTICE FOR NATIVES ?

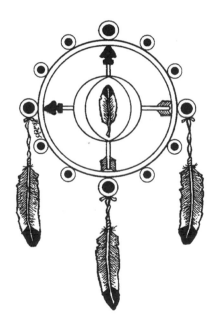

PANEL ONE
BARRIERS TO JUSTICE

TOBY MORANTZ

Toby Morantz is an associate professor in the Department of Anthropology at McGill University. Her research and writing have focused on the fur trade period in eastern James Bay, specifically looking at the 18th and 19th Century social organization of the Cree and what accommodations were made to incorporate the fur trade. She has written several books and a number of articles looking at this and related questions.

THE JUDICIARY AS ANTHROPOLOGISTS

I began this paper on December 11, 1984 when I first heard of the judgment in the Temagami case, at which time Justice Donald Steele of the Ontario Supreme Court declared that the Temagami People were not an "organized society". His pronouncement startled me, since as a social scientist I knew that the word "society" in itself means organized. I became alerted to the fact that the legal profession lacked a basic understanding of society, in general, and Native societies, in particular.

I would like to review the Temagami case, present a quick tour through the intricacies of the type of social organization that in anthropology is called "band societies" and then examine more closely Judge Steele's findings. On a note of nomenclature, the people refer to themselves as "Teme-augama Anishnabay" but to avoid confusion with the written documents they will herein be referred to as the Temagami.

The Temagami Case

In August 1973, three legal cautions on some four thousand square miles of land were filed on behalf of the Bear Island People to prevent the Ontario Crown from selling or leasing any land in an area they had recently designated for further development as a recreational area with "discreet resource production". Economic development by southern interests of this Temagami region had been on-going since the turn of the century: first, with logging, then mining and tourism. Although the filing of cautions was followed by some negotiation, the Ontario government nonetheless filed proceedings against the Temagami People in May 1978, and hearings began in mid-1982.

According to Judge Steele, the basic dispute before the court was "whether Ontario is the owner of certain lands, free of any Aboriginal rights claimed by the Indians, or whether the band or registered band has Aboriginal rights in the lands that prevent Ontario from dealing with the lands until those rights are properly extinguished".

The findings

Justice Steele sets out eight findings in his judgment of December, 1984:

1. He claimed that the area was not covered by the *Royal Proclamation, 1763* but that the respective rights of the Indians and Crown were dealt with in common law as though they were *Proclamation* lands, except that the relevant date for determining Aboriginal rights is the arrival of settlers.

2. He concluded that the *Royal Proclamation* and common law gave to the Indians only the Aboriginal right to continue using the lands for the purposes and in the manner enjoyed in 1763, and not to subsequently put the land to any new uses.

3. He found that the Bear Island Temagami failed to prove that in 1763 their ancestors were sufficiently organized to be recognized as a band; that as an organized society, they had exclusive occupation of the area claimed in 1763; or that as an organized society, they had continued to exclusively occupy and make Aboriginal use of the land claim area from 1763, or the time of settlement, to the date legal action commenced.

4. He found that the *Constitution Act, 1867* did not give Indians any independent right to self-government.

5. He found that the effect of the *Robinson-Huron Treaty* was to extinguish Aboriginal rights in the land claim area, and that the ancestors of the defendants having the authority to sign were party to this treaty in 1850; or, in the alternative, had adhered to it in 1883.

6. He found that the Province of Canada prior to Confederation and Ontario after Confederation had enacted legislation with the intent and effect of opening the land claim area to settlement and extinguishing Aboriginal rights.

7. He then found that the Province of Canada, prior to 1867, was constitutionally competent to enact legislation and enter into treaties which had the effect of extinguishing Aboriginal rights in the land claim area.

8. Finally, he ruled on the *Statute of Limitations.*

Two of these findings, numbers three and five, which made reference to concepts of organized society in relation to the treaty formation, contradict basic anthropological principles and knowledge. It is this discrepancy on which I would like to focus.

A brief historical review

Archaeological evidence points to human occupation in the Temagami region about five thousand years ago and there is evidence of occupation from the Archaic to the Late Woodland Period (Hodgins and Benidicks 1989:9). As the period of contact with Europeans approached, the people in the Temagami Lake region were already occupying an area criss-crossed by fur trade routes to the Huron. Close by were the Nipissing, who dominated the area as strong trade partners of the Huron. After the Huron were dispersed in 1849, the Nipissing became middlemen to the Cree and the West (Harris 1987:Pl. 35). As for direct documentary evidence, the Temagami are mentioned in French documents and maps as "Outemagami" or "Outimagami" (Heidenreich 1971:241).

After 1640, the Temagami are not again mentioned in European records until the Hudson's Bay Company established an outpost at Lake Temagami in 1834 (Hodgins and Benidicks 1989:29). In the intervening years, the post at Temiskaming, through the French and the North West Company, dominated the fur trade in the region. Evidently, the ethnohistorian, Charles Bishop, used the prolonged absence of any reference to Temagami to argue that they had dispersed in the 1660s due to Iroquois raiding (Ibid:304, f.n. 37), and again in 1725 due to exhaustion of game caused by over harvesting (Ibid:305, f.n. 56). His conclusions were refuted by William Eccles, who found that Bishop's analysis rests "on no analysis at all", and that "lack of records cannot be equated with lack of trade or lack of a people with whom to trade" (Ibid:21).

However, the key event to the court's findings is the signing of the *Robinson Huron Treaty* in 1850 at Sault Ste-Marie. The fact that the Temagami were neither present at the treaty discussions or at the signing of the treaty is not in dispute. However, on September 13, 1850 the Canadian government did distribute "government presents" through the Indian superintendent at Manitowaning on Manitoulin Island, and one of these presents through George Ironside, the Indian superintendent, went to the "Naibanagonai of Temaguming" (Ontario Factum 1991:Vol. 2, App. 8, no. 5).

Incidentally, the anthropologist Frank Speck visited the Temagami People in the summer of 1913, and besides recording family hunting territories, he also listed chronologically the Chiefs of the "Timagami Band". The first Chief, who dated back to the "time of the white man's coming", was Ne'bone'gwun'e, meaning "feathers all over" (Speck 1915:23). He also lists a second Chief named Ke'ke'k, meaning "hawk", who is also noted in the 1850 distribution list (Ibid:no. 9).

An organized society

I would like to return to the third finding of Justice Steele, relating to the concept of an organized society. Although it seems arrogant and presumptuous to anthropologists that a judge should pronounce on whether a society was "organized", there may be a partial explanation. In 1980, in the Inuit land rights case *Baker Lake*, Justice Mahoney set out several tests which had to be met in order to claim Aboriginal rights under common law:

1. The Aboriginal group making the claim and their ancestors were members of an organized society.

2. The organized society continued to occupy the specific territory over which Aboriginal title was being asserted.

3. The occupation was to the exclusion of other organized societies.

4. Their occupation was an established fact at the time sovereignty was asserted by England (Baker Lake 1980:542).

Mahoney based his reasoning on the 1973 Nishga case judgment of Justice Judson of the Federal Supreme Court, *Calder* v. *Attorney General of British Columbia*. Justice Judson claimed that the plaintiffs must prove they were "organized in societies". This concern with "society" can probably be traced back to the landmark 1832 Cherokee case, *Worcester* v. *the State of Georgia*, in which Justice Marshall refers to Indian nations as being distinct and describes them as "having institutions of their own and governing themselves by their own laws" (Ibid:543). However, Mahoney finds that the rationale for the "organized society" test stems from the following dicta of the Privy Council in *Re Southern Rhodesia* (1919):

> The estimation of the rights of Aboriginal tribes is always inherently difficult. Some tribes are so low in the scale of social organization that their usages and conceptions of rights and duties are not to be reconciled with the institutions or the legal ideas of civilized society. Such a gulf cannot be bridged. It would be idle to impute such people some shadow of the rights known to our law and then to transmute it into the substance of transferable rights of property as we know them ... (Ibid:543)

Therefore, it seems that Steele drew his inspiration from this 1919 decision as well as the testimony of Charles Bishop, who claimed that fires, game shortages and epidemics in the 1840s led to depopulation of the area and that the Temagami People only regrouped as a "trading post band" in the 1860s (Hodgins and Benidicks 1989:307, no. 10).

The Temagami People are classified by anthropologists as Ojibwa speaking and are similar to other southeastern Ojibwa occupying eastern Ontario, north of the Great Lakes. They exploited different food resources throughout the year and therefore shifted camps a number of times each season. During the early Fall months, large numbers of southeastern Ojibwa met at Sault Ste-Marie, where they fished extensively at the rapids. The winter months were spent inland hunting and fishing. They did not always have sufficient food: the Jesuits speak of how in the 1640s the Indians were sometimes forced to eat the inner bark of trees or to make soup from mooseskins and moccasins (Rogers 1978:762).

The sociopolitical organization termed as a "traditional band" refers to social units that corresponded in size to the availability of game. The hallmark of a band society was flexibility: it decreased in size when game was scarce and increased when game was more abundant. During the winter, the band would divide into smaller winter hunting groups, and then in the spring and summer months, they would re-congregate once the fishery could support greater numbers of people.

The arrival of Europeans and the fur trade generated other types of band structures. The "trading post band" developed once missionaries in the late 1800s began congregating Native Peoples at the trading post for a period of time in the summer. Traditional bands that came together to trade at one post, often remaining for the summer, eventually coalesced into a "trading post band", although its components remained the traditional bands. At Mistassini in the James Bay region, the anthropologist, Edward Rogers, noted that the missionaries despaired of being able to persuade the five bands present at the Mistassini trading post band "to take collective action" (Rogers 1963:24). It is these trading post bands that were recognized as "government bands" under the *Indian Act*, and controlled through regulation of band membership and residence.

Leadership existed at several levels of native sociopolitical organization: a head of family, a head of the winter hunting group and a head of the band. In all cases, the leadership was best described as *primus inter pares*, or "first among equals". The leader had influence rather than authority, and was acknowledged as leader for his supernatural powers that provided him with expertise and power.

Contrary to popular belief, the northern Algonquian speaking Peoples did not wander aimlessly over the land, but held customary rights over large tracts of hunting territory. We know from Speck's work at the turn of the century that these hunting tracts were further subdivided into family hunting territories; territories to which winter hunting groups returned yearly. Studies such as those done of the James Bay region (Morantz 1983:108-128) show that these family hunting territories existed at least as far back as the mid-1700s, according to the records of the Hudson's Bay Company. For a variety of reasons, they may date well back into the precontact period.

Although we do not have extensive documentation on the Temagami, the pattern and variety of social institutions for this region have been so well-established that it is reasonable to assert that the Temagami and their neighbours adhered to similar patterns of social organization.

To return to the Temagami case

Although I have only read a few of the sixty-eight volumes of testimony presented during the trial, the testimony of Edward Rogers, a long-standing student of band societies in Quebec and Ontario, permits us to assume that the judge was indeed introduced to the finer points of Algonquian social organization: nuclear and extended family, winter hunting group, local group, traditional band and trading post band.

Nevertheless, Steele either chose to ignore this commentary or was confused by the intricacies of flexible social organization. On the one hand, he speaks of giving the Temagami the "benefit of the doubt", by allowing that in 1850 the ten families may have been a "band" rather than "just a group of families", but then he adds:

> I believe that they were a very loosely-knit organization, without any strong or real central leadership. In fact, the Temagami band was merely beginning to emerge as a cohesive and increasingly larger group around the Nebenegwune family because of the treaty-making process and the present-giving process (Bear Island Case Judgment 1984:161).

It is obvious that Steele did not understand the nature of band leadership, and that his understanding is ethnocentric. Essentially, bands do not begin to emerge: they either exist or they do not. Nor would an essentially subsistence-based sociopolitical organization of the mid 1800s come into effect because of treaties or presents.

It is even harder to accept the reading given by both Steele and the Ontario lawyers of the region's history. It is undisputed that the Temagami People were not signatory to the *Robinson-Huron Treaty*. No Temagami are identified as present at the negotiations or listed among the thirty-eight chiefs signatory to the treaty. Nor is there a reserve in the Lake Temagami area among the seventeen reserves actually set aside by the Treaty (Morris 1971:306-308). In fact, the federal government has also consistently denied that the

Temagami were party to this treaty; first in 1870 (Hodgins and Benidicks 1989:46), and most recently in 1980 (Ibid:267).

One might well ask why the Temagami were not signatories. One possible answer comes from Chief Dokis of the Nipissing, son of the signatory for the Nipissing in 1894, given when the federal government was investigating treaty payments to the Temagami at their request. He simply said that "Peter Naban-Nay-Quan-Nay did not go to the *Robinson-Huron Treaty* because I think he was not invited and said he did not know anything about the treaty until it was over". (Appellant's Factum 1991:26)

In the early depositions made in 1982, the government of Ontario claimed that a non-Temagami chief had signed for the Temagami as their representative. A connection between this chief and the Temagami was so hard to substantiate that by the time the Ontario government went to trial, Ontario had picked another "representative", namely Chief Tagawinini (Diane Soroka, pers. comm, March, 1991). Tagawinini was resident on Manitoulin Island from 1848 onwards, and did not come from the Temagami region but in fact from southern Ontario, in an area between present-day Sarnia and Owen Sound. The linguist, John Nichols, testified that the Temagami and Ojibwae from Southern Ontario did not even speak the same dialect. Furthermore, Tagawinini himself had successfully claimed a share of proceeds from the sale of lands in the Fort Sarnia region (Ontario Appeal Court Judgment 1989:19), but under the Treaty, his band received a two square mile reserve at Wanabitibing, near Lake Nipissing (Morris 1971:307). The Wanapatei band today continue to occupy this land and are clearly distinct from the Temagami at Bear Island.

Why did the Ontario lawyers not declare Dokis, Chief of the nearby Nipissings, the supposed progenitors of the Temagami, as the bona fide representative of the Temagami in 1850? Why did they choose Tagawinini as their "missing piece" in the puzzle? The answer seems to be that the law firm representing Ontario, Soloway, Wright and Howston, found that Tagawinini was not linked to any part of the ceded land. Nor could they determine what he was doing at the treaty discussion since his now ceded lands were not part of the negotiations. Their pairing of the Temagami with Tagawinini seems to follow from their declaration that Nebanagonai (who later became chief of the "emerging band") and Tagawinini considered that they had in common a "certain secondary nationality" (Ontario Factum 1991:App. 10, no. 10). They based their choice of Tagawinini on the following statement in the report of the commissioners who negotiated the Treaty, Vidal and Anderson: [i]t occasionally happens that a Chief possessed of superior information, intelligence or cunning assumes or obtains authority to act for others (Ontario Factum 1991:19). They were right about Tagawinini's intelligence and cunning because he managed to obtain two square miles and treaty rights for land that had never been his. Nevertheless, there is no evidence to substantiate that he had acted for the Temagami People nor any convincing reason for why he ought to have done so. The decipherment of Temagami leadership by the lawyers is one based purely on convenience for constructing their case and totally at odds with Algonquian notions of leadership, as earlier noted.

The only other connection that the lawyers were able to make between the two men, Temagami and Nebanagonai, was that both appear on the same list, one after the other, for payments received on September 13th, 1850. These payments, by the way, could not have been treaty payments since these were paid at the signing of the treaty at Sault Ste-Marie. It is likely that the 1850 payments were government presents given to Upper Canada Indians as part of a military strategy to keep them "loyal". Surtees, in his study of the history of Indian policy, notes that the government never clearly distinguished military presents from annuities (Surtees 1969:59), however, payments to the Temagami ceased in 1855, when military presents were no longer considered necessary.

In the 1880s, the Temagami petitioned the government for a reserve and for an annuity of four dollars per year, the sum also accorded by the *Robinson-Huron Treaty* annuity, and in 1883 they were added to the annuity list, although they had not signed an adhesion to the treaty. They received annuities until 1979, when a band council resolution determined that they should be returned. They did not receive a reserve on Bear Island until 1943, after decades of forestry and mining operations on their lands.

As for whether they had signed the Treaty of 1850 and therefore ceded their Aboriginal rights to their lands, Steele noted that Robinson, the commissioner, "was aware of Nebenegwune and persons residing in the Temagami community ... Nebenegwune did not sign the Treaty, but I find that he was not of sufficient importance as a chief or headman to warrant his signing ... I find that Tawgaiwena represented Nebenegwune and that his signature bound Nebenegwune and his group". (Bear Island Case Judgment 1984:1951)

The Ontario Appeal Court came to the same conclusion in their judgment of February 28, 1989. Their decision, which often relies on circular reasoning, held that it made little sense to argue that Tawgaiwene represented none but himself. They concluded

> There can be no doubt on the contemporary evidence available that Robinson and the government of the day regarded Tawgaiwene as the spokesman for those Nipissing Indians that included Nebenegwune and the Temagami Indians even though, while an Ojibwa, he was not of a Nipissing-area band himself ... (Ontario Appeal Court Judgment 1989:20)

> [T]here is no contemporary evidence of Nebenegwune or any members of the Temagami Band attempting to disassociate themselves from Tawgaiwene's actions ...

The court also thought it unlikely that the other chiefs would permit Tawgaiwune to play such an active role if he were not recognized by them as a chief with representation in the Treaty area (Ibid:21). Again, the Justice's pronouncements on the Temagami's "borrowed" leadership and on the chaotic functioning of band society flow from legal principles that have absolutely no bearing on understanding or interpreting the political organization of a hunting society.

The Supreme Court of Canada delivered a minuscule decision of four double-spaced pages on August 15, 1991. They found against the Temagami Band, claiming that:

> [T]heir Aboriginal right was surrendered whatever the situation on the signing of the *Robinson-Huron Treaty*, by arrangements subsequent to the treaty by which the Indians adhered to the treaty in exchange for treaty annuities and a reserve.

The Supreme Court also expressed some disagreement over the legal findings based on the facts. In particular, they wrote:

> [T]he Indians exercised sufficient occupation of the lands in question throughout the relevant

period to establish an Aboriginal right (Supreme Court Judgment 1991:3).

A reasonable interpretation of this statement is that the Supreme Court recognized them as "an organized society".

The Algonquians are not the only victims of the judiciary's lack of basic knowledge about social organization. One could fill textbooks documenting the injustices that this ignorance has brought about in other cases, most recently for the Gitskan-Wet'swet'en Peoples in present-day British Columbia. In the *Delgamuukw* case, Justice Allan McEachern of the British Columbia Supreme Court presents a number of findings that are at variance with anthropological principles of social organization, not to mention the Gitskan's. One simple example pulled from this judgment illustrates how court procedures have produced barriers to justice rather than justice itself. In regards to the maintenance of the Gitskan-Wet'swet'en institutional organization, McEachern writes:

> I do not accept the ancestors ... behaved as they did because of "institutions". Rather I find they more likely acted as they did because of their survival instincts (Delgamuukw Case Judgment 1991:213).

To conclude

It is obvious that far too many judges have interpreted Native society from either an ethnocentric viewpoint or from some legal conception of hunting societies that is, from the viewpoint of an anthropologist, and more importantly for the Native Peoples, gravely ignorant. The result has been decisions that are highly unjust. This ignorance is truly a barrier to justice and I believe it is the moral responsibility of anthropologists, in cooperation with legal scholars, to re-educate the legal profession.

OWEN YOUNG

Owen Young received his Bachelor of Arts (cum laude) at the University of California, Los Angeles, 1969, and his Bachelor of Law at University of Toronto 1976. He is currently a member of the Ontario bar. He is also affiliated with the Montreal firm of O'Reilly & Associates, which has considerable experience in acting as counsel for Aboriginal Peoples. Owen Young also acted as one of defence counsel at the trial of Ronald Cross, Gordon Lazore and Roger Lazore, three Mohawk Warriors.

THE OKA TRIAL

One of the major prosecutions of Warriors who were involved in the Oka crisis has just come to an end. Sentence has not yet been passed, so I would ask you to understand that there are some issues I cannot address today.

The first step in defending a case like the one against Ronald (Lasagna) Cross, Gordon (Noriega) Lazore and Roger (20/20) Lazore, three Mohawk warriors, is to make sure that you know where your clients stand philosophically. Understand that a Native sovereigntist sees no role in his or her life for Canadian legal institutions. A Native sovereigntist would not go voluntarily to the courts of Canada and does not expect justice from them. For the sovereigntist, treaties are not creatures of Canadian domestic law, and Canadian courts are without legitimate power or authority to interpret and apply them to Natives. The enshrinement of Native treaties in the Canadian constitution is only marginally relevant to their claims.

The Mohawks at Kanesatake based their negotiations on the sovereignty of their nation. Thrust into a Quebec courtroom facing criminal charges being prosecuted under Canadian law forced some hard decisions on them – and on their lawyers. We were all weighing the prospect of conviction and jail against being true to the Mohawk world view and political position. We found ourselves searching for defence strategies that would accommodate both the legal needs and political demands of our clients.

It may be that sovereignty can only be asserted politically in order to be effective. It may be that the issue of Native sovereignty is simply not a justiciable one. Going to a Canadian court – particularly to a criminal court – to ask for a declaration that one is sovereign is a meaningless exercise. However, as legal counsel for the three Mohawks warriors, we found ourselves in a courtroom defending individual men who justified their actions at Oka on the basis of Mohawk sovereignty.

We faced several questions. Should we approach the case legalistically by asserting a national or international legal right before the courts, as was done in the *Temagami* case? Should we try to meld our clients' political views with existing concepts of *mens rea*? Even if we adopted a more political approach, should we turn the case into a showpiece, a kind of "Barnum and Bailey" of the Superior Court, or should we try to take Native political notions and fit them into the box that is Canadian legal thinking? Ultimately, we had to decide on a fixed philosophical base for our arguments. Otherwise the case would have been impossible to handle.

As a starting point to the Oka trial, we decided to slide the defences into existing notions of Canadian legal thinking through the concept of a subjective state of mind. It was a difficult approach, but we felt it was important to work through the Canadian criminal legal system, and push it to operate at its optimum. We felt this might be possible since our trial and its issues were very public so the trial would be closely scrutinized. In effect, it would be like trying the case in a fishbowl, with everyone on their best behaviour. Unfortunately, that did not happen.

First of all, we began the case expecting the prosecution evidence to deal with the serious facts underlying the Oka crisis, but the Crown side-tracked the issues with trivial details. That left us trying to convince Mohawks to put forward their nationhood and sovereigntist principles as excuses to answer petty charges – crimes such as people "stealing" and riding lawnmowers to cut an absentee homeowners' lawn. This was tantamount to asking the Mohawks to desecrate the importance of their People, values and traditional law for a trivial purpose. That was the first problem.

The second problem arose because of the interplay of personalities amongst Crown, defence, and judge. I found nothing whatsoever in the jury's deliberations that I could point to as suggesting that they were motivated in any way by racism or prejudice. As you may know, the jury was all-white and English-speaking, although much of the evidence was a mixture of English and French. They took this incredible task on, and the strain of it showed in their faces by the end of the case.

The defence began with the objective of achieving a fair trial, and with the attitude that, whatever the result, we would simply have to live with it. However, that objective was soon compromised when the Crown started off the first round of the trial with a battle over which language would be used by the prosecution. This somewhat acrimonious struggle to have the trial in English went as far as the Court of Appeal. Mohawks found themselves in the unfortunate position of recognizing the importance of culture and language in Quebec, and yet having to assert a right to use English. They were uncomfortable doing so, but found it necessary to protect their position.

A third problem was that the Crown misunderstood its obligations to the public as well as to the accused – although I say this with respect for the individuals involved. There was a consistent lack of disclosure, such that the judge gave the defence the right to call back over twenty of the thirty prosecution witnesses. Imagine that a judge says at the end of a trial, "You can bring back twenty people and ask them a bunch of questions that you didn't know you should have asked at the beginning, because the Crown forgot to disclose that evidence".

Worst still, because of this lack of disclosure, two major counts, rioting and obstruction, were stayed by the judge. For our clients, that was a major defect in the trial; namely, that the counts which could have served as springboards for sovereigntist and jurisdictional arguments were now gone. Essentially, these charges were the only basis upon which the confrontation between the Mohawk as a collective body and the Canadian state could have been represented before the courts.

There was also a tendency throughout the judgments, I regret to say, to favour expediency over full consideration of the issues. To his credit, Justice Greenberg gave some very powerful decisions in this case – some of them compassionate and well-reasoned; and it is always an arduous task to deal with opposing sides fighting constantly and even viciously for eleven months. Nonetheless, it seemed that there was an attempt to salvage the trial at any cost. The result was three motions for mistrial.

Just to illustrate the point, His Lordship commented that the decision on language involved serious constitutional questions. Yet, after only a weekend of contemplation, he delivered his verdict while observing that the matter should have been given more study and reflection. The same issue was then argued two or three weeks later before Justice Tannenbaum, also of the Superior Court, and he ruled the opposite way. It is extraordinarily difficult for three accused sitting in a prisoners' box to hear one judge say, "I should have taken more time" and then hear another judge, only a few weeks later, decide the exact opposite way. In such circumstances, the accused could be forgiven for thinking that "right" may be less important to the legal system than the mere appearance of justice. As Roger Lazure commented, "Even though I was acquitted, the process was not fair. That process didn't allow me to be judged for who I am and what I did. It simply was a lot of manoeuvring over principles I don't understand and have no feeling for."

On the defence side, I would argue that there were no obvious mistakes that affected the fairness of the trial, although that remains to be seen. As you may know, none of the accused were called to give evidence. Of course, it is up to the defence to raise sovereigntist or political arguments. No defence was called because, on the one hand, the prosecution's evidence was dreadful and, on the other, we had hoped to separate out offenses that were "political" in nature from others that were less so. This attempt to split the issues failed and we were stuck with the untenable choice of calling witnesses to give evidence on "political" offenses, but then having them cross-examined on everything. Our concern was that the accused would be exposed to a wide-open, wide-ranging cross-examination, possibly proving the Crown's very weak case out of their own mouths. The problem was further complicated by conflicting objectives between the Native collective and the individual over the question of protecting the individual from self-incrimination.

So, we began with this great hope that we would actually see the system operating at its optimum, and that everybody could be satisfied – perhaps not with the result, but at least satisfied that justice had been done. However, the only measure of our success was that everybody was unhappy. The most positive reading was that perhaps we had done something right since, as in any compromise, nobody was able to get exactly what they wanted. I followed the press afterwards and there was dissatisfaction, to say the least, among the French and the Mohawks, while the English seemed to leave it alone. It is difficult for me to assess the trial objectively, since it is still so close. However, at this point I would have to say that our experiment was a failure.

The reason it was a failure was that we did not, even in this fabulous crucible of a case, have an opportunity to see whether the system itself could produce a result that Natives and non-Natives alike could consider just – not whether they were happy with it, but whether they could consider it just. Furthermore, all other considerations aside, the way our system plays itself out through individuals such as lawyers and judges undermines the possibility of a result that will ever satisfy a collective society such as the Mohawks. While I hesitate to throw out the whole system, this experience drove home the near impossibility of making such a system work fairly for Natives.

QUESTION PERIOD: PANEL ONE

Question: LYNN WILSON
Law student, McGill University

I am just wondering how you would slide the sovereignty defence into notions of criminal law, such as *mens rea*.

Answer: OWEN YOUNG

First of all, we looked at the conflict as a problem that required a Canadian legal solution. And in the context of Canadian law, we saw the need to bring in the teachings of these people, including their history, culture, and law to show how this all-encompassing world explained their actions. We needed to help the courts hear the voices saying "defend the land, they are attacking it". A defence based on a subjective state of mind is not based on a colour of right or a new legal notion, but is simply based upon the fact that these people do not have criminal intent. And that is in fact what they were saying – "we are not criminal".

Question: STUART MYLOW
Mohawk of Kahnawake

Did this case set a legal precedent of jurisdiction over Native Peoples?

Answer: OWEN YOUNG

No.

Question: STUART MYLOW

How can you say "No" when they have already found Natives guilty – and in a case clearly out of the jurisdiction of non-Native courts?

Answer: OWEN YOUNG

You have asked whether it sets a precedent. To a lawyer that means will this case be brought up in a subsequent case to see how it was decided, and then it would be followed. In that context, the answer is no. This case, literally, means nothing to another case coming along. We were able to obtain a ruling for the second case that the validity of treaties was to be determined initially by a jury. So, buried away in the middle of our pre-trial motion we have this important ruling. It is important since if those questions go to the jury, they will decide the issue regardless of how other cases were decided in the past. However, a jury decision itself has no significance as a precedent.

Question: STUART MYLOW

They brought Natives into that judicial system, not as a collective Mohawk nation, but as individuals. So right there, it is a statement to Native society and Canadian society that, first, they are not recognizing any treaties, and second, they are not recognizing Mohawks or any other Natives as a collective group. Therefore, you might as well be tearing up those treaties in front of everyone's eyes.

So, they brought them into that judicial system as individuals, just like non-Natives who are subject to the judicial system as individuals and not as a collective. Non-Natives do not have collective right, it has only been the Natives who have had such a right, but now it is clearly established that it does not exist by simply giving the decision into the hands of a group of people, a jury, who do not know the political structure of those treaties. When you give it into the hands of a group of people like that, the government is saying "Well, here, we don't want to deal with it. You attempt to deal with it and, in the process you will be the ones who will be guilty of taking away the collective rights of the Natives." There is a precedent, whether lawyers agree or not – and it will always be pointed to, throughout time, as law. The precedent is that the collective rights of the Natives are no longer recognized.

When we look at the whole spirit of the treaties, the treaties were not two-sided deals, they were one-sided. There was always this stipulation in the treaties that, "It is as the Natives understand them". So it was not two-sided. People forget the way they were brought about. They forget that there were actually wars, because there seems to be peace all around us today. But the whole reason for those treaties was that our two societies were at war. The white society, today the melting-pot society, found that they could not conquer our people. And our people, right from the beginning, did not want to war with anyone, and respected the rights of other people to live in freedom. So when you look at what these treaties were built on, they were built on the fear of that melting-pot society that they would be wiped out, even though our people would have also been wiped out in the process. However, ever since the treaties were established, we have been in constant battle. But now it is a legal battle.

The Canadian government knew that our people had to live by our word, but they did not have to live by their word, this melting-pot society. The proof is all around you – the government steals land for themselves. You people do not even come close to realizing the truth at Oka. Canadian society has become subject to this conspiracy to steal land and eventually people are going to find out that it effects them very deeply.

As long as you have a judicial system that creates barriers from the natural world, then you have a barrier that keeps you in your own little bubble. Just like you sit in this class – you do not actually know what is happening on the outside. When you fall into this judicial system, you do not actually know what is happening outside in the real world. And this is what is going to effect every person in Canadian society because they are making judgments upon people, and these people do not fit within that bubble.

The spirit of those treaties was always two separate societies. In reality, there are no peers to these men in this melting-pot society. But I was wondering if you could comment on the selection of the jury. I found it phoney that there was no argument against the jury selection and that it went so fast. It seemed that you just allowed the first twelve on the list.

Answer: OWEN YOUNG

The jury selection process actually took ten days, and it is probably one of the longest in a Canadian trial. And, in fact, we were allowed challenges "for cause" which has not been done in any previous case in Canadian history. We were allowed a range of questioning that delved into political beliefs and attitudes in a way that is not permitted normally.

It is quite true that there was only one Mohawk on the jury panel, and that Mohawk asked to be excused because she felt that she might be too close to the case. If by "peers" you mean Mohawk, that is a very difficult question to which I do not know the answer. I do know from Mohawk communities that if Mohawks were on the panel, it would be likely that they held strong opinions in advance. They would likely be excluded simply because they were not able to say when they looked into their hearts that they could judge these people without bringing preconceived notions to bear.

So, after ten days, we managed to pick a jury of people that generally, to a person, said that they were sympathetic to the Mohawk position, although concerned about the method the Mohawks chose to assert their right. So if there was a bias, at least as expressed, it was in favour of the Mohawks.

Question: STUART MYLOW

I suppose that, from a non-Native point of view, you could say the jury was sympathetic. But when you talk about a jury of one's peers, you are not talking Mohawks or all Natives, you are talking about idealists – people who do not put the dollar before all things.

At Oka, there was no leader telling these people what to do, it was a collective understanding that when the natural world is attacked in such a manner, there comes a point where you have to stand up for it. So, no matter how much the jury was in favour of the Mohawks, their society has no similar idealists. People value things that are not living. They fall under policies that either have no effect on the natural world, or effects it negatively.

So from the viewpoint of the Native person, it is true what my Elders said – there is no justice whatsoever. Because when you talk about the justice that your society has created, you talk about a justice that dates back to medieval England when a woman was thrown in the water and if she did not drown, she was a witch, if she did drown, she was not a witch. From our viewpoint, it is still the same kind of system.

Answer: OWEN YOUNG

It is true that no non-Native jury could ever look into and understand the Native mind. We did not try to approach the case as a way of determining whether or not the system was a perfect justice system for Natives because that would require an entirely different effort. What we were trying to determine is whether or not the system itself could produce a result that everybody could feel was just, not perfect. But it is true that a non-Native could never so transform himself as to go into the Native mind and understand it completely, and that's a limitation that we were faced with.

LEGAL ISSUES: CONTINUING RELATIONS

MICHAEL HUDSON

Michael Hudson was, at the time of the conference, Senior Counsel, Indian Affairs and Self-Government, Legal Services, at the Department of Indian Affairs and Northern Development. He is presently Senior Counsel, Legal Services, Department of Health Canada.

CROWN FIDUCIARY DUTIES UNDER THE INDIAN ACT

When I was first contacted, the working title of this panel was "The Ties That Bind", and I cringed a little bit at that description of the *Indian Act*, appropriate though it may be. I was somewhat relieved to see the new title "Continuing Relations" as I hope that it captures the position we are in today.

It is probably an understatement to say that we are in the midst of great change in the juridical framework of the relationship between Canada's Aboriginal Peoples and Canadian society generally. The *Indian Act* is only one element of that framework handed down to us from the 19th century. Anyone who has read through the *Act* can see how it is imbued with concepts dating from an era when the Crown was viewed as being almost a parent to Indian communities.

Our society has evolved considerably in the last hundred years, as has the view and place of Aboriginal Peoples in the Canadian legal system. Nonetheless, we still work within the *Indian Act* today, although it may eventually be removed. In fact, I would be somewhat surprised if it lives out this century in its present state. Reforms to the current *Act* are being considered, and some communities have agreed to sit down with the federal government to discuss new administrative arrangements for greater control over their own affairs. There are also a number of legislative alternatives to the current *Indian Act* proposed by Indian groups across the country. Over the last few years, various committees of chiefs have met to discuss new approaches in specific areas such as land management, monies management, and of course, constitutional principles.

In the midst of these great changes, we can nonetheless recognize a key element of the relationship between the Crown and Aboriginal Peoples which has come down to us through the centuries, namely the idea of the fiduciary relationship. The concept of the fiduciary relationship was recently clarified in Supreme Court decisions such as *Guerin* and *Sparrow*, but in some ways, it is like a veil being lifted off of a concept that had always been there. When we look back through time, although Crown officials two hundred years ago may not have thought in terms of a fiduciary relationship with Aboriginal Peoples, we can in fact see that there has been an element of continuity in Crown policies. What I would like to do is examine the concept of this fiduciary relationship in the context of the *Indian Act*, although underscoring that the *Indian Act* is only one small part of the overall relationship between the Crown and Aboriginal Peoples.

In 1984, the Supreme Court of Canada in *Guerin* recognized the existence of a Crown fiduciary obligation in its dealings with Indian reserve lands. It should be remembered that throughout the 1960s, 1970s, and the early part of the 1980s, there was scarcely any debate on the existence of such an obligation, and certainly until *Guerin* was decided, this relationship was unclear. *Guerin* was thus an important milestone in Canadian legal history.

Guerin concerned a band's decision to surrender reserve lands for lease on the basis of information provided by the Department of Indian Affairs and Northern Development (DIAND). DIAND officials had withheld vital information from band members at the time they voted to surrender their lands, and the same officials also failed to follow the band's directives as expressed through the surrender vote. Not too surprisingly, the Court found that the Crown had a role of a fiduciary through the surrender process and had failed to meet that duty. As a consequence, a heavy award of damages was imposed against the Crown in favour of the band.

More recently, the same court in *Sparrow* elaborated on the fiduciary relationship in a case concerning the obligations of the Crown with respect to Aboriginal and treaty rights protected by section 35 of the *Constitution Act, 1982*. Based on *Sparrow*, we can see that the fiduciary duties acknowledged in *Guerin* are only one aspect of a broader fiduciary relationship between the Crown and Aboriginal Peoples. I like to describe this fiduciary relationship as an arch – two stones of which are *Guerin* and *Sparrow*. This arch between the Crown and Aboriginal Peoples is imbued with the duty of the Crown to act in an honourable fashion in its dealings with Aboriginal Peoples. *Guerin* and *Sparrow* are just two instances where the courts have acknowledged that such a relationship can give rise to very specific legal obligations.

The obligations in those two cases were quite distinct because of the different contexts, even though both recognize the concept of an underlying fiduciary relationship. Each calls into play duties that are appropriate to the particular situation. It is also important to note that not all the obligations between the Crown and Aboriginal Peoples are fiduciary in nature – although I tell my client, DIAND, that every single interaction that they have with an Aboriginal community must be respectful of the fiduciary relationship and ensure that the Crown is seen to be acting in an honourable fashion. A note of caution, however, is that the entire spectrum of common law rules developed in relation to fiduciaries may not be applicable to all aspects of the relationship.

A comparison with the common law trust

If we examine the *Guerin* type of fiduciary relationship, we find that is similar, but not identical to a classic trust or fiduciary obligation recognized in common law. We must begin by distinguishing the special or *sui generis* nature of the Crown's obligations to Aboriginal Peoples from that of a true trustee in common law. One important difference is that the latter relationship is based on the supposition that the beneficiary either will not or cannot handle their own affairs, such as in a trust for the benefit of a child. An Aboriginal community is obviously in a very different situation. While the courts are still struggling with the fundamental ideas of the fiduciary relationship, we see an evolution reflecting the desire and ability of Aboriginal communities to increasingly manage their own affairs.

On the other hand, there are certain elements that do come within the common law notion of a trust. A *Guerin* type of fiduciary obligation relates to those situations under the *Indian Act* where the Crown is holding the assets of a community or of an individual, controlling it through a statutory framework, and where the beneficiary cannot access the assets, at least under the current confines of the *Indian Act*. We find that under common law, the fiduciary obligation arises when three elements are present:

1. An obligation of a person, the fiduciary, to act on behalf of another, the beneficiary, who benefits from the obligation.

2. The fiduciary has sole power to effect the beneficiary's legal interests.

3. The beneficiary is vulnerable to the exercise of that power.

In the case of designations under the *Indian Act*, as in the *Guerin* context, all three elements of this test are present. Indian reserves are lands generally held by the Crown for the use and benefit of an Indian band. Under the *Indian Act*, lands can only be surrendered for sale or designated for lease by an Indian band with the approval of the Governor in Council. In addition, as was demonstrated in *Guerin*, band members are extremely vulnerable to an improper or incorrect exercise of the Crown's power.

The same elements are present in the power held by the Crown over Indian monies under the *Indian Act*, with respect to both capital funds that are held for the band as a whole and individual accounts held for individuals. As with reserve lands, these monies are held by the Queen in a consolidated revenue fund; the funds remain separate only in the sense that they are coloured by this fiduciary relationship. An Indian band can usually only access its monies with the approval of the Minister of Indian Affairs and Northern Development through mechanisms set out by the *Indian Act*. Thus, in this respect, we again see the first and the second elements of a trustee relationship. And since the Indian band is extremely vulnerable to the actions of the Minister in relation to the monies, the third element is also present.

Since the 1960s, there has been a great deal of litigation relating to the management of lands by the Crown. The last time I counted, there were well over three hundred cases against the Minister of Indian Affairs and Northern Development across the country, many in regards to alleged breaches of fiduciary obligations. The management of monies is also becoming a common element in litigation, and it could easily be a growth area for litigation in the 1990s. Again, it is not too surprising considering how much money is actually held for bands. There is approximately two billion dollars at stake – much related to specific oil-rich bands in Alberta. Therefore, the potential for claims of Crown liability is great.

How far is the Crown required to meet the obligations of a common law trustee in its dealings with Indian assets? In *Guerin*, the Supreme Court of Canada was careful to say that the Crown's obligations vis-a-vis Indians cannot be defined as a trust *per se*. This does not imply that the Crown's obligations are unenforceable, rather that its dealings with Indian lands do not amount to a trust in the private law sense. These comments are important to underscore in that it is misleading to assume that the Crown will have exactly the same duties as a true trustee at common law in its handling of Indian assets. The most significant difference, as I alluded to earlier, is that an Indian band has significant powers in relation to its own affairs. The other important difference is the general, overarching duty of the Crown to act honourably in its dealing with Aboriginal Peoples.

One comment following the first panel was that the Canadian legal system is unable to grasp concepts arising within a different juridical system and society, and has difficulty fitting them into familiar concepts of Canadian law. In the past, we have seen this difficulty in the efforts of the courts to try and translate the Indian interest in reserve lands into terms recognizable to European-trained lawyers in the nineteenth century and Euro-Canadian lawyers in this century. My sense is that we are seeing the same problem in the ongoing efforts to try and capture the fiduciary relationship between the Crown and Natives. We know it is there and are struggling to describe its attributes. Part of that process of exploration is the courts taking up the concept of the fiduciary, probably under the influence of American jurisprudence.

It will likely be many years before we see clear statements from the courts describing in a complete and comprehensive fashion the nature of these attributes. Indeed, the answers may not lie within the Canadian court system and the courts in recent years have challenged both the Crown and Aboriginal Peoples to develop the concept of the fiduciary relationship through negotiation, rather than turning to the courts for solutions. The challenge ahead is to work out these issues in a collaborative rather than confrontational manner.

YAN LAZOR

Yan Lazor is the Director of Legal Services at the Ontario Native Affairs Secretariat where he is responsible for providing legal support for land claims and self-government negotiations. Mr. Lazor also is Ontario's negotiator in the negotiations concerning the unsold surrendered Indian Reserve lands in the Bruce Peninsula. Mr. Lazor obtained his law degree from the University of Ottawa and was called to the Ontario Bar in 1979. His past work experience includes representing children in personal rights matters in all levels of court in Ontario. He has provided legal services for the Human Rights Commission and the Ministry of the Solicitor General. He was chief negotiator for Ontario in talks leading to a policing agreement between the Akwesasne community, Quebec, Canada and Ontario.

TOWARDS A NEW RELATIONSHIP BETWEEN FIRST NATIONS AND ONTARIO

I would like to focus on a recent political document, the *Statement of Political Relationship*, developed in Ontario between First Nations and the provincial government, since it is a good example of modification in the system of political and legal relations between Aboriginal and Canadian government. I would like to look at some of these changes and their practical implications. The *Statement* itself should also be of great interest to Native law scholars for the topical legal and social questions it raises. Finally, as we have heard previously in this conference, we know that we cannot leave current problems to the justice system to resolve, and I find that the *Statement* is an example of how to use political action to take some of the current problems out of the courts, and to strengthen the political will to resolve current problems cooperatively.

The major significance of the *Statement* is that it recognizes that First Nations have an inherent right to self-government. Self-government, of course, is an issue at the forefront of media attention and constitutional discussions, and a central concern to Native Peoples. The focus has been largely on entrenchment of an inherent right to self-government in the *Constitution*, however, the *Statement* is an example of how provincial relations can move in that direction.

The *Statement* came about as the result of several months of negotiations and discussions between representatives of the First Nations in Ontario and the Ontario government. It was signed by Premier Bob Rae, the Ontario Minister for Native Affairs, the Regional Chief of the Chiefs of Ontario, thirteen chiefs representing regional First Nations organizations, such as the Union of Ontario Indians, and independent First Nations, such as the Mohawks of Akwasasne. It should be noted that the *Statement* extends to all 127 First Nations represented by the Chiefs in Assembly.

The basic principles of the *Statement*

Beyond recognition of the inherent right to self-government, the *Statement* is based on five principles. The first is that the First Nations exist in Ontario as distinct nations, with their own governments, cultures, languages, traditions, customs and territories. I found a speech given by Premier Rae at an Assembly of First Nations banquet in 1990, where he spoke on the substance of this principle. The first point, which is so obvious, yet needs to be said over and over again, is that Native Peoples were here first. And that has profound implications for the relationship between and among us as fellow citizens of this country. He then went on to quote from the *Calder* case, which was one of the first breakthroughs in the Supreme Court for dealing with the idea of distinct nations in a more understanding way. Premier Rae relied on the *Calder* decision to reiterate that when the settlers came, the Indians were established societies, occupying the same land as their forefathers had done for centuries. The strength of this approach is the recognition that before Confederation in 1867, before the *Royal Proclamation* was signed in 1763, and even before European settlers arrived, societies already existed with their own systems of law and power, and that these societies negotiated with the British and French governments as they arrived.

The second principle states that the government of Ontario recognizes that its relationships with the First Nations are to be based on Aboriginal and treaty rights recognized and affirmed in the *Constitution Act, 1982* including those formally recognized in the *Royal Proclamation of 1763*, and in the treaties and agreements with the Crown. Although section 35 of the *Constitution Act, 1982* recognizes and affirms the existing Aboriginal treaty rights of the Aboriginal Peoples of Canada, namely the Indian, Inuit, and Metis Peoples of Canada, the question remains as to the content of those rights. The courts to date have not given us a comprehensive definition of Aboriginal rights. Nonetheless, we can say that there are at least two principal features. Firstly, these rights are exercised by an organized society, and secondly, the exercise of these rights is an integral part of Aboriginal life. As a general principle, Aboriginal rights arise from the cultural, social and political characteristics unique to Aboriginal Peoples.

The third principle is that Ontario's commitment to and participation in the *Statement* is subject to the limits on provincial constitutional authority, an acknowledgement of the division of powers between the federal and provincial governments provided under the *Constitution*. The *Constitution* under section 91(24) empowers the federal government with legislative authority with respect to Indians and lands reserved for Indians. However, this separation of powers should not be interpreted so as to prevent provinces from making progress in their relations with Aboriginal Peoples. The *Statement* is an example of the progress that can be made within constitutional limits.

The fourth principle is to minimize conflicts between Ontario and the First Nations. I believe that the way to accomplish this is by communicating, by sharing visions and working towards common goals. This is the direction that the *Statement* is pointing towards.

The final principle of the *Statement* is that both the First Nations and Ontario recognize the need for mutual understanding to govern relations between governments. There are three points I would like to make in regards to such a government-to-government relationship and the *Statement*. First, Ontario recognizes that First Nations exist in Ontario as distinct nations, as societies with specific territories. Second, First Nations are not recognized as special interest groups or stake-holders in the Ontario government, but as governments in their own right. Third, the *Statement* recognizes the need for further efforts to define the government-to-government relationship between Ontario and First Nations.

Certain provisions of the *Statement*

Based on these five principles, the First Nations and Ontario agreed to specific clauses, of which I will focus on the first two. The first finds that the inherent right to self-government of the First Nations flows from the Creator and the First Nations' original occupation of the land. In the second paragraph, Ontario recognizes that under the *Constitution*, the First Nations have an inherent right to self-government within the Canadian constitutional framework, and that the relationship between Ontario and the First Nations must be based upon a respect for this right. The question, of course, as to the nature of an inherent right to self-government remains for Aboriginal Peoples and other Canadians to resolve.

At this point in time, we are able to distinguish the source of such a right and its content. The source reflects a view of history respecting the arrival of Europeans to North America and the pre-existence of organized societies governing the continent. Does this imply that the right to self-government and whatever it encompasses does not depend on federal or provincial endorsement or authority? The actual content or meaning of "inherent right" will probably be determined through the course of negotiations and through the constitutional discussion process. If not, it likely will be determined in Ontario through discussions between the Ontario government and the First Nations.

The *Statement* also provides that the First Nations in Ontario – involving the Government of Canada where appropriate – are committed, to facilitating the further articulation, exercise and implementation of the inherent right to self-government within the Canadian constitutional framework through the respect of existing treaty relationships and through the various means acceptable to First Nations and Ontario, such as treaty-making or constitutional and legislative reform. The *Statement* thus recognizes that the further articulation, exercise and implementation of the inherent right to self-government within the Canadian constitutional framework may require constitutional and legislative reform. Implicit in this recognition is the view that one does not have to wait for the courts to make judicial pronouncements and that we are able to look at other means to further develop government-to-government relations. For example, we have a round table process underway in Ontario, where representatives of the Ontario government and the First Nations meet with respect to issues relating to the constitutional discussions on the inherent right to self-government. Closely related are other issues dealt within the *Statement*, such as accountability, funding, priority setting, third party interests, and on and off reserve matters. Finally, the *Statement* also clearly establishes that it shall not be construed as determining Ontario's jurisdiction or diminishing Canada's responsibility towards First Nations. It is an expression of the political commitment of the First Nations and Ontario and as such it provides direction rather than legal solutions.

The influence of the *Statement* on intitiatives and negotiations within Ontario

Ontario would like to see the inherent right to self-government entrenched in the *Constitution*. However, with or without constitutional amendment, the *Statement* will affect a wide range of negotiations including Native harvesting agreements, Native commercial fishing, tripartite education negotiations, Aboriginal family violence strategies, First Nations policing agreements and arrangements, Whitefish Bay self-government negotiations, and land claim negotiations, to name just a few.

There are also justice initiatives agreed to by both the First Nations and the province, such as a pilot project with the Attawapiskat First Nation, a community located on the north-west coast of James Bay. It is a community-based justice initiative, whereby an Elders' panel chosen by the chief and band council sits to hear cases diverted to it by the provincial court in Ontario and by the justice of the peace following consultation with the Crown attorney and project coordinator. The hearings before the Elders are entirely in Cree, without the intervention of a prosecutor or defence counsel. The Elders also have a panel which acts as an advisory sentencing panel to the provincial court presiding at Attawapiskat.

Another example is the Sandy Lake First Nation justice project, which is again a community-based justice initiative. In this project there is also an Elders' panel, selected by the chief and council, that sits as an advisory sentencing panel to the provincial court judge and justice of the peace when presiding in Sandy Lake. The Elders are also involved in both pre-trial and post-trail counselling, working particularly with young people. The Sandy Lake First Nation is in north-western Ontario.

Another matter I would like to speak about is Akwasasne. Akwasasne is a community located in Ontario, Quebec, and in the state of New York. I was Ontario's negotiator for the negotiations concerning the Akwasasne policing agreement involving the governments of Akwasasne, Quebec, Canada, and Ontario. Grand Chief Mike Mitchell impressed upon me (and he can be a very impressive person) early in the negotiations that Akwasasne is a unique community. For example, the average Canadian is generally subject to three sets of laws: municipal, provincial, and federal laws. The residents of Akwasasne are subject to Akwasasne Mohawk council bylaws, to the by-laws of the American Tribal

Council, and to the Great Law of Peace. They are also subject to New York State Law, United States federal law, Quebec provincial law, Ontario provincial law and Canadian federal law.

The Akwasasne policing agreement is between the governments of Akwasasne, Quebec, Canada, and Ontario. An explicit goal is the eventual transfer of policing responsibility to Akwasasne. In order to ensure that it was truly a document by and for the Akwasasne community, a lot of time was spent listening to people from the community. We heard the priorities: a sound police force, law and order in the community, and responsibility and accountability in the police force. The agreement was struck in such a way that Akwasasne now controls certain portions of policing and will eventually take total control over the course of subsequent agreements. Following the signing of the agreement, a multi-jurisdictional policing committee met regularly at Akwasasne to share information and to talk about policing problems. It has listened to concerns of the Akwasasne people and has looked at ways of dealing with policing and prevention. Akwasasne saw this project as an historic event, since all governments concerned had representatives from their policing agencies participate in this committee, something that had never happened before. This committee included representatives from the Ontario Provincial Police, the R.C.M.P., the Sureté du Québec, the F.B.I., the New York State troopers, the Mohawk police of Akwasasne, the American Tribal Council, and other agencies. The committee was an expression of the commitment of all these parties to work together to improve policing. Although the Akwasasne agreement was negotiated prior to the signing of the *Statement*, it illustrates that parties can and should work cooperatively towards self-government even in unique and complex communities.

In terms of the *Statement*, it is clear that it has had, and will continue to have, an impact on how the province of Ontario deals with First Nations, in light of the fact that it recognizes a government-to-government relationship and the inherent right to self-government of First Nations. It is no longer a relationship reflecting delegated federal authority under the *Indian Act*.

Comment: STUART MYLOW
Mohawk of Kahnawake

You know, it is amazing how you people with all this education, you seem to think that we do not understand what you are doing. The *Royal Proclamation of 1763* is supposed to be very simple, and yet it seems that you do not understand the rights it gives. There is supposed to be a Governor General representing the Queen – this is the person that is supposed to make sure you people conduct yourself in the proper manner. But how can he when he has been appointed by your Parliament over here? In other words, they do the bidding and he carries everything out.

I can see there are people becoming honest. What I have been seeking up to this day is the truth. But what these students are learning here today is how to be hypocritical. You people continue to mislead these youngsters. They may be young, but I do not think they are stupid. We have got to wake up to reality and your reality is scheming to get land away from the Natives. You have no desire to do the right thing. You find every legal loophole by twisting up all the words. "Who's the smarter lawyer?" This is the way you people are playing. So these students better find knowledge elsewhere because what they hear here is two-faced and only beneficial to the government. The real facts are not at their disposal.

For example, I did not hear you refer to the traditional government. You spoke of First Nations but they do not represent the people. They are paid officials of the federal and provincial government. You mentioned Mike Mitchell; however, the tribal council has no right to the territory of the Five Nations. Anyone that accepts the dictates of the Canadian government, according to our law, alienates themselves from the territory and the people.

Question: JEREMY WEBBER
Professor, McGill Faculty of Law

I would like to ask Michael Hudson or Yan Lazor to comment on the notion of a government to government relationship. There is, as was suggested, a fundamental contest over whether the governments with whom Ontario is dealing are the legitimate representatives of Aboriginal Peoples. Have you wrestled with that issue?

Answer: YAN LAZOR

It is an issue that we are definitely aware of. When I was speaking about my experience in Akwasasne, I indicated that the people in Akwasasne are subject to three sets of laws: the Mohawk council by-laws, the laws of the American Tribal Council, and the traditional law which is the Great Law of Peace. Therefore, we recognize that traditional law has an important role to play.

The *Statement of Political Relationship* is a joint document – not Ontario's own document, nor a unilateral document. One hundred and twenty-seven First Nations from across Ontario, who are bands within the meaning of the *Indian Act*, took part in its drafting through regional governments, although some are dealt with on an independent basis. These communities are exploring the issue of traditional government and other forms of government. The key point, therefore, is that the issue of representation must be worked out within the Native community since it is certainly not something that the Ontario government or the federal government can impose.

Question: JEREMY WEBBER

Were the traditionalists involved in the negotiations as well or were you simply dealing with band council representatives?

Answer: YAN LAZOR

I really do not have the information to answer that question. We were dealing with representatives of the First Nations as I have defined it, and that includes the chiefs of Ontario which speak for the First Nations of Ontario.

Answer:

I would like to add that it would be presumptuous for us to comment on whether certain chiefs or councils are representative of a particular community – that is for the community to decide. I am more concerned with how community members wish to handle their assets – whether money or land. The *Indian Act* does recognize the potential for a dichotomy between the band council and the community itself when it insists, for example, that the surrender or designation of land be made on the basis of a community vote. Since the asset is held in trust by the Crown for the members of the community, it is appropriate to seek their views on what should be done with that asset.

Similar mechanisms are in place for comprehensive land claim agreements, for which communities exchange their claims to title for specific rights set out in the agreement. Again, the government turns to the membership of the collectivity to ratify the overall agreement and indicate their approval of the exchange, rather than simply depending on the representatives, who have negotiated the settlement on behalf of that collectivity.

I would also like to comment that the issue of representativeness is not unique to the Native-Crown relationship. In fact, you could raise the same question for any government – how representative are they of their people?

Question: JEREMY WEBBER

When you do have an expression of the collectivity through a referendum of the band members, for example, to what extent does that exhaust the Crown's fiduciary obligation? Is it appropriate to second guess the memberships' expression within Indian Affairs?

Answer:

No, there is no second guessing of the members' views. However, Indian Affairs officials must seek assurances that the decision of the community is on the basis of fully informed consent. While it would be unusual today to find a situation where Crown officials are capable of tricking a community into surrendering land, we still need assurances that the community knows what it is voting on, has had a reasonable amount of time to consider the choices, and has made a fully informed decision. Depending on the significance of the deal, we would also want assurances that the community has had access to independent legal advice, and where appropriate, independent financial advisers.

Question: JUDY BALK

I am just an interested observer with no legal experience. I do not think that I would like to live in Akwasasne, where so many levels of government having something to say about how their community is policed – the committee seems to be made up of so many people other than themselves. You gave quite a long list of representatives, and their own people seem outnumbered. How do they feel about that?

I would also like to know why the Canadian public is so poorly informed about Native Peoples – the public does not understand that the First Nations are not a part of Canada, and that they should be self-governed, taking care of their own land and health programs. How did we get to the point where we are so totally misinformed – and now we are being told that this "inch by inch" progress should satisfy us. Satisfy who? Some of us? It does not satisfy me.

Answer: YAN LAZOR

The multi-jurisdictional policing committee is an initiative that came from Akwasasne to bring together all of the policing agencies already involved in policing Akwasasne to share their concerns and to seek solutions for multi-jurisdictional policing problems. As I have already mentioned, it involved the Mohawk police of Akwasasne, the Akwasasne police commission, the American Tribal Council, and the traditional Mohawk government. So there was a lot of participation from Akwasasne. Akwasasne wrote-up their annual report on the multi-jurisdictional policing committee with the comment that the committee was not only worthwhile, but also historic. The basic advantage is the opportunity for communication – people come together to talk and to listen to each other's concerns. I believe that the committee, in those terms, is working quite well.

Question: JUDY BALK

Does it seem like a step forward because in the past we have made so little progress? I have sat in on a number of these conferences over the past two or three year and it has been an amazing education but I still feel terribly uninformed. Perhaps if I were a Mohawk, I would feel every bit as upset and confrontational. I find the situation of ignorance quite unbelievable and I wonder why we have been so poorly educated in our own history or why our leaders still give us the kind of responses we hear in the media.

Answer: YAN LAZOR

A lot of people share your frustration both within government and within Aboriginal communities. I am not making an apology. There is a lot of history to undo, three or four hundred years of history, and it is not a relationship that you change in ten years or even a lifetime.

If it is any consolation, if we look at where we are today, and compare that to where we were thirty years ago, there has been a fundamental change in the attitude of policy-makers within government.

Question: JUDY BALK

Because of the Native Peoples' absolutely confrontational attitude?

Answer: YAN LAZOR

Again, if we have come this far in thirty years, I am hopeful that we will go even further in the next ten or fifteen years.

Question: CARL TRUDEAU

Ma question s'adresse peut-être plus particulièrement au représentant du gouvernement de l'Ontario. J'aimerais savoir plus concrètement ce que implique en réalité le document: the *Statement*. Le gouvernement fédéral, et aussi le gouvernement québécois, parlent d'un gouvernement autonome, d'autonomie politique également. Autrement-dit, en quoi la politique du gouvernement de l'Ontario se distingue de la politique fédérale ou de la politique québécoise? Concrètement, ici au Québec, il y a un problème politique entre les Mohawks de Kahnawake et le gouvernement du Québec.

Les Mohawks de Kahnawake ne tiennent pas à ce que la Sûreté du Québec ait autorité sur les "Peacekeepers". Le gouvernement du Québec croit le contraire et même à un moment donné a dénoncé le gouvernement fédéral pour avoir financé les "Peacekeepers" et a dénoncé le fait que les Peacekeepers ne relevaient pas du Ministère de la justice.

Concrètement, en Ontario, est-ce que ça signifie – ce principe-là – que la police provinciale de l'Ontario, n'aurait plus de juridiction sur les polices amérindiennes dans les réserves. Est-ce que, par exemple, si vous êtes devant un problème semblable à celui qui existe à Kahnawake, est-ce que votre position politique ferait en sorte que vous adopteriez une autre position que celle du gouvernement du Québec présentement?

Answer: MICHAEL HUDSON

Est-ce que la question est sur l'administration de la police de Akwasasne qui travaille avec l'O.P.P. ou sur les Mohawks de Akwasasne?

Question: CARL TRUDEAU

Est-ce que vous accepteriez, au niveau du gouvernement de l'Ontario, que le Ministère de la justice n'aurait plus juridiction sur un territoire indien en Ontario? Est-ce que vous accepteriez ça?

Translation: JEREMY WEBBER

For the benefit of anglophones, the question is what distinguishes the position of the Ontario government from that of the Quebec government. For example, with respect to policing services: does it mean that the Ontario government would take a very different position with respect to the jurisdiction of the Ontario provincial police over Indian reserves? In Quebec, although some autonomy has been given to the Peace Keepers on the Kahnawake reserve, the Sûreté still retains jurisdiction over Indian lands.

Answer: MICHAEL HUDSON

His question is complex because it is comparative. The Akwasasne policing agreement, which involves Quebec, was negotiated prior to the *Statement of Political Relationship*, and points in the direction of greater responsibility and accountability. In other words, we anticipated that Akwasasne would gradually take more control over policing, which meant developing appropriate mechanisms, such as an operating police commission, which they now have, and mechanisms for financial accountability.

Question: STEEL JOHN

When the *Indian Act* came in, the people of Kahnawake were against it. When the government man came down to Kahnawake, my grandfather told me that eight were for it, and the rest of the people were against it. But when the government man went back to Ottawa, he said the majority wanted the *Indian Act*, and only eight were against it. So, how can we trust the government man in Kahnawake? How can we trust the provincial government or the provincial police? Remember what happened in 1972, what happened in 1979, and what happened in Kanesatake.

As far as I am concerned, the people in Kahnawake and places like Akwasasne were never really organized. They had no police. They did not even know what your word "organized" meant. But the people of Oklahoma learned how to "organize" and they went further than anybody thought they could. Today, like them, we have our own police, but Ryan says that we need the protection of the provincial police. I think he is full of it. We do not want help from those people because we do not forget how the harassment in 1972 and in 1979 hurt all the people of Kahnawake, and still hurts us right down here. Back in 1979, when the provincial police made trouble for us, we called on the federal government and they told us they had no jurisdiction. Now, we ask them, "What are you doing over here?" and they answer, "We have jurisdiction". How can we believe them when one day they do not, but when they feel like it, they do? That is the mentality of these government people – and that is what the people of Kahnawake, Akwasasne, and Kanesatake do not care for. So, when Ryan comes along and says that we have to be trained by the provincial forces, we ask him to teach his own people how to respect our people. As far as I am concerned, our police protect us, not the provincial or the federal police.

The mentality I am speaking about also describes what is said to the Canadian public. For instance, the newspapers only described one side of the crisis at Kanesatake. The papers would not write about the other side, which was honest and true. I was interviewed about seven times during the crisis but nothing I said was put in the papers or on television. Maybe because I hit them below the belt, but I had to say what was true. The newspapers said that the people of Kahnawake were only looking for war. We do not want to fight, but neither do we step back when someone attacks us. The provincial government knows that and the federal government knows that.

There are many things I would like to say to the Canadian people. We are human beings like anybody else. It hurts. I have been called to go to many places around this country to speak about what has happened at Kahnawake and Kanesatake, and I hear how the Mohawks are spoken of. When I was young, the books told me that the Five Nations were bad. Now, we make our own books, and we talk with people of all the nations, not just the Five Nations, since all of us have a part of this world. Still, when I look in the newspapers, I see nothing on the Five Nations. All they talk about is the Assembly of First Nations, the band council, or the chiefs. The Five Nations are over five thousand years old – the Assembly of First Nations is only about fifteen years old, yet, they want to control all of the People. That is not right. We, the Five Nations, feel that they do not represent us and that they have never represented us. What use are their treaties? The band council is controlled by the government through money. So is the First Nations. They are not controlled by the people. They are going to go down – I honestly believe that the Creator Himself will fix that. Because the honest truth is that the First Nations do not act from the heart. No, not from the heart. They act from what they think people should get. They do not listen to the people.

The Five Nations comes from the people, the people themselves. Before any chief can go out and speak, he has to get the answers from the people. He cannot say more or less than that. He has to do what the people tell him to do. That is not how the band council operates. And so I say to the band council, get out!

PANEL THREE
MODELS FOR CHANGE

MURRAY KLIPPENSTEIN

Murray Klippenstein is a partner in the firm of Iler, Campbell, in Toronto and has practiced mainly in the field of litigation, with an emphasis on First Nations groups, non-profit and community organizations, and environmental groups. He has assisted various First Nations and Aboriginal organizations in political and corporate matters and in negotiations on claims settlement and self-government.

CO-MANAGEMENT: SHARING THE LAND

The topic "Co-management: Sharing the Land" speaks to an issue of justice in a different way than politics or law. "Sharing the land" is a phrase we hear quite often, and I would like to explore and give content to it. However, part of the discussion depends on the notion of group rights or collective rights, which remains a topic of vigorous debate. The dominant liberal democratic political ideology has particular difficulty with the concept. I believe that group rights are crucial to understanding First Nations and my discussion assumes that such rights do exist.

Further, I am more interested in talking about relationships than rights, and so I focus on a way of structuring relationships between groups called co-management. Co-management is based on cooperation between groups rather than competition, and a structured relationship rather than unstructured. It is an important topic since the relationships between groups, including First Nation groups and others, are being reconstituted in major ways from constitutional negotiations to everyday bureaucratic encounters.

Co-management and similar ideas are relevant at all points in the spectrum of such relationships.

What is co-management? Co-management is participatory joint decision-making in which two or more political communities share the management of natural resources by means of a specific institution. It is a way of sharing power and responsibility. For the present, a co-management institution typically consists of a committee with mixed representation. An example might be a committee of six members, with three members appointed by a First Nation group, two by the federal government, and one by the provincial government. That committee might work on management of wildlife and fishing, through information gathering and control of access by the allocation of hunting, fishing and trapping licenses.

An important function of co-management is bringing together traditional and scientific knowledge, as well as traditional and state resource management methods. Co-management committees attempt to combine these very different, and sometimes oppositional approaches. Another common feature of a co-management system is preferential or exclusive access to resources, thereby limiting harvesting to certain territories or species in the interest of conservation.

Some concrete examples of co-management are found under the *James Bay and Northern Quebec Agreement*, which has a Hunting Fishing and Trapping Coordinating Committee with representatives from the Cree, the Inuit, the Naskapi, the provincial government, and the federal government. Other examples are found under the *Inuvialuit Final Agreement*, which has both a wildlife management and a fisheries joint management committee composed of representatives for the Aluit, Canada, and the North-West Territories. A final example is the Temagami stewardship council. In spite of litigation between Ontario and the Temagami at Bear Island, on-going negotiations have led to the establishment of a stewardship council equally comprised of members appointed by the First Nation and the provincial government. One significant agreement was that no forestry licenses would be granted without the approval of this joint committee.

Some advantages and disadvantages to co-management

Both advantages and disadvantages have resulted from existing co-management systems. An important advantage is the creation of a formal and recognized role for traditional harvesting knowledge. The people who live on the land and know the land are recognized as being a unique source of knowledge. Another advantage, which I would like to emphasize, is that the co-management structure establishes a continuing relationship, in which negotiations and discussions can take place. Regular meetings of the different groups create opportunities to discuss issues of mutual concern, and in such a structure, the groups can search for mutually advantageous solutions to problems. More discussion quite simply increases the chances that the groups can discover mutually advantageous routes or solutions which otherwise they would not have the time to discover.

Another element of a continuing relationship is that theoretically you can build trust between the individuals involved in the process. You know that the last time you worked together, the other person promised to do X and followed through by actually doing X, therefore you trust her to do Y if she promises it. You also know that even if a concession on a particular issue is made, the other side may reciprocate by making a concession on another issue in the future. It is true that there are certain elements of game theory in my examples, since we can observe patterns in the way people approach collective decision-making.

Although these theoretical advantages sometimes become real advantages, co-management institutions that have already been established have definitely not been optimal for achieving these goals. For a number of reasons, I would say that they have been an interim step. First, they usually arise as a solution to a crisis, such as when the wildlife or the resource is almost depleted, and the pressure to resolve the crisis is extreme. It may also be the result of a political crisis, such as the Temagami stewardship council, which arose in response to land claim litigation. When the process is initiated as an ad hoc solution to a crisis, there are bound to be serious limitations.

Second, co-management committees often rely upon delegated authority from the federal or provincial government, and have little autonomy. Indeed, most present co-management institutions only have an advisory function, so that the concerned minister is under no obligation to implement their recommendations. This indicates a lack of real power in the co-management structure.

One study of co-management structures under the *James Bay Agreement* identifies some of these concerns. The participants criticize the fact that government representatives are generally at a low level in their bureaucracy. They also complain that there is not enough reliable data on wildlife, nor the funds to generate data. They say that there is too much travel for Native participants, and that it is often awkward and ill-timed. The diversity of languages involved makes large meetings difficult, and the meeting format alienates the hunters and trappers on the committee.

My own experience is that an attempt at co-management of resources often becomes adversarial. This is partly due to the fact that the context is usually one of crisis. For example, in a proposal for an open-pit mine in a traditional hunting territory, there was the initial difficulty of bringing together the necessary First Nation participants for a series of meetings. On top of that, the serious lack of data led to the suspicion that the truth was being hidden. Native Peoples felt that they had a deep concern, and all they were receiving were bland assurances that the mine would not be a problem, yet, there was no data to back up that claim. In the end, we came to a seemingly satisfactory solution. When I last spoke with the ministry official, he said, "Well, you know, it was tough. Hopefully we have learned something. We are all new at this game. So, hopefully next time we can do it better." Frankly, I am not sure what will happen in the future.

Co-management as cooperation

Moving away from a description of existing co-management institutions, I would like to focus again on an aspect I mentioned earlier, namely that co-management is an example of cooperation between groups with collective rights, for their mutual benefit. When you examine the political landscape, there are very few political institutions which are set up for that type of on-going relationship. Basic constitutional and political structures, such as the fundamental division of powers between federal and provincial governments, are based on a system of parallel, independent, and exclusive powers. There is no national institution for dealing with conflict between governments exercising their respective powers. It is just not something that is built into our system of government. An interesting part of the *Meech Lake Accord* was that it sought to institutionalize an annual meeting of first ministers in an attempt to move beyond total separation of powers.

Beyond that general observation, I have identified a common fallacy, which I call the "the self-government fallacy". When we talk about relationships, particularly between governments, there seems to be an assumption that the only issue is defining the rights assigned to the group. Once we lock into place that particular regime of assigned rights, we will simply negotiate or work on the basis of those assigned rights. There is little or no discussion of how the groups will inter-relate in the future. Nor do we do consider the structure as a relationship. We assign rights and then "let the machine go".

The future relationship between groups is a crucial issue. There seems to be a shared assumption that, all things being equal, self-government will be advantageous to Native groups. However, the qualifier "all things being equal" is important. Greater self-government for one group does not necessarily result in better relationships between that group and other groups. In fact, it is possible that greater self-government for one group might worsen relationships and have the net result of making the overall situation worse. This "fallacy of self-government" is usually overlooked, and should be addressed when looking at future relationships.

When I talk about co-operation between groups and the use of co-management techniques, I do not mean to ignore the importance of a competitive relationship, or of collective rights. There will be times when co-operation is not fruitful, and litigation or forms of political pressure are necessary. In these instances, rights held by the group can be important, such as in the litigation over the *James Bay Agreement* on the necessity of a joint environmental assessment. That dispute arose from specific provisions in the *Agreement* which said, "There will be a federal assessment; there will be a provincial assessment; and if all three parties, including the Crees, agree, those assessments can be joined". Although this provision clearly opened the way to co-operation, it did not materialize because of what you might call "duplicity" on the part of the federal government. Thus, the rights held by the parties according to their agreement became crucial.

If we are to use existing co-management institutions as models of change in the future, we must therefore be aware of the difficulties they have faced. Speaking from experience rather than theoretical knowledge, I have observed that co-management institutions are rarely equipped to deal with conflict between major uses, such as conflict between harvesting and resource extraction. These conflicts are fundamental, yet it is unclear how a co-management committee could handle them, although we have somehow managed to deal with them up to now. For example, in one committee, the conflict was between mining and harvesting rights. As a litigator, I was obliged to focus on ways of stopping the mine, whereas the wisdom of some of the chiefs and trappers was to look at the actual proposal. It turned out to be an area that was not heavily harvested, so in practical terms, the loss was minimal. The length of time involved in the ore sampling activity would be relatively short and with limited impact, although still significant. In the end, we agreed to let it proceed on certain conditions.

Another practical problem with co-management is timing. A government body will often want to move quickly when it is presented with a particular problem, whereas the First Nation members want to consult their community. Related to this is the importance of consensus decision-making. In a study of James Bay co-management committees, it was found that a First Nations chairperson would operate on consensus, and therefore decisions were made more slowly. When the chairperson was non-Aboriginal, decisions were made more quickly by the use of a majority vote, but dissatisfaction resulted among certain members.

Are co-management models of any use? One of the fundamental problems of asking such a question is that it can only be answered by actual experience. Each continuing relationship must deal with its conflicts through negotiations and meetings. However, the alternative to co-management may be major confrontation, which again requires some form of conflict resolution. I believe, therefore, that a co-management relationship has long-term benefits for groups attempting to live together and share the land.

FRANÇOIS ROBERT

François Robert is a lawyer practicing in Aboriginal, environmental and municipal law. He previously worked for the legal services of the Grand Council of the Crees (of Quebec) / Cree Regional Authority.

A CREE SYSTEM OF JUSTICE: IMPLEMENTING CHANGE IN THE JUSTICE SYSTEM

Although the title of this conference is "Justice for Natives?", I suggest, based on my experience of working with the Cree in the North, that a more appropriate title would have been "No Justice for Natives". We must be concerned when we hear the former Minister of Justice, Kim Campbell, state that there will be no separate justice systems for the Native Peoples of Canada. The use of the word "separate", after all, raises a question of degree, much like "distinct" in "distinct society". Indeed, the federal government and Quebec have already agreed to a separate or distinct justice system for the Cree in the 1975 *James Bay and Northern Quebec Agreement*. In fact, sections 18 and 19 of the *James Bay Agreement* reflect a commitment from governments of Canada and Quebec to adapt the justice system to the Cree way of life and customary values.

I will review in this paper the recent history of the Cree justice system and a Cree justice project undertaken by Carol Laprairie, Jean-Paul Brodeur, and Roger McDonnell as the basis for a discussion of models of change. I will then continue with some thoughts on introducing change into the justice system.

In the 1970s, the Crees had their traditional lands flooded for hydro-electric projects, and now in the 1990s, the warning bells are ringing again. The twelve years that followed the signature in 1975 of the *James Bay Agreement* between the Cree, the Inuit, Quebec, and Canada were marked by frustrated attempts by the Crees to implement the provisions of the treaty. Consequently, in 1987, the Cree decided to hold a summit on a Cree system of justice in Mistissini, Quebec, with the participation of all interested parties. The consensus reached at the summit was that the justice system for the Cree was a failure.

The recommendations of the task force for a Cree system of justice

The Cree chiefs then appointed a task force to draft a proposal for a Cree system of justice. The task force consulted with the Cree bands throughout 1989 and their proposal was accepted at the Cree Nation annual general assembly in 1990. The document was based on a systemic approach, in which all components of the justice system were taken into account, as well as the effects of an action taken by one component of the system on another component. In order to further expand from the proposal, the Cree chiefs initiated a research study under an interchange program with the Department of Justice Canada. Dr. Carol Laprairie thus worked for the Grand Council of the Crees (Quebec), taking a year and a half to complete her work, and was later guided by Dr. Jean-Paul Brodeur and Roger McDonell.

The research is divided into three parts. The first part is a study of interviews, court data and police records in Cree communities. The second part consists of an analysis of the Cree police system, which is defined and empowered by the *James Bay Agreement*. The final part examines Cree customary values as they relate to justice. The studies' main recommendations include the following:

1. There should be an increase in police manpower to reflect a more appropriate level of services required by the community.

2. The career prospects for police must be up-graded to improve the morale of the police force.

3. An extensive public education campaign on police and justice matters should be undertaken.

4. There should be continuing education and training for Cree police.

5. Cree constables should not be provided with a side-arm (a contentious issue among the police force because some want to wear a side-arm while others do not).

6. Consideration should be given to the appointment of community relation officers in each community to act as messengers, negotiators, and mediators between individuals in cases of conflict.

7. In each community, there should be a panel designated as the Community Justice Authority composed of three or more individuals selected by the community to make decisions on local disputes. Elders or people familiar with

Cree customs could sit on these panels. The jurisdiction would be determined by the communities.

8. The position of Justices of the Peace could be incorporated into the local justice authorities with clearly defined roles and responsibilities. The Community Justice Authority of each community could receive a mandate to perform police performance assessment, where they could evaluate the police work.

9. Two circuit lay courts should be in place; one for coastal and one for inland communities. They would be composed of members of each local community justice Authority. The existing itinerant court should be maintained for serious indictable offenses, which the community has considered too problematic to handle locally. The itinerant courts and community courts must have available a range of dispositional options which are more relevant, acceptable, and effective than those that are in force today. Intermediate sanctions could be selected and used. For the well-being of the communities, it is important to form priority prosecution that is adopted for dealing with persistent, repeat offenders, who are not involved in offenses of a serious or semi-serious nature.

10. The itinerant court judges should be fluent in English, and English should be spoken at all times, unless Cree is required and requested by the accused. Presently, the crown attorney, the judge, and council for the defence often speak in French when discussing a legal question, and in English when addressing the witnesses, which is then translated into Cree.

11. Legal education should be an integral part the school curriculum.

12. The lack of options for the victim must be remedied, but the solution must be based on what the community feels useful.

With these recommendations in hand, further consultations took place with the Cree bands in order for them to identify the problem and propose pilot projects suited to their particular needs. It is apparent that these recommendations will lead to greater control by the Crees of their government.

Any major change to a complex system such as the justice system requires motivation from everyone involved in order to overcome the initial reluctance to depart from familiar procedures. We must therefore understand the dynamics of that change, so that we can plan the charge accordingly.

The components of change

The task of implementing change in the justice system involves many organizations. The most important parties are: the Cree bands, their members, the Band Councils, the Cree Regional Authority, the Grand Council of the Crees (of Quebec), the Cree Trappers Association, the Cree Health Board and Social Services, the Cree School Board, the Federal and Provincial Departments of Justice, the Public Security Department, the Solicitor General of Canada, and the Department of Indian Affairs. All of these organizations can be seen as part of a mechanism that takes input and transforms it into output. In the context of a Cree justice system, the transformation process is composed of inputs such as the facts concerning a particular case, the legislation, the *James Bay Agreement*, Cree custom, the Cree legislators, the federal and provincial legislators, jurisprudence, procedure, personnel, lay judges, lawyers, court clerks, and the administration. All of these inputs in a justice system are interdependent and together lead to the output, namely a panel or court decision. From the perspective of the transformation process of an organization, we will analyze the implementation of change in the justice system. We must first look to the major components of any organization. The components are: its tasks, the individuals who will perform these tasks, their formal arrangements (structures, processes, and systems), and their informal arrangements (communication, power, influence, culture, and values). Each of these four components interact in a delicate balance.

So, how can we implement change in a system of justice? The transition between the status quo and the proposed future state is critical and must be managed carefully. It is important to remember the expectations of each organizations involved in the process. All this must also be accomplished without undue cost to either the organizations or the individuals. Although transitions cannot always be managed systematically, guidelines can constructively help implement change. As these changes occur, new and different types of organizational control will be needed to replace mechanisms that have become irrelevant. During the transition period, there will also be changes in the power structure that must be addressed. Each of these concerns will need special attention in order to increase the probability of success.

It is clear that the Cree have concluded that the present justice system in the North is a failure. The Courts and the Department of Justice have not expressed their dissatisfaction as clearly, but I am convinced are also frustrated by the present system. One solution to address the delicately balanced input during the transition period is to ensure that adequate salaries encourage participation and recruitment of Crees in the new system. Another one is to develop a transition plan and have it implemented by a manager or justice coordinator. For the Cree, the transition plan is to use the recommendations of the research study and to let the community develop their own solutions. Another important element to the success of the system is to develop feedback mechanisms to keep the right balance. For example, the local judges will have to report to the Cree government as well as to the federal or provincial government to ensure that the decisions rendered are harmonious with the well-being of the community and are enforceable outside the Cree system. Finally, leadership will play a key role in overcoming resistance to change and in generating support for the new justice system. Leaders are great symbols and creators. Their use symbols and language can contribute to the successful implementation of change in the justice system. Further, in the turbulence of change, people seek stability in a number of ways, including the anchor that leaders can represent.

In conclusion, some aspects of this analysis may seem self-evident, but we need to return to these basic elements to sort through the great difficulties we face. The implementation of change to a system such as the justice system involves many organizations, each having its own distinct culture. It is indeed a great challenge and a unique opportunity to implement major changes in a system of justice, and we can but hope that it will benefit to the northern justice system.

LEROY LITTLE BEAR

Associate Professor, Department of Native American Studies, University of Lethbridge

AN INDEPENDENT NATIVE JUDICIARY

Shakespeare once said that if you want change, first of all, kill off all the lawyers. I could leave you with that thought, but I would like to talk about a couple things. Toby Morantz spoke to you about the judiciary as anthropologists. My talk could be titled, "The Judiciary as Philosophers", or another thought that came into my mind was simply to call the talk "Don't Underestimate the Difference".

Let me start by sharing some stories with you. One time, I was talking to this elder on a reserve. I was wearing a watch, and when I am wearing a watch, I have a very bad habit of looking at it. And you know, he noticed me looking at it. He said, "Are you in a hurry? Have you got something to do?" And I said, "No, it's a nice day; I've got all day." And he says, "What do you keep looking at your watch for?" And I replied, "Oh, I just want to find out what time it is." And he says, "No, that's not true. You're looking at your time to find out what time it isn't!" And I did not know what he was getting at, so I asked him, "What do you mean?" And he says, "Well, to a large extent, you've adopted the white way of thinking about time. You look at your watch to find out what time it isn't. Like in the morning you say: it isn't eight o'clock – I got time for another cup of coffee. Because if it was eight o'clock you'd be at work, wouldn't you? You look at your time to say: hey, it isn't coffee break yet, I can push another piece of paper across the desk. Because if it was ten o'clock, you know, you'd be taking your break, wouldn't you?"

You know, he caught me off guard, so I said, "Well, what about you? You're wearing a watch." And he was. And he says, "Well, me, I don't have no schedule to follow. There's some things I want to do around my house, my little cabin, but I'm the one, you know, that really wears the watch to find out what time it is."

That leads to another story about the notion of time. I need to give you a little bit of background for this. Some of you may have heard of or visited the Smith Hashton Buffalo Jump, a United Nations heritage site in southern Alberta, where I'm from. Well, it seems that in the minds of anthropologists, buffalo jumps are the only way of hunting buffalo by Plains Indians, but in fact that's not true. It was only one way of hunting, and there were other ways. The Plains Indians were very practical people, and as you all know, being out on the plains, there wasn't always a cliff handy. So, the Indians, for instance, used to chase buffalo into gumbos and sloughs where the buffalo would get stuck, and then they would come after them.

Well, one of the Elders on my reserve – his name was Long Jim, because he was a big, tall, lanky guy like Too Tall Jones – was being asked by these young punks, "Hey, Long Jim, how old are you? When were you born?" And he didn't think that was very important, so he didn't really bother to answer them. But they were persistent and they kept asking him, "How old are you? When were you born?" Finally, he kind of mumbled under his breath, "Oh, well, they wouldn't understand." And so he told them, "Well, you want to know when I was born. Do you remember the last time we got the buffalo stuck? I was born the Wednesday before."

A look at some underlying assumptions

I tell you these stories because they serve as very important indicators of a very different way of looking at the world. The problem with the justice system is that everybody is trying to make these little fine tunings, here and there, hoping that it will accommodate Aboriginal Peoples and some of the problems they have with the justice system. When in reality, those minor, fine tunings of the system are not going to lead anywhere. Why? Because, if you were to look at the existing justice system, if you were able to just step back outside of it for a while and look at it objectively, you would find a whole bunch of unarticulated assumptions and presumptions underlying the system. These are the things we take for granted. Sometimes those unarticulated beliefs are so accepted that it's hard for somebody like a lawyer or a judge to even think that anybody could look at justice in any other way.

Well, let me tell you a little bit about these underlying assumptions. When you look at Western European society, thinking is very linear. The concept of time is a good example of linear thinking: when you go from A to B to C to D, you're going down a one-way street and nothing ever returns. What if you were to try to picture this idea of time? When I am thinking in English, I think, "There's something like a river flowing past me – my back is to the past and I'm looking into the future." There is a constant one-way flow. Well, just stop and think about that. What implications, what ramifications would arise if you were simply to turn around and have the future at your back instead of the past? In other words, play around with the concept a little bit. What ramifications are there for the underlying belief system?

I don't know if some of you have read, for instance, Kurt Vonnegut's writings. *Slaughterhouse Five* was an interesting book about time. Vonnegut talks about how Billy Pilgrim becomes unstuck in time, and in the book, time is actually still and it is the human beings that are moving up and down the time line. Now, that's a very different concept of time, with very different implications.

When we look at Aboriginal Peoples' notion of time, we find that time is not dynamic, every day is not a new day. Every day is the same day repeating itself. And we talk about phases in the year as something continuous, as opposed to nice, neat little units like months and days of the week and so on. The day to day aspect of time for Aboriginal Peoples is not very important, but at a cosmological level we are very exact. This is the reason, for instance, for the existence of things like medicine wheels. Those phasings are marked so that certain things, certain ceremonies, take place when a certain phase goes by. I could say more about that, but the example serves to show a very different way of thinking about time. One way is linear, while the other is cyclical.

Another aspect of a linear way of thinking is either/or propositions, or what I refer to as polarized thinking. There is good/bad, saint/sinner, day/night, black/white. The dichotomizing that takes place in polarized thinking is water-tight. If I were to draw a dichotomy of good and evil, and I said: which side of the dichotomy would you put widgets on – widgets are those fictional things that somehow exist in law school classrooms only – or let me give you something you're probably all familiar with, and then think about which side of the dichotomy you'd put it on. Are you ready? Sex. Which side of the dichotomy is sex on, good or evil? The thing is, especially in Christian homes, many of us were told as kids that sex was sinful, but somehow when we've grown up and gotten married, we go through a rite of passage to penetrate the dichotomy, and cross the imaginary boundary. In the Aboriginal way of thinking – in Blackfoot, my Native language – that type of dichotomizing doesn't occur. Good and evil are probably the two outside extremes. Most things exist in a grey area. These two ways of thinking, a linear versus a holistic, cyclical way of thinking, result in very different premises for things we take for granted and for what we think exists for everybody.

Along the same lines, we find in Western European society the value of specialization. If I were to ask people out on the street "Who are you? What are you?" I'd probably get answers like "I'm a lawyer", "I'm a teacher", or "I'm a plumber". In other words, we identify with a specialty. Among Aboriginal Peoples, being a "Jack-of-all-trades – master of none" is valued. In other words, Aboriginal Peoples are generalists as opposed to specialists. Again, that has many implications. For instance, we've all heard about the lazy drunken Indian and statements like "Indians don't stay with a job". Well, that's because employers don't understand that most jobs are specialized. You do one thing, day in, day out. Well, an Aboriginal person might come along and do one thing until he's experienced, and then say, "Well, now I know what this is all about. I think I'll move on and do something else." In other words, over a period of a person's life, we want many different experiences because of our generalist way of thinking.

In Western European society, there's a very heavy emphasis on "product". And we think about the justice system as though it were a product that we can shape. When Aboriginal Peoples think of the justice system, they really talk about process. For instance, Native languages, to a large extent, express that difference. In Blackfoot, most words are verbs or action-oriented words, as opposed to English, which is very noun-oriented or product-oriented. English is a good language for identification, but it's not a good language for describing processes or action. So, we see that these contrasts highlight very different world-views and underlying assumptions that are usually taken for granted.

When we talk about justice, you can see how the justice system as it exists today is really a Western European product of a linear, specialized way of thinking. The law embodies all of these underlying assumptions, which remain unarticulated in a particular situation. The problem is that the underlying beliefs and premises of a Native world view are not part of the existing system, and that's where all the misunderstanding and frustration comes from. We lay out a nice neat little plan and we try it out on a Native community, and then we find that it just doesn't work and people just don't respond. That is because the existing system does not embody the Native way of thinking.

The assumptions inherent in the existing criminal justice system

Without going into each premise, here are some of the underlying assumptions of the existing criminal justice system, which I will compare to some of the underlying assumptions of Aboriginal concepts of justice. The existing system takes for granted that crime is a violation of the state. In other words, if we were to talk in terms of public law and private law, the existing criminal justice system goes on the basis that criminal law is public law. And, therefore, when a little kid lifts a bag of potato chips from the local 7/11 store, the whole state takes action, since the kid has committed a crime against the whole society. However, for Aboriginal Peoples, crime is a violation of one person against another, which means that most criminal law is private, and only those people who have been wronged need be involved. Usually the extended family will negotiate with the other extended family to bring about a resolution, rather than involving the whole tribe in the settlement of a rather trivial act.

The focus in the existing criminal justice system is to establish blame or guilt. In other words, when you appear before a judge, he asks you, "Did you or did you not commit the crime you've been charged with?" Remember the either/or thinking? You either did or you didn't do it. Now, let me give you an example of what we heard in the Alberta Commission, which I served on. We'd go to the inmates in the penal institutions, in fact, we visited all of the institutions, and the inmates would say, "I was charged with assault." And we'd ask them, "Did you commit the assault?" And they'd say something like, "Yes, I committed the assault, but I beat the hell out of the guy 'cause I saw him beating up an old man, so I stepped in for the old man." Now, for the judge it's simply either/or. The larger contextual situation is never taken into consideration. In an Aboriginal justice system, the larger picture will be taken into consideration. And it may be that they do not find that the person committed a wrong because they recognize that he had justification. In other words, under the existing criminal justice system, you cannot mitigate guilt. You can only partly mitigate through sentencing. But in Aboriginal justice, you can mitigate the guilt by showing some reason for the action. However, there is no set pattern that says that if you do certain things that result in bad behaviour, then those things are wrong, because there is no absolute wrong in Aboriginal concepts of justice.

290 Leroy Little Bear

Truth in the existing justice system is found through an adversarial relationship between the offender and the state. In other words, the adversarial approach is considered the best way to find justice or truth. Have we ever had a judge admit to misinterpreting the facts? I don't think there are too many that would confess to that, but somehow the truth comes out from two opposing stories. In an Aboriginal system, dialogue and negotiation are used to eliminate bad feelings between the parties, but in the Canadian justice system today, there's no such thing as the elimination of bad feelings. The goal of most traditional justice systems, in contrast, is to bring about harmony and group balance.

The community does not play much of a role in the existing justice system. Once a person is charged, the whole machinery of the state comes into operation, but even the victims get left out. Nobody ever asks the community, "Well, what do you think? What should we do in this particular case?" Aboriginal Peoples think, "We have to have a balance, we have to have group harmony, so therefore the group has to get involved." And to a very large extent, it's usually the group that negotiates and makes sure that any bad feelings that arose are put aside, and that the people move on.

Another difference is that in the existing system, once you've got a criminal record, the state never forgets. So, even if you become a one-hundred percent, law-abiding citizen, you will always have a criminal record, and it will haunt you throughout your life. Amongst the Plains Indians, once the person is forgiven, once a person has corrected the problem, every move is made to re-incorporate that person into society. Past wrongs are forgotten, and nobody talks about them anymore.

The examples I've given show the embodiment of basic beliefs into institutions. They also show how Native beliefs and world-views have been excluded. The result is that:

> It is now a judgment of many bands that the price
> inherent in adopting our process (the criminal jus-
> tice process) is too great in light of its failure.
> Many want us to leave, taking our unproductive,
> perhaps destructive judicial system with us. More
> voices join the call for self-government.

If we hope to bring about fundamental justice, the Aboriginal world-view will have to be included. The inclusion of that

Aboriginal world-view and its underlying premises may, to a large extent, bring about the changes required in the existing system. Separate Native justice systems is the solution called for by most First Nations because of the lack of embodiment. They would not call for separate justice if their belief systems were taken into consideration.

When it comes to social problems, such as the economy, we have a tendency to blame the government for all our wrongs. Well, I'm not one to let the government get off lightly, but there are other groups of people that nobody ever says a thing about, who are just as responsible. Corporations are very good at milking the system, but nobody ever says anything about the corporate world. Everybody simply blames the government.

In the same way, I think law schools are partly responsible for the existing justice system. Everybody looks at the state, with its police, prosecutors, judges, and correctional institutions, and all the other side "industries" that have evolved, like legal aid. Nobody ever says anything about law schools and the education they're putting out. I think it's time that law schools examine these issues, so legal practitioners will be more sensitive. However, for the foreseeable future, as we stated in our report, law schools show little likelihood for change. Only when they start to put out a even a slightly different product can we be more hopeful for changes in that larger system out there.

QUESTION PERIOD: PANEL THREE

Question: RONALD SKLAR
Professor, McGill Faculty of Law

The comment about the need to kill off all the lawyers in order to bring about change made me think, not about self-preservation, but about how lawyers are obstacles to change. Lawyers are the defenders of the status quo. We are conditioned, like Pavlovian dogs, to defend the system we have been trained in.

I reacted in this fashion to a quote by Owen Young of one of the accused at the Oka trials: the trial was not about who I am, but what I did. Automatically, I thought that, of course, no criminal trial goes into who the accused is. Its function is only to determine what was done and why it was done. It does not go into the person's world view. If a person wants to say who he is, then he should go into psychoanalysis, not a criminal trial. However, after some reflection, my opinion has changed. It is permissable for us to ask if this is the right approach to a criminal trial, and, as Bobby Kennedy said, "Perhaps envision an entirely different system and ask why not?"

You gave an example of a shoplifting case in which the problem might be worked out in negotiations between victim and offender, rather than in a criminal trial, which is the way western society would resolve it. For trivial offenses this may be feasible, but what if the crime was sexual assault or armed robbery, which potentially endangers the public? Could this also be resolved out of court by negotiation?

Answer: LEROY LITTLE BEAR

The tribe in traditional justice systems would take the whole picture into consideration. For example, they would consider whether the incident would affect the balance of the tribe as a whole, or if it would mainly be an individual matter. Each crime has a different impact, so that something that seems as minor as a stolen bag of potato chips may actually result in tribal imbalance. In this case, the group that gets involved will be larger than if the crime does not upset the tribe. It is a matter of relativity and there are no clear-cut lines.

Question:

I think that everybody recognizes a need for change to the existing system. There has also been a statement from the Native point-of-view demanding an independent system. The question I have bears on this independent system. What are the possibilities of *Charter* challenges to this system, and does the *Charter* apply to Native Peoples in terms of Aboriginal rights?

Answer: MURRAY KLIPPENSTEIN

As mentioned earlier, I am on the board of the Aboriginal legal services of Toronto. We are just starting to implement a pilot project for a community council to act as an Aboriginal court in Toronto. Our first hearings start in a few weeks and we have already been notified that there is a *Charter* challenge against the project. The challenge has been raised in another case by a non-Native accused who claims he is being discriminated against because he does not have the same option to go to a community council type of system. Without having examined the details, I suspect that an initial issue is that the community council system is funded by the Attorney General and it is a community initiated project. In this sense, it is not a question of discrimination, rather that the claimant's community has not developed a similar system yet. I do not know what the result of the challenge will, but I am not too worried.

Furthermore, we spent a great deal of time working out rules of procedure for this community council. Naturally, we decided that every person who appeared in front of the council would have the right to be represented by a lawyer, although the lawyer does not have the right to speak.

Answer: FRANÇOIS ROBERT

In respect to the Crees, the situation is different from the rest of the Aboriginal Peoples in Canada in that they already have a separate, or alternative justice system. It is included in the *James Bay Agreement*, and recognized by the *Constitution* and the *Charter*.

Answer: LEROY LITTLE BEAR

Currently there is a debate over the application of the *Charter* to self-government. If the inherent right to self-government was to be recognized in the *Constitution* in this constitutional round, would the Charter apply? The National Chief, Ovide Mercredi, has said, "No, we don't want the *Charter* to apply." The reason for this is the nature of a charter or a bill of rights. It is a notice by the people to their government that the state cannot abrogate certain sacred things, such as freedom of speech and freedom of religion. The notion of a charter is in direct opposition with the idea of parliamentary supremacy. However, our constitution includes section 1, which we refer to as the Mac Truck clause because it can run over everything. It is certainly not going to be the individual who determines what is reasonable in a free and democratic society – the government will make this determination. The notwithstanding clause also weakens the *Charter*.

There are two reasons against having the *Charter* apply to Aboriginal self-government. First, as I have indicated, the *Charter* is rather weak. Second, a charter is an instrument to protect people in a very hierarchical society. The people at the bottom of the hierarchy need protection from those up on top. If you look at most Aboriginal societies in Canada, you will find that their societies are horizontally structured. In these societies we make references to circles, such as talking circles, consensus-making, and so on. In a horizontally structured society, everybody is equal – nothing is done until consensus is reached and everybody's views are taken into consideration. A charter is somewhat redundant in this kind of situation. We are not against the application of a charter. There may be some need for a charter in a horizontally structured society, but we should not try to apply an instrument that was developed for a hierarchically structured society.

Question:

Could you give some concrete examples of how an independent Native judiciary could work in relation to the Canadian legal system, particularly in a situation that involves both Natives and non-Natives? Which forum would it go to? Who would decide on jurisdiction?

Answer: LEROY LITTLE BEAR

Speaking from an Alberta point-of-view, in the Native communities it is felt that if a non-Aboriginal person were to commit what we could consider a wrong in our community, then that person should be responsible to the community. Similarly, once I cross the boundary into Quebec, I cannot argue that Ontario laws should continue to apply to me. I should abide by the standards of the community I am in.

However, there are further considerations. If, for instance, a non-Aboriginal person was apprehended on an Indian reserve, we are considering whether he should have the option to use the Native system or their own court. In fact, that option is being studied right now by the Alberta government. The idea is to establish a Native circuit court, which will travel from community to community to give that option to Native offenders.

The experience of a system already in operation, the South Island Tribal Council on Vancouver Island, is telling. Where an offender is brought before a panel of Elders, the Elders decide on the punishment. Usually the punishment is not a jail sentence, it is something much harsher. The people that have gone through both systems are opting out to go through the justice system, pay their fines or serve their term in jail, and get it over with. The alternative punishment imposed by the Elders often involves a community service. Someone who has kicked in a person's window will not only have to replace the window, but will have to work for the owner for a whole week, and stay with the family for a whole week in order to correct the bad feelings arising. The offenders are finding it very difficult to face the victims.

Answer: MURRAY KLIPPENSTEIN

Present plans for the community council in Toronto allow offenders of property crimes the choice of whether or not to participate in the community council. We anticipate that there will be quite a few non-Aboriginal victims appearing before us, and we will also be going further than the non-Aboriginal system by taking the views of the victims into account. In fact, we are planning on paying the victim fifty dollars to come to the court for his or her trial in attempt to make them feel wanted and valued.

Question:

You mentioned the possibility of a charter in a horizontal society. Would you accept equal rights between men and women in such a charter? I understand that this is one of the main issues in the *Charter* application debate.

Answer: LEROY LITTLE BEAR

I do not think that would be a problem for the men. In fact, in many Aboriginal systems, the women play a more important role than men. In the Iroquois system, it is the women who appoint the chiefs and act as the government. Moreover, in a horizontally organized society, the system is based on equality so there would be no problem in accepting equality for men and women in that kind of a system.

Question:

Leroy Little Bear mentioned the issue of process versus product. How would this link to a codification of your separate system? Would codification make it static, and if that is the case, how would you go about codifying a separate legal system so that it would be understandable, not only to you, but to the other people who would have to interact with it?

Answer: LEROY LITTLE BEAR

Aboriginal society and the Aboriginal way of thinking is largely process oriented, and in that orientation, there is constant change. What is today may not necessarily be tomorrow. We cannot say that any particular action is right or wrong in advance of its occurrence. Any action could be wrong, any action could be right, depending on the context. We could codify, but it would be a codification of broad principles as opposed to a very specific, product-type of codification.

Answer: FRANÇOIS ROBERT

I agree with this, and, if I may quote a judge of the Supreme Court of the Navajo Nation, he said that one can codify the process, but if the customary rules are codified they are put in a tight jacket and will not evolve as they are meant to.

Question:

All members of the panel talked about co-operative councils, co-management, and now a separate system for Native justice. Canada still has a role in all of this. However, for some of the Native nations, the goal is to be sovereign and to deal with Canada as international partners. If some nations are sovereign, how will Canada's role be different than its current dominant one?

Answer: FRANÇOIS ROBERT

I can only say that my clients have already signed an agreement, the *James Bay Agreement*, in which both Canada and Quebec do recognize self-government. Although this poses some problems, it is signed to reflect this position.

Answer: LEROY LITTLE BEAR

In the current constitutional round, the position of First Nations such as my own tribe, the Blood Tribe in southern Alberta, is that we were independent and sovereign and we entered into a relationship with the Crown. That relationship was made explicit through a treaty agreement, which deals with land and the exchange of land for a number of benefits. Those benefits included free education, free health services, exclusive use of certain pieces of land (reserves), a continuing right to hunt year-round even outside of the reserve. There was no mention of self-government or about justice systems. One small section provides that the tribe was to bring to justice to anybody that may have committed a crime within the area covered by the treaty. The Blood Tribe interprets this to mean that we can establish our own police and develop correctional institutions. This is presently occurring.

Our position is that we already have an agreement and what Canada does with their own constitution is their business. Our interference amounts to coming into your house and telling you how to arrange your furniture. We do not want to do that; we want to keep peace and good relations between our two houses. However, we want to remind you that while you are doing your renovations, do not forget about the treaty relationships that exist between our two nations. This is the reason First Nations are heavily involved in this constitutional round – in order to ensure that Canada does not misinterpret or unilaterally interpret this relationship.

EPILOGUE
OPENING REMARKS
THE YEAR OF THE INDIGENOUS PEOPLES:
OKA REVISITED

JONG QUISHO (OREN LYONS)

Faithkeeper Turtle Clan
Onondaga Nation
Fire Keepers of the Haudenosaunee

It is 1993 and the international year of the world's Indigenous Peoples has come and gone, along with the 1992 Earth Summit in Rio de Janeiro and for most Indigenous Peoples it has been a disastrous time.

The homeless street children of Rio were purged to present a clean face to the estimated forty thousand delegates attending the Earth Summit. Agenda 21, the environmental world plan for the 21st century, was purged of meaningful direction for the issues of energy and population and the term "Sustainable Development" became the euphemistic cry of the status quo, meaning "how to have your cake and eat it too". The United States led the way as the Bush administration set the amoral parameters by declaring that the United States standard of living was "not negotiable".

Where were the Indigenous Peoples in all of this?

In the way.

In the way of hordes of gold miners tearing up Indigenous lands of Kiapos and Yanomomies in Brazil. In the way of the Shining Path of Peru are the slaughtered Ashaninkas on the border of the Amazon basin. In the way of U.S. nuclear policy are the Western Shoshone led by the Dann sisters and David Yowell, who continue their seventeen year struggle for their lands under the Ruby Valley Treaty in Nevada. In the way of international mining corporations in the Indigenous lands of the Aboriginal Peoples of Australia. In the way of Japanese supported logging corporations in British Columbia, Alaska and the North West forests of the United States. In the way of the Malaysian government as trees and Indigenous Peoples are uprooted simultaneously.

In the way of "sport" fishermen on the East and West coast of North America as salmon runs get thinner and thinner and the last chinook to make it up to its ancient spawning grounds is stuffed and hanging on the wall of the Governor of Oregon, who just now sees the light and says "That ain't right!"

Indigenous Peoples are in the way of the University of Arizona and the Holy See of Rome, who are partners in a scientific venture that placed an interstellar telescope named "Columbia" on the sacred mountain of the Apaches that the Vatican declared not sacred.

In the way of commercial whaling by Norway and Japan, as the rest of the world shuffles, hitches up their pants and looks the other way as they negotiate trade agreements.

More? In the way of the North American Free Trade Agreement as Indians in Chiapas, Mexico rebel against their poverty, neglect and the taking of their lands and resources by big business on both sides of the border.

We the Haudenosaunee are in the way of the Governor of New York who wants state jurisdiction in our lands and territories that lie between New York and Canada. He wants to tax our Peoples and lands.

We are in the way of so-called Iroquois businessmen who are willing to help the Governor do that so that they can continue to accrue personal fortunes at the expense of their Peoples' sovereignty.

We are in the way of State of New York gaming compacts that demand New York state police presence on our territories twenty-four hours a day.

We are in the way of businessmen who want to bring the Bureau of the Indian affairs elective system into our free territories and land so that they can use their fortunes to control the lives of our people.

And what about Kanesatake, they who were the centre of the conflict in 1990 that brought the Canadian Army onto Haudenosaunee Mohawk lands?

Not much has changed there as the people still struggle to come to an agreement amongst themselves as to the best direction to take concerning the return of the lands to the Mohawk people.

The understanding of what took place during that time was described by the Haudenosaunee External Affairs Committee to the members of the Standing Committee on Aboriginal Affairs. I submit extracts of that report herewith:

— EXTRACTS –

MINUTES OF PROCEEDINGS
THE STANDING COMMITTEE ON ABORIGINAL AFFAIRS

HOUSE OF COMMONS
WEDNESDAY, FEBRUARY 20, 1991
ISSUE NO. 48

Chief Lyons (Six Nations Iroquois Confederacy):

[...]

When our Confederacy meets with the Crown, as it has been doing for more than three centuries, it has always been our custom before turning our thoughts to immediate problems to do two things: first, we give thanks to the Creator for the earth and all things in and on it and for all the parts of the natural world that allow us to continue to live by keeping to their instructions from the Creator.

This thanksgiving reminds us of our duties as Peoples with responsibilities, not only to ourselves but to future generations and to the entire natural world. This thanksgiving is how we begin and end our meetings.

The time you have allotted us will not permit us to begin our meeting properly and we regret that.

Second, there is what we call the ceremony of condolence in order for us to put our minds together to listen to each other with respect and clarity and to be of good mind. Our minds must be clear of the emotions and grief that are the enemies of reason.

Since the beginning of our Confederacy, long before most of your ancestors arrived here, we have used the words of condolence to clear our minds before opening any council with another nation, and especially if blood has soiled the clarity of our relations, as it has recently. The time you have allotted us will not permit us to begin our meeting properly, and we regret that. We want you to know that we mean no disrespect to you, to our Confederacy, to our ancestors and children when we begin this meeting with you today in such haste and with so little regard for the rules that should govern our behaviour. We are taught that for lawmakers there is always enough time in this world to do things right. We have learned that for you, time is of the essence.

[...]

We believe we have an important message to deliver here today to the lawmakers of Canada. First, we want to explain carefully the factors that have led to the problems we face. Second, we want to state that these problems have not gone away. They remain immediate and serious, and we need to address them together.

We suggest an approach based on principles of fairness, reason, respect and peace. We suggest that this approach, given the broadness of the problems, requires a broader approach and a greater vision than has been given to date. One part of the problem dates back to the 1880s, when the Government of Canada decided that Iroquois communities, as advanced Indians, required governments chosen by election and structured like your own system. The result of that imposition of band councils under the Indian Act in almost every one of the communities has not been the destruction of our traditional form of government. Our traditional government has been weakened over time, it is true, but the band council has not been able to establish the respectability and vision needed to deal with the issues that confront our communities.

Canada and Quebec complained this summer that the traditional government of the Confederacy lacked the authority to impose order in the communities. We replied that for more than a century, it has been Canada's deliberate policy to ensure that our governments have been weakened and their authority attacked. It is not for you to complain now that you do not like the alternatives you have created.

[...]

Canada has failed to develop a policy for dealing with what it calls "native land claims" that follow principles of fairness, justice, or generosity. In the wake of the many blockades and confrontations of the summer of 1990, we see that the Government of Canada is tending toward changing the amount of money made available to deal with the claims and perhaps the process. We echo the feelings of almost every group your government has consulted – the problem also lies in the policies that are being used, and without a fundamental shift in the policies, improved processes and increased funding will still lead to bitterness.

For example, part of the policy suggests that Canada will not be responsible for anything that occurred before 1867. We have been told that Great Britain accepts no responsibility; it says it sent everything to Canada. We are told that provincial governments are not responsible since they did not exist before 1867. There is no part of the Crown that is willing to accept clear Crown responsibilities.

Another part of the policy suggests that the Crown has no responsibility for compensation of Aboriginal rights in southern Quebec and the maritime provinces. Though this may be legal, we see the institutionalized theft of land as repugnant to our sense of justice.

Another part of the policy suggests that though procedural and technical legal defences should not be used to refuse a claim, they can be used to discount the compensation offered. Generally, the discount is 50%. Canada refuses to provide reasons for its reduction for what it considers to be fair compensation.

In the next few weeks we expect Canada to announce changes in its approach to claims. Unless basic policy questions are addressed, the changes will lack the vision necessary to bring about real headway.

The factors that gave rise to the problems of the summer have not gone away and have not yet been addressed by the government. We see that Canada intends to begin local negotiations in Kanesatake without giving that community time or resources to heal itself internally and to find its own internal harmony.

The communities and their people have suffered and continue to suffer real trauma. We see a need for counselling, for a time to reason and meet and think. By insisting on a single representative group in Kanesatake, for example, the Government of Canada has pressured the community in ways that may satisfy Canada's short-term goals but may not promote long-term peace.

The Confederacy remains willing to discuss resolution of these difficult issues with the Government of Canada. Like our laws, our approach is based on respect, reason and peace. We hope that Canada will take up our invitation once again, recognize the legitimacy of the Confederacy, and face the issues that will only result in more crises unless we resolve them together. ...

[...]

I might add a little history. In the beginning of the Confederacy in our country a tremendous war of attrition was going on among our people, and even among families. It was a terrible time. Our people had forgotten our original instructions and it had deteriorated to that point.

It was at that point that we received this second message we call the Great Law. The Great Law was brought by an individual. This individual, along with the help of another now very famous person, who may be called at some time Hiawa-

tha... Together, they moved about and they brought peace to these nations one by one. They changed the minds of these individuals, finally – and this is a long story and I am just quickly cutting through it – eventually, coming to Onondaga and dealing with the most recalcitrant of all of them. Taradaho was a very evil man, incarnate, and they were able to convince him about this great peace. They sat on the shores of Onondaga Lake and at that point he instructed the Confederacy on how to set their government up and under what principles they were going to operate. There were peace, power of the good mind and righteousness, justice and equity. Those were the principles, the first principle being peace.

After this long time – and no one really knows how long this effort took, some say it could have been a hundred years – at one point they finally were all gathered. They all agreed, and at that time the peacemaker – we call him the peacemaker, this great messenger – said "I plant now as the symbol of this Confederacy the Great Tree of Peace, the Great White Pine. It has four white roots that reach out in the four cardinal directions of the earth, and those people who have no place to go can follow those roots back to the source and sit under this great tree of peace, under its protection, by obeying its laws of peace, justice, equity, and righteousness."

After saying all of that and after presenting the process, and after everybody understanding what the process was of raising the clan mothers and the faith keepers and the chiefs, he said, "I now uproot this great tree and I command you to pass by and throw your weapons of war into this hole" – which they did. He said, "These weapons of war will be carried to the four dark directions of the earth, undercurrents of the earth". Then he replanted the tree. Thus, he had buried the warrior. He said, "In this place we now have a governing body of law, this Great Law".

We had great peace from this Confederacy, and many nations have stood at one point or another under this great tree, including the fledgling Government of the United States. But the principle we are talking about now is that this was now a Confederacy, a governance of law. As Chief Longboat said, in the case of defence then it was up to the men, as any nation has a right to defend itself, and has, as you know, in the history of this country. The Haudenosaunee has stood firm, and still stands.

So those principles we talked about, the democratic principles, are really the fundamental basis of the Government of the United States. In 1987 the Congress and the Senate of the United States passed two agreements saying that they recognized the contribution of the Haudenosaunee to the Government of the United States – these fundamental, basic principles of democracy.

So it is based on peace, and it is a very important definition in this discussion, because our people have been people of law and recognize that. This is what we are attempting to reassert to calm these troubled waters.

Chief Longboat: [...] I feel that this whole situation that we have between federal governments and Native governments, whatever they may be, is a form of attitude.

I think once the non-Native Peoples take the attitude that we are people too, and that we have the capabilities as people to look after ourselves, and we will look after ourselves, and give us the chance and the things that are necessary to be able to do that and to make our own decisions and to make our own mistakes, I think we have to get to that attitude first, because I think one of the oldest phrases of the old Indian Act is that Native Peoples are other than human, and in many of my relationships and dealings with non-Native Peoples I feel that way, that you do not give me that opportunity as a person equal to you to do for my people what I feel my people want.

So if I were Prime Minister that is what I would do first, or whatever, our Minister of Indian Affairs – say that we have to have an attitude change in dealing with Native Peoples.

Chief Lyons: I think we have another comment from Mr. Williams on that subject, much more to the point.

Mr. Williams: You asked specifically what our recommendations were. Very briefly, if there had been a fair process and fair policies for dealing with land rights issues, and I say land rights and not land claims – that is an attitude word too – if there had been a fair process there would have been no blockade in Kanesatake and there would have been no confrontation. There is still no fair process.

The discussions the minister has had to date, and it has been quite a while, are focused on procedural rather than substantive changes in the claims policies for the most part, and that is distressing.

What we can see is that the symptoms of the problems are being addressed but the causes are not, and we would really want to address ourselves to the underlying causes. Gambling and smuggling are symptoms of the fact that the communities do not have viable, appropriate economies. Canada needs to address itself to the fact that there need to be proper, viable, appropriate economies.

We see that these issues do not just stop in three Mohawk communities in Canada, they affect every Iroquois community on both sides of the border. We are suggesting to Canada and to the United States, and to Ontario and Quebec and New York, because we deal with those jurisdictions too, that they should consider dealing with one proper appropriate government of all those communities. There is a need for regulation of commerce. We suggest it should be done jointly.

We suggest the first thing that Canada should do is recognize the spirit of the treaties the Crown made and the promises that were made, because if we cannot trust you to keep your promises it is very difficult for us to begin accepting further promises. Again, this is a matter of respect.

These communities have suffered a great deal of trauma and they need resources and they need time to do healing. We do not see that pressuring them to unify their governments, pressuring them to establish negotiating mechanisms, is necessarily very helpful. They need the time to heal.

The other thing concerns the negotiations this past summer. We came very, very close to a full agreement. The issue they broke down over was the question of what kinds of activities were actually criminal and how fair trials might be conducted. What we suggested initially was that we did not have time in the 48 hours that we were given to reach a negotiated agreement before the army went in. We did not have time to sit down and say this man is a criminal, this man is not. We suggested that there should be an independent review of the kinds of activities that should result in prosecution and the kinds that should not.

Quebec refused. They said they did not want anything that might bind their attorney general's discretion in the field of criminal law. We wanted guarantees of procedural and other fairness in trials. We had difficulty getting that.

We are still concerned. There are trials going on now. We are concerned about the fairness of them. We are concerned about the appropriateness of what are essentially political trials. Those are issues that still have not been dealt with and are continuing to go on even as we speak. In our negotiations we tried to address the underlying causes of the problems rather than the symptoms. We find that people are continuing to address symptoms and not the things that led to the crisis itself.

This is a personal observation of mine. I do not want it to be taken as anything else. If you look at the history of North America in terms of Aboriginal crises, you find they take place in the summertime. The wintertime is basically a time of hunkering down and surviving. I would not want Canada or anyone else to think that because nothing is happening in the winter, nothing is going to happen in the summer. We have time to do some work now, time to do some thinking and some healing. But the underlying issues have not been addressed, have not been dealt with, and they need to be addressed properly. [...]

[...]

Mr. Blondin (Western Arctic): Because you did not have the opportunity to give your condolences, I want to just start by saying... *[Mr. Blondin continues in Native language].*

I want to thank you for coming here. I am really curious, because I come from an Indigenous background, and I believe the root of many of these problems we experience with internal fragmentation in the community and conflict has to do with how our people have always governed themselves. I feel strongly about it, because my grandfather was the chief who signed Treaty 11. My grandmother was the matriarch. We never have a chief and the matriarch marry, because they are two sources of power, but I come from a strange family.

Having said that, the whole idea of the Longhouse and the Confederacy has a very complicated history the average Canadian does not appreciate. You have given us some explanation, but I am interested in the idea of a referendum that we now have floating around Kanesatake. I know Mrs. Bourgault is involved with that. You also have leadership under the Indian Act. You now have a coalition; they are supposed to be the spokespeople for... Then you have a number of versions of what the Longhouse should be, like the Hanson Lake and the Parker versions. These are all things the average Canadian does not understand.

According to my understanding of the tradition of Kanesatake and the Mohawks, there is a last message from the great peacemaker, and it is *Kariwiioi*. Could you tell us what that is? Is that what should guide leadership in that community? What do you feel about the other things I mentioned, such as the coalition and the referendum?

Chief Lyons: I am looking at the time.

The Chairman: You have the time.

Chief Lyons: The third message of the *Kariwiioi* came to us around the beginning of the 19th century. It was delivered to an individual who later on recounted this experience. The message was how to deal with the white man. The laws we had originally – the Great Law, the Great Peace – dealt only with Indians, because there were no white people here. When the white man came, he brought a lot of things

with him that were destroying the nations.

They talked about four elements the Indians had to deal with. One was strong drink. They said you must not use the strong drink, the liquor. One was witchcraft: they said it came over with them on the boat, and to stay away from that. One was the Bible: they said that you had your instructions; abide by them, go back to them. What was the fourth one? Oh yes, gambling. The fourth one was gambling. They said that those things will destroy your people unless you deal with them.

That was essentially the message. That came in 1799 or 1800, and without that message we would not be standing here today talking to you. It gave us the instructions we needed to carry on, and they said at that point that these were our last instructions. We would not receive any more.

So the original instruction was the first message, the Great Law was the second message, and *Kariwiioi* was the third message, the good word, and has sustained our people up to this point. It is a very powerful, very complex knowledge that has been handed down to us. It continues, and it has been the strength of the Longhouse in all of our territories.

So we have a broad perspective and we have very direct instructions. What they said was that the duties of the chief, number one, were to see the ceremonies were carried out at the proper time, in a proper way, and then to sit in council for the welfare of the people, among any others.

But essentially, to answer your question, yes – that is what it was.

[...]

Mr. Thorkelson: Who do you recognize as the legitimate leadership? Do you deal with different factions on different issues?

Mr. Williams: In the negotiations we were involved in, I should say we were dealing with as many people as we could, because our instructions were to seek consensus as much as possible. To the extent that it was allowed, there were community meetings with people in the community and people who had left the community. There was a real effort to meet with as many people as possible and come to one mind as much as possible.

Mr. Thorkelson: Who do you consider to be the legitimate leadership today?

Chief Longboat: As far as the Confederacy and the Six Nations Council is concerned, we look to Samson Gabriel, the chief. It says in our language that this is where our minds have to go in that community. That is our obligation. We became involved when he invited us to a council by use of the wampum. Traditionally we are not to interfere in that community until they ask for help.

Chief Lyons: It should be noted that at the same time he brought the wampum, there was a representative of the non-traditional community there representing, as they said at that time, 80% of the people. They were there together saying that they were of a common mind that they wanted help.

Mr. Ferland (Portneuf): Thank you, Mr. Chairman. I am very happy to welcome you here today because I have a feeling that you and me have inherited a history although we have no say in its making. We must however write today's history which will be read tomorrow.

I would like you to explain further to me why you resorted to arms in a country where everyone is indeed equal before the law, a country which has always shown patience, maybe

learned from you, in discussing and finding solutions to really serious problems.

Many people in Quebec and in Canada had the feeling that this outburst had not been anticipated. Everyone seemed surprised when the barricades went up and when they saw kalashnikov in your hands. We were not used to seeing Natives act that way. I would like you to explain to us why you decide now, after the Meech Lake Accord has been rejected, to resort to arms which goes against your philosophy, I think.

Mr. Williams: I have three very brief points. The Confederacy did not condone taking up weapons. The Grand Council of the Confederacy cannot condone that. You are asking for an explanation from outside the minds of the people who did take up the weapons.

You say that the law is equal for everyone in this country. One would think that after the experience of the past three or four years – the Donald Marshall inquiry, the Manitoba Native justice inquiry, the events a couple of weeks ago in the Prison for Women in Kingston, and so on – one would realize that the law may be written the same for everyone in the country, but its effects are certainly not equal for everyone.

In the case of the land issue in Kanesatake, the people believed, honestly and consistently, for over 150 years that was their land. They had the wampum belt, the documents, and the promises to prove it.

Although the law is written equally for everyone, it does not do the same justice. It was available having neither political processes nor legal avenues to secure fairness that led to the frustration.

That is one the factors. The land issue and the inability to deal with the land issue in any other way is one of the factors that led to people taking up arms. There are several others, but it would take a long time to explain them.

I think you are wrong if you think that just because the law is written the same for everyone it is an equally just law. It is not. Again, it was not the Confederacy who decided to take up the arms or to condone that. That was not the way we would have preferred to deal with things.

Chief Lyons: That does raise the question of where a nation can go when the laws of a country forestall any attempt to move in a legal manner to protect one's self when an issue of principle is not being met. I think that is why the first blockade went up, but I am merely guessing at this point because we were not there. When the laws of a country are used to cut off all legal avenues of the people who are being pressured, it leaves them no alternative but to stand if they believe they are right.

Everyone knows that if you go into someone's house you invite whatever happens, and you were coming into a house when you went into a nation's territory. They had to defend themselves. This has been the history of our country. Our people have forever been defending themselves. It is a common history. I think the mayor of Oka's clever use of that avenue – to close off the legal avenues first and leave no other recourse but to surrender – to build a golf course, is unconscionable. And Mr. Ciaccia advised against it. He advised the mayor not to do it, but he went ahead anyway.

[...]

Mr. Wilbee: [...] What do you see as the relationship between the Mohawk people you represent and the Government of Canada? I am talking here about the sovereignty issue. How do you see the relationship between the two groups, jurisdiction, that type of thing?

Chief Lyons: We have probably what we call the grandfather of all our agreements, the Kaswenda, or the Two-Row Wampum. It is the first agreement between Indian nations and, shall we say, Europeans around 1613. It was a request from the Dutch to trade in our areas. They wanted some kind of a document that would allow them to travel in peace and so forth. The response was, well, why do we not just sit down and have a discussion as to how we are going to deal with one another because it is quite apparent that you people keep coming; you are not going to leave, and we do not have an association here? Let us sit down and make one.

From this agreement, around 1613, they sat down at what is now Albany, New York, and they discussed the issues and the principles of agreement. Essentially what they did was produce a belt, a two-row belt, on a field of white denoting peace, friendship, and two purple rows side by side, neither meeting. They said that this is our canoe, our people, our government, our way of life; this is your boat, because you have a much larger group of people. Your people, they have many colours; your religions, you have many religions; your way of life; your government. We will travel down this river of life side by side, in peace and friendship, for as long as the grass grows green, as long as the water runs downhill, as long as the sun rises in the east and sets in the west, and as long as the earth itself shall be here.

This was a document of great humanity, because at the time our people were very powerful and these people were very small, but in the document, as you see it, they are equal, as we believe all people are equal.

We believe that in the creation and the way we are taught that all life is equal and that you are a manifestation of creation. The Creator put you here as well as he put us here, therefore we must respect you as part of creation and everything that is in it. Those concepts were in this agreement.

Then there was a covenant chain with three links; peace, friendship, forever, and this covenant chain you will find in your history, in the American document history, again and again and again. They made the covenant chain of silver so that it would require polishing. In other words, we must periodically sit down and polish this chain, our agreement, refresh ourselves, let ourselves know what is going on.

Obviously this has not been going on and the result of it is what happened at Oka. But this discussion, what is the position? This is the position that we predicate all of the subsequent treaties on. The Dutch held us; the French held us; the English held us; the Americans held us. All held this belt and agreed on these principles.

From that time on there were other great documents and treaties and agreements, but the principles that were put down in that first one is what we try to keep forward. This is what I think we are looking for in our relationship – respect for one another's people, territory, our position. We want to respect one another; we want to work together, because we do have the agreement, the agreement is there. It has been stretched pretty hard, but it has been stretched before.

These people said in their wisdom that there was going to come a time when these two, this boat and this canoe, will be separated by a great wind. You will find that there will come a time when people will have one foot in the canoe and one foot in the boat. When this separation comes, people will fall into this river, and there is no power on this side of the creation for us to help those people. They said this would come about. Who knows when or what?

But I think that, in dealing with one another, these are our concepts. We have never varied and, as you well know, every time you meet with Haudenosaunee, with the Confederacy, you always talk about the Two-Row Wampum Treaty. But that is fundamentally what it is, a reminder of our association. How we do this, how we are able to develop this and make this work in these times and context is what we are about today. But I think if we can have, from your perspective, that respect for our position, we can go a long way. I think that, in terms of Canada itself, this must be applied to every Indian nation that is in Canada.

You and I have a long way to go. There are great problems in this world today, as we know. We are going to need one another and our combined experiences to survive. We talk about the seventh generation. What they tell us is that every decision that you make must reflect on the welfare of the seventh generation to come. That is one of the basic, fundamental rules that is told to our leaders and we do that when we sit in council – we look ahead and we also look back. So our perspective is quite long. We have a broad context here. We easily jump to these different times and different treaties because we believe they are all relevant and it is an ongoing context.

A lot of work has been done beforehand. These treaties have come and so forth. It reflects upon us today to make them continue and to make them work. So what we want from you is this respect.

[...]

Ms Blondin: What should the government do?

Chief Lyons: We really must develop a process first of all – a group, a committee. Maybe this is it; I do not know. It seems like a very reasonable forum here to begin the discussion on how we develop that process.

Have you seen the agreement that we were...? Oh, you have. In the agreement there is a real effort toward this process. We really outline what to do. Perhaps you should take a look at this agreement and see where we can work. There was a real effort to come to this conclusion, because we were not thinking just of the Mohawks at Kanesatake, but of the Indians in Canada. We know the problem remains.

You have to have a better formal process to deal with this. The heavy attitude of police is not the best way. We need a little breathing room at this point. As I say, efforts are being made for coalescence. If we can indicate to our nation, to our people, that we can have the support and patience this is going to take, such patience at this point would be much more productive than trying to come to conclusions immediately. We really have to continue discussions, I would say.

Mr. Thorkelson: To Mr. Williams. I asked about your negotiations and you said you have bogged down on the issue of fair process. In your mind, someone who had taken a gun to protect his land – I think those were your words – and pointed it in the air should not be subject to criminal trial. I understand you to mean that those people who did not fire their weapons, whether they were automatic weapon or other weapons, should be given amnesty. Is that the position of the Six Nation Iroquois Confederacy?

Mr. Williams: I was trying to give an example of the spectrum of people's thoughts about what might be criminal and what might not be. I was not trying to suggest that we had any pre-conceived notions about what is criminal and what is not. In fact, we did not. We did discuss the concept that a person who has injured no one and acted in good faith, and in what he believed was self-defence or defence of his community, might not be a criminal.

We did not want to pre-judge what kind of actions are criminal and what kind are not. We were merely trying to set up some way for someone other than ourselves, with more time than 48 hours or the 12 hours that were left, someone who everyone would listen to and respect, to go off and come back later – I think we said within a month – and tell us what is a criminal act and should be dealt with in a criminal way, and what is not criminal. We are not talking about amnesty, or forgetting. We are talking about people not being prosecuted or dealt with in any way if they are not criminals.

Mr. Thorkelson: If they are not criminals, what was your position on the demands for amnesty by those in the Treatment Centre?

Mr. Williams: You would have to ask them.

Mr. Thorkelson: No, but what is your position? Did you agree with that? For those people who, let us say, met your definition.

Mr. Williams: Well, we did not have a definition. We did not want to get into a name-by-name examination of individuals because that might pre-judge any fairness in dealing with them in any possible trials. It is not just for the people in the Treatment Centre. A lot of other people have been charged, including in Kahnawake. What we were really trying to say was: let us try to find some fair, reasonable, respectable way of determining what is a criminal act.

Mr. Thorkelson: Outside of the Criminal Code.

Mr. Williams: Outside of a Quebec government functionary who might have his own agenda in making those decisions unilaterally, because whether he was fair or not, we would end up questioning his motives. By September 16 we were suggesting a special prosecutor – because that got around the question of the Attorney General of Quebec having the feeling that his jurisdiction was invaded – mutually acceptable and immune from any kind of political interference, conducting these hearings.

Mr. Thorkelson: So you had no position on whether or not –

The Chairman: I am sorry, Mr. Thorkelson, I am afraid we will have to stop you there. We will have one short question from the last member who has not had a chance to ask a second question.

Mr. Ferland: A quick one. If I understand you, you reject the capacity of the Attorney General of Quebec to implement the Criminal Code which is the same from coast to coast in this country. It is what you are telling me or at least it is what I understand. Finally you say that the minister of Justice in Quebec is incapable of implementing the Canadian Criminal Code. Is it what you are saying? I am trying to understand what you say; "We will decide what is criminal and what is not".

The Canadian Criminal Code is the same for everybody whether you live in Quebec, in British Columbia or in the Canadian Great North. It is the same Criminal Code. And it is the Attorney General of each province who has to enforce it whether it be in Quebec, in Manitoba or elsewhere.

You are telling me: we consider that shooting with kalasnikovs is not a criminal act. But if I were to shoot that weapon, tough luck, for it is a criminal act and I will be prosecuted as any other Mohawk, Algonquin or anglophone. It is the same Criminal Code which is applicable to everybody.

I would like you to elaborate on that point. I feel that you are trying to negotiate what appears to me hardly negotiable, that is to define what is or is not a criminal act, whereas the code is the same for everybody.

Mr. Williams: There is a difficult question underlying this, and that is that there are treaties that govern the question of criminal jurisdiction. For the purpose of these difficult negotiations we decided not to put these treaties into question, but we reserved the right to raise those treaties later on in any criminal proceedings.

At no time did anyone say that we reserve the right to decide who are criminals and who are not. What we were saying was that in the political climate that existed at that time, with the antagonism that existed at that time, and had existed in fact since April in Akwasasne, we could not convince Mohawk people that the Government of Quebec would deal with them fairly if left to its own political choices. The decision on whether or not to prosecute someone does come through the Criminal Code, but it is essentially in many ways a political decision. We were trying to depoliticize that decision to allow a neutral body to make recommendations on who should be prosecuted and who should not. Anything less than that – a series of decisions by the Attorney General of the province when the Attorney General had already taken positions on the morality of Mohawk actions – simply would not be politically acceptable to the Mohawks. It would not cause people to put down their guns if we could not assure them that they were going to be fairly and objectively dealt with. We are not saying that some people should not be criminals, or which ones should not be considered criminals; we are saying that the decision about who to prosecute has to be done fairly and without bias. We were trying to find a way for that decision or those recommendations to be made.

* * *

EPILOGUE
CLOSING REMARKS

The Grand Council of the Haudenosaunee offered to hold the lands in question for the Mohawk Peoples at Kanesatake while they determined how they would function as a concerning group. This was to remove the lands from the Canadian governments hands while this internal determination at Kanesatake took place. The offer still stands.

Both the Canadian and American governments should deal very specifically on a government-to-government basis with the governing bodies of the Haudenosaunee and Indian nations.

The first instruction given to us by the peacemaker as he presented the Great Law to us was "Peace". Peace among ourselves.

"Peace" brought his second great instruction and that was "United". United we stand, divided we fall. Today the divisive activities of both Canadian and United States governments have promoted this disunity. Their activities have produced many bitter and confused Haudenosaunee people.

We now have our own individual people promoting the position of the whiteman to accrue personal wealth and to put the nations, our nations, welfare second to the individual. This not only destroys unity but will eventually destroy our sovereignty.

The peacemaker instructed us to put aside our self-interest and our families self-interest for the health and welfare of the seventh generation to come. To hold for them what we have and en-joy today. Thus we survive and carry on the mandates of peace and freedom for our lands and its Peoples.

It is in our hands, money is not sovereignty as some suggest, lands and its Peoples are sovereignty, and unity is the necessary principle to insure our lands against all outside interests.

What will be the epilogue of the seventh generation? That will be written by our generation, today.

DRAFT UNITED NATIONS DECLARATION ON THE RIGHTS OF INDIGENOUS PEOPLES

As agreed upon by the members of the U.N. Working Group on Indigenous Populations at its eleventh session, Geneva, July 1993. Adopted by the U.N. Subcommission on Prevention of Discrimination and Protection of Minorities by its resolution 1994/45, August 26, 1994. U.N. Doc. E/CN.4/1995/2, E/CN.4/Sub.2/1994/56, at 105 (1994).

Affirming that indigenous peoples are equal in dignity and rights to all other peoples, while recognizing the right of all peoples to be different, to consider themselves different, and to be respected as such,

Affirming also that all peoples contribute to the diversity and richness of civilizations and cultures, which constitute the common heritage of humankind,

Affirming further that all doctrines, policies and practices based on or advocating superiority of peoples or individuals on the basis of national origin, racial, religious, ethnic or cultural differences are racist, scientifically false, legally invalid, morally condemnable, and socially unjust,

Reaffirming also that indigenous peoples, in the exercise of their rights, should be free from discrimination of any kind,

Concerned that indigenous peoples have been deprived of their human rights and fundamental freedoms, resulting, *inter alia*, in their colonization and dispossession of their lands, territories and resources, thus preventing them from exercising, in particular, their right to development in accordance with their own needs and interests,

Recognizing the urgent need to respect and promote the inherent rights and characteristics of indigenous peoples, especially their rights to their lands, territories and resources, which derive from their political, economic and social structures and from their cultures, spiritual traditions, histories and philosophies,

Welcoming the fact that indigenous peoples are organizing themselves for political, economic, social and cultural enhancement and in order to bring an end to all forms of discrimination and oppression wherever they occur,

Convinced that control by indigenous peoples over developments affecting them and their lands, territories and resources will enable them to maintain and strengthen their institutions, cultures and traditions, and to promote their development in accordance with their aspirations and needs,

Recognizing also that respect for indigenous knowledge, cultures and traditional practices contributes to sustainable and equitable development and proper management of the environment,

Emphasizing the need for demilitarization of the lands and territories of indigenous peoples, which will contribute to peace, economic and social progress and development, understanding and friendly relations among nations and peoples of the world,

Recognizing in particular the right of indigenous families and communities to retain shared responsibility for the upbringing, training, education and well-being of their children,

Recognizing also, that indigenous peoples have the right freely to determine their relationships with States in a spirit of coexistence, mutual benefit and full respect,

Considering that treaties, agreements and other arrangements between States and indigenous peoples are properly matters of international concern and responsibility,

Acknowledging that the Charter of the United Nations, the International Covenant on Economic, Social and Cultural Rights and the International Covenant on Civil and Political Rights affirm the fundamental importance of the right of self-determination of all peoples, by virtue of which they freely determine their political status and freely pursue their economic, social and cultural development,

Bearing in mind that nothing in this Declaration may be used to deny any peoples their right of self-determination,

Encouraging States to comply with and effectively implement all international instruments, in particular those related to human rights, as they apply to indigenous peoples, in consultation and cooperation with the peoples concerned,

Emphasizing that the United Nations has an important and continuing role to play in promoting and protecting the rights of indigenous peoples,

Believing that this Declaration is a further important step forward for the recognition, promotion and protection of the rights and freedoms of indigenous peoples and in the development of relevant activities of the United Nations system in this field,

Solemnly proclaims the following United Nations Declaration on the Rights of Indigenous Peoples:

PART I

Article 1

Indigenous peoples have the right to the full and effective enjoyment of all human rights and fundamental freedoms recognized in the Charter of the United Nations, the Universal Declaration of Human Rights and international human rights law.

Article 2

Indigenous individuals and peoples are free and equal to all other individuals and peoples in dignity and rights, and have the right to be free from any kind of adverse discrimination, in particular that based on their indigenous origin or identity.

Article 3

Indigenous peoples have the right of self-determination. By virtue of that right they freely determine their political status and freely pursue their economic, social and cultural development.

Article 4

Indigenous peoples have the right to maintain and strengthen their distinct political, economic, social and cultural characteristics, as well as their legal systems, while retaining their rights to participate fully, if they so choose, in the political, economic, social and cultural life of the State.

Article 5

Every indigenous individual has the right to a nationality.

PART II

Article 6

Indigenous peoples have the collective right to live in freedom, peace and security as distinct peoples and to full guarantees against genocide or any other act of violence, including the removal of indigenous children from their families and communities under any pretext.

In addition, they have the individual rights to life, physical and mental integrity, liberty, and security of person.

Article 7

Indigenous peoples have the collective and individual right not to be subjected to ethnocide and cultural genocide, including prevention of and redress for:

(a) Any action which has the aim or effect of depriving them of their integrity as distinct peoples, or of their cultural values or ethnic identities;

(b) Any action which has the aim or effect of dispossessing them of their lands, territories or resources;

(c) Any form of population transfer which has the aim or effect of violating or undermining any of their rights;

(d) Any form of assimilation or integration by other cultures or ways of life imposed on them by legislative, administrative or other measures;

(e) Any form of propaganda directed against them.

Article 8

Indigenous peoples have the collective and individual right to maintain and develop their distinct identities and characteristics, including the right to identify themselves as indigenous and to be recognized as such.

Article 9

Indigenous peoples and individuals have the right to belong to an indigenous community or nation, in accordance with the traditions and customs of the community or nation concerned. No disadvantage of any kind may arise from the exercise of such a right.

Article 10

Indigenous peoples shall not be forcibly removed from their lands or territories. No relocation shall take place without the free and informed consent of the indigenous peoples concerned and after agreement on just and fair compensation and, where possible, with the option of return.

Article 11

Indigenous peoples have the right to special protection and security in periods of armed conflict.

States shall observe international standards, in particular the Fourth Geneva Convention of 1949, for the protection of civilian populations in circumstances of emergency and armed conflict, and shall not:

(a) Recruit indigenous individuals against their will into the armed forces and, in particular, for use against other indigenous peoples;

(b) Recruit indigenous children into the armed forces under any circumstances;

(c) Force indigenous individuals to abandon their lands, territories or means of subsistence, or relocate them in special centres for military purposes;

(d) Force indigenous individuals to work for military purposes under any discriminatory conditions.

PART III

Article 12

Indigenous peoples have the right to practice and revitalize their cultural traditions and customs. This includes the right to maintain, protect and develop the past, present and future manifestations of their cultures, such as archaeological and historical sites, artifacts, designs, ceremonies, technologies and visual and performing arts and literature, as well as the right to restitution of cultural, intellectual, religious and spiritual property taken without their free and informed consent or in violation of their laws, traditions and customs.

Article 13

Indigenous peoples have the right to manifest, practice, develop and teach their spiritual and religious traditions, customs and ceremonies; the right to maintain, protect, and have access in privacy to their religious and cultural sites; the right to the use and control of ceremonial objects; and the right to the repatriation of human remains.

States shall take effective measures, in conjuction with the indigenous peoples concerned, to ensure that indigenous sacred places, including burial sites, be preserved, respected and protected.

Article 14

Indigenous peoples have the right to revitalize, use, develop and transmit to future generations their histories, languages, oral traditions, philosophies, writing systems and literatures, and to designate and retain their own names for communities, places and persons.

States shall take effective measures, whenever any right of indigenous peoples may be threatened, to ensure this right is protected and also to ensure that they can understand and be understood in political, legal and administrative proceedings, where necessary through the provision of interpretation or by other appropriate means.

PART IV

Article 15

Indigenous children have the right to all levels and forms of education of the State. All indigenous peoples also have this right and the right to establish and control their educational systems and institutions providing education in their own languages, in a manner appropriate to their cultural methods of teaching and learning.

Indigenous children living outside their communities have the right to be provided access to education in their own culture and language.

States shall take effective measures to provide approriate resources for these purposes.

Article 16

Indigenous peoples have the right to have the dignity and diversity of their cultures, traditions, histories and aspirations appropriately reflected in all forms of education and public information.

States shall take effective measures, in consultation with the indigenous peoples concerned, to eliminate prejudice and discrimination and to promote tolerance, understanding and good relations among indigenous peoples and all segments of society.

Article 17

Indigenous peoples have the right to establish their own media in their own languages. They also have the right to equal access to all forms of non-indigenous media.

States shall take effective measures to ensure that State-owned media duly reflect indigenous cultural diversity.

Article 18

Indigenous peoples have the right to enjoy fully all rights established under international labour law and national labour legislation.

Indigenous individuals have the right not to be subjected to any discriminatory conditions of labour, employment or salary.

PART V

Article 19

Indigenous peoples have the right to participate fully, if they so choose, at all levels of decision-making in matters which may affect their rights, lives and destinies through representatives chosen by themselves in accordance with their own procedures, as well as to maintain and develop their own indigenous decision-making institutions.

Article 20

Indigenous peoples have the right to participate fully, if they so choose, through procedures determined by them, in devising legislative or administrative measures that may affect them.

States shall obtain the free and informed consent of the peoples concerned before adopting and implementing such measures.

Article 21

Indigenous peoples have the right to maintain and develop their political, economic and social systems, to be secure in the enjoyment of their own means of subsistence and development, and to engage freely in all their traditional and other economic activities. Indigenous peoples who have been deprived of their means of subsistence and development are entitled to just and fair compensation.

Article 22

Indigenous peoples have the right to special measures for the immediate, effective and continuing improvement of their economic and social conditions, including in the areas of employment, vocational training and retraining, housing, sanitation, health and social security.

Particular attention shall be paid to the rights and special needs of indigenous elders, women, youth, children and disabled persons.

Article 23

Indigenous peoples have the right to determine and develop priorities and strategies for exercising their right to development. In particular, indigenous peoples have the right to determine and develop all health, housing and other economic and social programmes affecting them and, as far as possible, to administer such programmes through their own institutions.

Article 24

Indigenous peoples have the right to their traditional medicines and health practices, including the right to the protection of vital medicinal plants, animals and minerals.

They also have the right to access, without any discrimination, to all medical institutions, health services and medical care.

PART VI

Article 25

Indigenous peoples have the right to maintain and strengthen their distinctive spiritual and material relationship with the lands, territories, waters and coastal seas and other resources which they have traditionally owned or otherwise occupied or used, and to uphold their responsibilities to future generations in this regard.

Article 26

Indigenous peoples have the right to own, develop, control and use the lands and territories, including the total environment of the lands, air, waters, coastal seas, sea-ice, flora and fauna and other resources which they have traditionally owned or otherwise occupied or used. This includes the right to the full recognition of their laws, traditions and customs, land-tenure systems and institutions for the development and management of resources, and the right to effective measures by States to prevent any interference with, alienation of or encroachment upon these rights.

Article 27

Indigenous peoples have the right to the restitution of the lands, territories and resources which they have traditionally owned or otherwise occupied or used, and which have been confiscated, occupied, used or damaged without their free and informed consent. Where this is not possible, they have the right to just and fair compensation. Unless otherwise freely agreed upon by the peoples concerned, compensation shall take the form of lands, territories and resources equal in quality, size and legal status.

Article 28

Indigenous peoples have the right to the conservation, restoration and protection of the total environment and the productive capacity of their lands, territories and resources, as well as to assistance for this purpose from States and through international cooperation. Military activities shall not take place in the lands and territories of indigenous peoples, unless otherwise freely agreed upon by the peoples concerned.

States shall take effective measures to ensure that no storage or disposal of hazardous materials shall take place in the lands and territories of indigenous peoples.

States shall also take effective measures to ensure, as needed, that programmes for monitoring, maintaining and restoring the health of indigenous peoples, as developed and implemented by the peoples affected by such materials, are duly implemented.

Article 29

Indigenous peoples are entitled to the recognition of the full ownership, control and protection of their cultural and intellectual property.

They have the right to special measures to control, develop and protect their sciences, technologies and cultural manifestations, including human and other genetic resources, seeds, medicines, knowledge of the proterties of fauna and flora, oral traditions, literatures, designs and visual and performing arts.

Article 30

Indigenous peoples have the right to determine and develop priorities and strategies for the development or use of their lands, territories and other resources, including the right to require that States obtain their free and informed consent prior to the approval of any project affecting their lands, territories and other resources, particularly in connection with the development, utilization or exploitation of mineral, water or other resources. Pursuant to agreement with the indigenous peoples concerned, just and fair compensation shall be provided for any such activities and measures taken to mitigate adverse environmental, economic, social, cultural or spiritual impact.

PART VII

Article 31

Indigenous peoples, as a specific form of exercising their right to self-determination, have the right to autonomy or self-government in matters relating to their internal and local affairs, including culture, religion, education, information, media, health, housing, employment, social welfare, economic activities, land and resources management, environment and entry by non-members, as well as ways and means for financing these autonomous functions.

Article 32

Indigenous peoples have the collective right to determine their own citizenship in accordance with their customs and traditions. Indigenous citizenship does not impair the right of indigenous individuals to obtain citizenship of the States in which they live.

Indigenous peoples have the right to determine the structures and to select the membership of their institutions in accordance with their own procedures.

Article 33

Indigenous peoples have the right to promote, develop and maintain their institutional structures and their distinctive juridical customs, traditions, procedures and practices, in accordance with internationally recognized human rights standards.

Article 34

Indigenous peoples have the collective right to determine the responsibilities of individuals to their communities.

Article 35

Indigenous peoples, in particular those divided by international borders, have the right to maintain and develop contacts, relations and cooperation, including activities for spiritual, cultural, political, economic and social purposes, with other peoples across borders.

States shall take effective measures to ensure the exercise and implementation of this right.

Article 36

Indigenous peoples have the right to the recognition, observance and enforcement of treaties, agreements and other constructive arrangements concluded with States or their successors, according to their original spirit and intent, and to have States honour and respect such treaties, agreements and other constructive arrangements. Conflicts and disputes which cannot otherwise be settled should be submitted to competent international bodies agreed to by all parties concerned.

PART VIII

Article 37

States shall take effective and appropriate measures, in consultation with the indigenous peoples concerned, to give full effect to the provisions of this Declaration. The rights recognized herein shall be adopted and included in national legislation in such a manner that indigenous peoples can avail themselves of such rights in practice.

Article 38

Indigenous peoples have the right to have access to adequate financial and technical assistance, from States and through international cooperation, to pursue freely their political, economic, social, cultural and spiritual development and for the enjoyment of the rights and freedoms recognized in this Declaration.

Article 39

Indigenous peoples have the right to have access to and prompt decision through mutually acceptable and fair procedures for the resolution of conflicts and disputes with States, as well as to effective remedies for all infringements of their individual and collective rights. Such a decision shall take into consideration the customs, traditions, rules and legal systems of the indigenous peoples concerned.

Article 40

The organs and specialized agencies of the United Nations system and other intergovernmental organizations shall contribute to the full realization of the provisions of this Declaration through the mobilization, *inter alia*, of financial cooperation and technical assistance. Ways and means of ensuring participation of indigenous peoples on issues affecting them shall be established.

Article 41

The United Nations shall take the necessary steps to ensure the implementation of this Declaration including the creation of a body at the highest level with special competence in this field and with the direct participation of indigenous peoples. All United Nations bodies shall promote respect for and full application of the provisions of this Declaration.

PART IX

Article 42

The rights recognized herein constitute the minimum standards for the survival, dignity and well-being of the indigenous peoples of the world.

Article 43

All the rights and freedoms recognized herein are equally guaranteed to male and female indigenous individuals.

Article 44

Nothing in this Declaration may be construed as diminishing or extinguishing existing or future rights indigenous peoples may have or acquire.

Article 45

Nothing in this Declaration may be interpreted as implying for any State, group or person any right to engage in any activity or to perform any act contrary to the Charter of the United Nations.

BIBLIOGRAPHY

1. LEGISLATION

Canadian Bill of Rights, 1960, R.S.C. 1985, App.III.

Canadian Charter of Rights and Freedoms

Civil Code of Lower Canada (1866)

Constitutional Act, 1791, reproduced in Morin, Jacques-Yvan et Ivoehrling, José, *Les Constitutions du Canada et du Québec* (Montréal: Editions Thémis, 1992) at p. 653.

Constitution Act, 1867, R.S.C. 1985, App.II, No.5

Constitution Act, 1982, R.S.C. 1985, App. II, No. 44.

Cree-Naskapi (of Quebec) Act, S.C. 1984, c.18. (James Bay Agreement)

Criminal Code, R.S.C. 1970, c. C-34.

Criminal Code, R.S.C. 1985, c. C-46.

Indian Act, R.S.C. 1970, c.I-6.

Indian Act, R.S.C. 1985, c. I-5.

Migratory Birds Convention Act, R.S.C. 1952, c. 179.

Migratory Birds Convention Act, R.S.C. 1985, c. M-7.

Quebec Act 1774, reproduced in Morin, Jacques-Yvan, *supra*, at p. 645.

Quebec Boundaries Extension Act, S.C. 1912, c. 45.

Royal Proclamation of 1763, R.S.C. 1985, App. II, No.1.

Sechelt Indian Band Self-Government Act, S.C. 1986, c. 27.

Young Offenders Act, R.S.C. 1970, c. 1-3.

Canadian Human Rights Act, Bill C-25, Acts of the Parliament of Canada, 1976-77, Vol. II, c. 33 (Ottawa: Queen's Printer for Canada 1977)

Divorce Act, 1985, Bill C-47, Acts of the Parliament of Canada, 1986, Vol. I, c. 4 (Ottawa: Queen's Printer for Canada 1987)

Indian Act, An Act to amend the, Bill C-31, Acts of the Parliament of Canada, 1985, Vol. I, c. 27 (Ottawa: Queen's Printer for Canada 1987).

Meech Lake Accord, reproduced in Morin, Jacques-Yvan, *supra*, at p. 897.

Robinson Treaty (1850), reproduced in *Consolidated Native Law Statutes, Regulations and Treaties, 1994* (Scarborough, Ont: Thomson Canada, 1993) at pp. 378 and 380.

Jay Treaty (1796), reproduced in *Consolidated Native Law Statutes, supra*, at p. 388.

Inuvialuit Final Agreement implemented by the *Western Arctic (Inuvaluit) Claims Settlement Act*, S.C. 1984, c.24.

International

International Labour Organization, *Convention Concerning the Protection and Integration of Indigenous and Other Tribal and Semi-Tribal Populations in Independent Countries*, (I.L.O. No. 107), 328 U.N.T.S. 247; concluded June 26, 1957; entry into force June 2, 1959 Convention No. 107.

United Nations, *Declaration of Human Rights*; adopted by the United Nations General Assembly December 10, 1948; GA Res. 217 A (III), U.N. Doc. A/810 (1948).

United Nations, *International Covenant on Economic, Social and Cultural Rights*, Canada Treaty Series 1976 No. 46; concluded December 16, 1966; entry into force January 3, 1976; in force for Canada August 19, 1976.

United Nations, *International Covenant on Civil and Political Rights*, Canada Treaty Series 1986 No. 47; concluded December 16, 1966; entry into force March 23, 1976; in force for Canada August 19, 1976.

United Nations, General Assembly, Resolution 1514 (XV) of 24 October 1970, AJIL 65 (1971) 243.

2. JURISPRUDENCE

Chief Robert et al. v. Attorney-General of the Province of Québec and the Québec Hydro Electric Commission

Musqueam (see *Grant* v. *B.C.* and *Grant* v. *Canada*).

MacMillan Bloedel v. *Mullin; Martin* v. *R.* in right of B.C., [1985] 3 W.W.R. 577, 61 B.C.L.R. 145. Leave to appeal to S.C.C. refused [1985] 5 W.W.R. lxiv.

A.G. Canada v. *Lavell*, (1973) 38 D.L.R. (3d) 481.

Appellant's Factum (Temagami case, see A.G. Ontario v. Bear Island Foundation et al.), Borden and Elliot, Toronto 1991, unpublished.

A.G. Ontario v. *Bear Island Foundation* (1984), 15 D.L.R. (4th) 321.

Baker Lake v. *Minister of Indian Affairs & Northern Development* [1979] 1 F.C. 487.

Baker Lake v. *Minister of Indian Affairs & Northern Development* [1980] 1 F.C. 518.

Calder v. *A.G. British Columbia* [1973] S.C.R. 313.

Canadian Pacific Ltd., a body corporate v. *Chief Winston Paul et al.* [1988] 2 R.C.S. 654

Canadien Pacifique Ltée c. Paul see *Canadian Pacific Ltd.*

The Cherokee Nation v. *The State of Georgia* (1831) 30 U.S. 1, 5 Pet.1.

Décontie v. *R.* [1989] R.J.Q. 1893.

Delgamuukw v. *British Columbia* [1991] 5 C.N.L.R. 1.

Dominion of Canada v. *Ontario* [1910] A.C. 637.

Grant v. *British Columbia* (sub nom. *Musqueam Indian Band* v. *British Columbia*) (1991), 57 B.C.L.R. (2d) 305, 48 C.P.C. (2d) 234 (S.C.)

Grant v. *Canada (Minister of Indian & Northern Affairs)* (1990), 31 F.T.R. 31, (sub nom. *Musqueam Indian Band* v. *Canada (Minister of Indian & Northern Affairs)*) [1990] 2 F.C. 351, (sub nom. *Grant* v. *British Columbia*) [1990] 2 C.N.L.R. 26

Guerin v. *R.* [1984] 2 S.C.R. 335.

Johnson and Graham's Lessee v. *McIntosh* (1823), 8 Wheaton 543.

Kruger v. *R.* [1978] 1 R.C.S. 104.

Lovelace v. *Canada* [1981] 2 H.R.L.J. 158 (U.N.H.R.C.).

Nowegijick v. *R.* [1983] 1 S.C.R. 29.

Ontario Mining Company, Ltd. et al. v. *Seybold et al.* (sub nom. *Seybold*) [1903] A.C. 73.

Paul v. *Paul* [1986] 1 S.C.R. 306.

Paul Band v. *R.* [1984] 2 W.W.R. 540.

R. v. *Arcand* [1989] 3 W.W.R. 635.

R. v. *Derriksan* (1976), 71 D.L.R. (3d) 159.

R. v. *Drybones* [1970] S.C.R. 282.

R. v. *Flett* [1987] 5 W.W.R. 115.

R. v. *George* (1968), 1 D.L.R. (3d) 113.

R. v. *Horse* [1988] 1 S.C.R. 187.

R. v. *Isaac* [1973] 3 O.R. 833.

R. v. *Isaac* (1975), 13 N.S.R. (2d) 460

R. v. *Sikyea* [1964] S.C.R. 642.

R. v. *Simon* [1985] 2 S.C.R. 387.

R. v. *Sioui* [1990] 1 S.C.R. 1025.

R. v. *Sparrow* [1990] 1 R.C.S. 1075.

R. v. *Stevenson* [1986] 5 W.W.R. 737.

R. v. *Syliboy* [1929] 1 D.L.R. 307.

R. v. *Taylor* (1981), 34 O.R. (2d) 360.

R. v. *White and Bob* (1966) D.L.R. (2d) 613.

Seybold see *Ontario Mining Company*

Sikyea v. *R.* [1964] S.C.R. 642.

Southern Rhodesia, Re [1919] A.C. 211 (Southern Rhodesia P.C.)

St. Catherine's Milling v. *R.* (1888), 14 App. Cas. 46.

St. Catherine's Milling v. *R.* (1885) O.R.V. x 196 (first instance)

Western Sahara Advisory Opinion, I.C.J. Reports 1975.

Worcester v. *Georgia* (1832), 31 U.S. 530.

3. AUTHORITIES

Harris, R. Cole, ed., *Historical Atlas of Canada, Vol. 1* (Toronto: University of Toronto, 1987).

Heidenreich, Conrad, *Huronia: A History and Geography of the Huron Indians 1600-1650* (Toronto: McClelland and Stewart, 1971).

Hodgins, Bruce W. and Benidickson, Jamie, *The Temagami Experience: Recreation, Resources, and Aboriginal Rights in the Northern Ontario Wilderness* (Toronto: University of Toronto, 1989).

Morantz, Toby, *An Ethnohistoric Study of Eastern James Bay Cree Social Organization 1700-1860* (Canadian Ethnology Service Paper 88) (Ottawa: National Museum of Man, 1983).

Morris, Alexander, *The Treaties of Canada with the Indians* (Toronto: Coles, 1971). The text was first published in 1880.

Rogers, Edward S., *The Hunting Group-Hunting Territory Complex Among the Mistassini Indians* (Anthropological Series 63) (Ottawa: National Museum of Canada Bulletin 195, 1978).

Rogers, Edward S., "Southwestern Ojibwa" in Bruce Trigger, ed., *Handbook of the North American Indians, Northeast Vol. 15* (Washington: Smithsonian Institution, 1963) at pp. 760-71.

Slattery, Brian, *Understanding Aboriginal Rights*, (1987) 66 Can. B. Rev. 727.

Slattery, Brian, *The Independance of Canada*, (1983) 5 Supreme Court Law Review 369.

Speck, Frank G., *Family Hunting Territories and Social Life of Various Algonkian Bands of the Ottawa Valley* (GSC Memoir 70, No. 8 Anthropological Series) (Ottawa: Department of Mines, 1915).

Surtees, Robert J., *The Development of an Indian Reserve Policy in Canada* (Ontario History 61(2): 87-98, 1969).